Memory and Mind

By the same author

Dreaming
Knowledge and Certainty
Ludwig Wittgenstein: A Memoir
Problems of Mind: Descartes to Wittgenstein
Thought and Knowledge

Memory and Mind

NORMAN MALCOLM

Cornell University Press

ITHACA AND LONDON

First published 1977 by Cornell University Press.
Published in the United Kingdom by Cornell University Press Ltd., 2–4 Brook Street, London W1Y 1AA.

International Standard Book Number 0-8014-1018-5
Library of Congress Catalog Card Number 76-28017
Printed in the United States of America by Vail-Ballou Press, Inc.
*Librarians: Library of Congress cataloging information
appears on the last page of the book.*

To Bruce Goldberg

Contents

■ □

Preface

I have worked on the topic of memory for a good number of years. The academic year 1960–1961, when I was a Fulbright Fellow at the University of Helsinki, was devoted to it and resulted in the publication of "Three Lectures on Memory," as part of my book *Knowledge and Certainty*. There are not many points of contact between the "Three Lectures" and the present book. The orientation of the earlier work was mainly analytical. The bent of this book is more historical, systematic, and destructive. It could be regarded as a critical study in the philosophy of mind, with primary attention to theories of memory.

A large part of the work on Part One was accomplished in 1968–1969, when I was a Fellow of the Center for Advanced Study in the Behavioral Sciences at Stanford. I am grateful to the Center for providing unparalleled conditions for intensive study, as well as a congenial atmosphere.

Part One was heavily revised, and the whole of Part Two was written, in 1975–1976, in London and Oxford, while I held a fellowship of the National Endowment for the Humanities. I thank the National Endowment for its support.

Chapter II, "Memory as Direct Awareness of the Past," is a slightly revised version of a lecture that I gave to the Royal Institute of Philosophy, at King's College, London, in May 1974. It was published in a volume of the Royal Institute entitled *Impressions of Empiricism*, edited by G. Vesey, Royal Institute of Philosophy Lectures, 9, 1974–1975 (London: Macmillan, 1976). I express my appreciation to Godfrey Vesey and to the Royal Institute of Philosophy for permission to reproduce that lecture.

I thank Nicholas Rescher and the *American Philosophical Quarterly* for permission to use ideas and examples taken from my article "Wittgenstein on the Nature of Mind," *American Philosophical Quarterly*, Monograph Series, edited by Nicholas Rescher, Monograph No. 4, Oxford 1970; and I also thank the Editor of *Noûs* for permission to make use of ideas and examples taken from my article "Memory and Representation," *Noûs*, IV, 1970.

I am particularly grateful to John Wiley & Sons for permission to include in the appendix to Chapter X generous quotations from Dr. Elliot S. Valenstein's book, *Brain Control: A Critical Examination of Brain Stimulation and Psychosurgery* (New York: John Wiley & Sons, 1973).

The quotation from *Mr. Sammler's Planet* by Saul Bellow, copyright © 1969, 1970 by Saul Bellow, is used by permission of the publisher, The Viking Press.

Finally, I express my gratitude to Cornell University for granting me sabbatic leave during the academic years 1960–1961, 1968–1969, and 1975–1976.

NORMAN MALCOLM

Ithaca, New York

PART ONE

MENTAL MECHANISMS OF MEMORY

If someone asked me, for example, "Have you ever before seen the table at which you are now sitting?", I would answer: "Yes, I have seen it countless times." And if further questioned I would say that I have sat at it every day for months. . . . What act or acts of remembering take place there? I do not see myself in my mind "sitting every day at this table for months". But yet I say that I remember having done this, and I can later prove it in various ways. Last summer too, for example, I lived in this room. But how do I know that? Do I see it in my mind? No. Then of what does the remembering consist in this case? If I inquire as it were into the ground of the remembering, there float up in my mind separate pictures of my earlier residence, but certainly not with their dates. And before they have floated up, and before I have called up in my mind various proofs, I say correctly that I remember having lived here for months and to have seen this table. Remembering, therefore, is certainly not the mental process which, at first sight, one would imagine. If I say, rightly, "I remember it," the *most different* things can occur, and even merely this: that I say it. And when I say here "rightly," of course I am not laying down what the right and the wrong use of the expression is; on the contrary, I am just characterizing the actual use.

Wittgenstein, *Philosophische Grammatik*

CHAPTER I

What We Remember

1.   At the start of his short treatise on memory, Aristotle says, "First, then, one must consider what sort of things the objects of memory are, for this often leads people astray." [1] Aristotle was himself led astray, as is shown by his next remarks: "For it is not possible to remember the future, which is instead an object of judgment and prediction. . . . Nor is memory of the present; rather, perception is. . . . But memory is of the past." [2] He adds: "No one would say he was remembering what was present, when it was present, e.g. this white thing when he was seeing it; nor would he say he was remembering the object of his theorizing when he was in the act of theorizing and thinking. . . . There is no memory of the present at the present. . . . But perception is of the present, prediction of the future, and memory of the past." [3] I take the question, What are "the objects of memory?", to mean: What sorts of things can rightly be said to be remembered? A little reflection on our actual use of language reveals that Aristotle was mistaken in supposing that "No one would say that he remembers the present, when it is present." On a long auto trip across the country I may exclaim, as we drive down the main street of a town in North Dakota, "I remember this town!" Or if I spot a familiar face in a crowded room, I may think to myself, "I remember that man." Or

---

1. Aristotle, *De Memoria et Reminiscentia*, 449b. Translation and commentary by Richard Sorabji, *Aristotle on Memory* (London: Duckworth, 1972).
2. Ibid.   3. Ibid.

if I am shown some object that I used in my youth (a toy, a clock, a stool), I may say, "Oh, I remember this!"

Aristotle was also mistaken in declaring that it is not possible to remember the future. I may wonder whether a friend remembers tomorrow's picnic or next week's wedding, and be assured by someone, "Yes, he remembers it." Now it may seem that our language is paradoxical here. But it is a correct way of speaking and rarely does it mislead anyone in ordinary life. One could rightly say that what this way of speaking means is that the friend remembers that there will be a picnic tomorrow. Granting this, then what is remembered is that there will be (or that there is supposed to be) a picnic tomorrow. But still, contrary to Aristotle, one cannot rightly say that this object of memory is in *the past*. Nor that it is in the future or in the present. That which is expressed by a propositional phrase of the form "that *p*," cannot be assigned any temporal location.

In the example of the picnic one vacillates between saying that what is remembered is that "there will be," or instead that "there is supposed to be," a picnic tomorrow. This is because picnics are notoriously dependent on the weather: the days are not *always* fine at Upper Buttermilk. And other contingencies may lead to the cancellation of a picnic. But it is easy to think of examples where no vacillation will be felt. Suppose the ship's navigator looked up the tide tables yesterday, and today he remembers that high tide will be at noon tomorrow. Or (another example) he remembers that in April there will be an eclipse of the moon. People don't cancel tides or eclipses. I believe there is no inclination to say that what the navigator remembers is that there is "supposed to be" an eclipse. Nor is it right to say that what the navigator really remembers is that *he read* in the nautical almanac that there will be an eclipse in April. He might not remember *reading* it there, nor even *that* he read it there. But he does remember that there will be an eclipse in April. And *what* he remembers (*that* there will be an eclipse in April) cannot be said to be in the past, the present, or the future.

Thomas Reid expressed a view about the objects of memory that is identical with Aristotle's. He says: "The object of memory, or thing remembered, must be something that is past; as the object of perception and of consciousness must be something which is present. What now is, cannot be an object of memory; neither can that which is past and gone be an object of perception or of consciousness." [4] Reid did not arrive at his view by carefully observing the actual grammar of memory locutions. For this grammar permits us to speak of remembering present and future things, and also things which cannot be said to be past, present or future. Under the latter category are to be included facts, names, numbers, formulae, how to make a good soup, where the flashlight is kept, when to water the garden, and so on.

One will feel, however, that there is truth behind the claim that what is remembered "must be something that is past"; or, as Aristotle puts it, that "memory is of the past." [5] Now indeed it is so that memory is of the past in the sense that if a person remembers something, then at some previous time he must have known, encountered, learned of, or experienced that thing. One cannot, today, remember tomorrow's cocktail party unless one had previous information of it. One cannot remember a face unless one has seen it previously, or remember the Greek alphabet without having ever known it before. This is a striking feature of the concept of memory. What memory and remembering require is, not that the object of memory be something that is past, but that the person who remembers that thing must have met, experienced, or learned of it in the past.

The inclination to assume that the objects of memory must be in the past may influence philosophical thinking about the "analysis" of various types of memory. There is, for example, the notion that some forms of memory are more *basic* than others, and also that the less basic may be *defined* in terms of the more basic. C. D. Broad held such a view. Broad willingly allowed that it can be quite cor-

4. Thomas Reid, *Works*, ed. W. Hamilton, 2 vols. (Edinburgh: Maclachan and Stewart, 1872), I, 340.
5. Aristotle, *De Memoria*, 449b.

rect to speak of remembering something that presently exists. "We can, and very often do, remember things which still exist and which we are now perceiving." [6] Broad thinks, however, that the memory of *past events* is the most *fundamental* form of memory.[7] And, he holds, some other forms of memory are reducible to the memory of past events. For example: "to remember a thing or a person simply means to remember certain past events and to regard them as incidents in the history of that thing or person." [8]

It is generally true that when a philosopher enters into the study of a concept (such as knowledge, belief, intention, memory) he assumes that the concept has a *unity* which can be disclosed by "analysis." In the case of the concept of memory there are a multitude of linguistic forms and locutions in which the noun "memory" and the verb "remember" are employed. The philosopher's normal assumption will incline him to suppose that one of these linguistic forms is preeminent, basic, or central, and that the other forms are offshoots from the central one. In some of my previous writing on the topic of memory I was influenced by this idea.[9] In the present work I believe I have freed myself from it. If I make an assumption, it is the opposite one. Wittgenstein's remark about the concept of "thinking" and the employment of that word in our language is very apt here: "It is not to be expected of this word that it should have a unified employment; we should rather expect the op-

6. C. D. Broad, *Mind and Its Place in Nature* (London: Kegan Paul, 1925), p. 224.

7. Ibid., p. 225.   8. Ibid., p. 224.

9. In my "Three Lectures on Memory" I distinguished several forms of memory (e.g., "personal" memory, "perceptual" memory, "factual" memory, and remembering *to do* something). I was inclined to think that "factual" memory (remembering *that p*) was central in at least the sense that all of the other forms of memory *entailed* factual memory. N. Malcolm, *Knowledge and Certainty* (Englewood Cliffs, N.J.: Prentice Hall, 1963), reprinted (Ithaca, N.Y.: Cornell University Press, 1975), p. 222. I had not much evidence but instead a prejudice in favor of there being *some* sort of unity. Acute criticism and counterexamples convinced me that this tentative opinion in favor of the centrality of factual memory was mistaken. See J. T. Saunders, "Does All Memory Imply Factual Memory?", *Analysis* (January 1965), Vol. 25, (Supp.) No. 3.

posite." [10] Since I do have this opposite expectation, my intention is not to achieve an "analysis" of the concept of memory.

To return to Broad: on the issue of whether to remember a thing or person "simply means" to remember "certain past events" and "to regard them as incidents in the history of the thing or person," it would appear that Broad is clearly wrong. If I am introduced to someone and his face seems familiar, I may say, "I remember your face although I can't remember where or when I saw you or anything about you." I remember his face, but I don't remember any past event in his history, let alone in the history of his face. I may recognize a coat or book or pipe as mine (recognition being a form of memory) without calling to mind some event in the history of the thing.

Broad realized that it is correct to speak of remembering some music one is *presently* hearing or a hat one *now* sees. I surmise that he was also attracted by the Aristotle-Reid view that what is remembered can only be something that is *past*. His mistaken claim that remembering some object of present perception really means remembering some past event in the object's history may have been an attempt to effect a compromise.

2. Let us turn now to one of the most puzzling attempts in philosophy to impose a severe restriction on the objects of memory. This is the conception that what we remember is always *mental* in nature. The objects of memory are called *ideas* or *sensations* or *impressions* or *perceptions* or *images*. Locke said that ideas are the *objects* of the understanding "when a man thinks." [11] These ideas are "in men's minds," and "every one is conscious of them in himself." [12] Ideas are conveyed into the mind by the senses, and also by the

10. Wittgenstein, *Zettel*, ed. G. E. M. Anscombe and G. H. von Wright; trans. G. E. M. Anscombe (Oxford; Blackwell, 1967), para. 112. Occasionally I modify the translation.

11. Locke, *Essay Concerning Human Understanding*, ed. A. C. Fraser (Oxford: Clarendon Press, 1894), Introd., Sec. 8.

12. Ibid.

mind's observation of its own operations.[13] *Memory* is "as it were the storehouse of our ideas." Locke goes on to say: "But, our ideas being nothing but actual perceptions in the mind, which cease to be anything when there is no perception of them; this laying up of our ideas in the repository of the memory signifies no more but this,—that the mind has a power in many cases to revive perceptions which it has once had, with this additional perception annexed to them, that it has had them before. And in this sense it is that our ideas are said to be in our memories, when indeed they are actually nowhere;—but only there is an ability in the mind when it will revive them again, and as it were paint them anew on itself, though some with more, some with less difficulty; some more lively, and others more obscurely. And thus it is, by the assistance of this faculty, that we are said to have all those ideas in our understanding which, though we do not actually contemplate, yet we *can* bring in sight, and make appear again, and be the objects of our thoughts, without the help of those sensible qualities which first imprinted them there." [14] Hume held a similar view. "All the perceptions of the human mind" may be divided into *impressions* or *ideas*. Those perceptions that enter the mind "with most force and violence" are impressions. Ideas are "the faint images" of impressions, which occur in thinking and reasoning.[15] Remembering, too, consists in the occurrence of ideas; but they are not so faint. When an impression you have had reappears and "retains a considerable degree of its first vivacity, and is somewhat intermediate betwixt an impression and an idea," this is memory. The ideas of memory have greater "force and vivacity" than do, for example, the ideas of the imagination. "When we remember any past event, the idea of it flows in upon the mind in a forcible manner; whereas in the imagination the perception is faint and languid, and cannot without difficulty be preserv'd by the mind steddy and uniform for any con-

---

13. Ibid., Bk. II, Ch. 1, Secs. 2–4.   14. Ibid., Bk. II, Ch. 10, Sec. 2.

15. Hume, *Treatise of Human Nature*, ed. L. A. Selby-Bigge, (Oxford, Clarendon Press, 1958), Bk. I, Pt. 1, Sec. 1.

siderable time." [16] Hume's view would seem to imply that the objects of memory are limited to impressions and ideas. And this surely was what he thought. For he says, "Now since nothing is ever present to the mind but perceptions, and since all ideas are deriv'd from something antecedently present to the mind; it follows, that 'tis impossible for us so much as to conceive or form an idea of any thing specifically different from ideas and impression." [17] If this is so, then we can remember nothing other than ideas and impressions.

With both Locke and Hume the limiting of the objects of memory to ideas and impressions was simply a consequence of what they thought were the limits of human understanding and perception in general. Many volumes have been written against what Thomas Reid calls "the theory of ideas," namely, the doctrine that the objects of perception, or at least the "immediate" objects, are always ideas, impressions, perceptions, images, or sense-data, in our own minds. I reject this doctrine, but will not undertake a criticism of it, since to do so would take me too far afield.

But also there have been writers to whom it has appeared that the objects of memory are limited by the nature of memory itself. St. Augustine may serve as an illustration. He says that many things perceived by the senses enter into the memory: light, colors, forms of bodies, sounds, smells, tastes, what is hard or soft, hot or cold, heavy or light. But then he corrects this statement in the following way: "And yet do not the things themselves enter the memory; only the images of the things perceived by the senses are ready there at hand, whenever the thoughts will recall them." [18] Augustine goes on to say that he has seen mountains, rivers, stars, and the ocean, and that he could not even speak of them unless he saw them "inwardly" in his memory. But he adds: "Yet did I not swallow them into me by seeing, whenas with mine eyes I beheld

16. Ibid., Bk. I, Pt. 1, Sec. 3.   17. Ibid., Bk. I, Pt. 2, Sec. 6.
18. Augustine, *Confessions*, trans. W. Watts, 2 vols. (Cambridge, Mass.: Harvard University Press, 1942–46), II, Bk. 10, Ch. 8.

them. Nor are the things themselves now within me, but the images of them only." [19] Among other things he remembers are the precepts of the liberal sciences. But here, he says, "nor is it the images of the precepts which I bear, but the sciences themselves," and he goes on, "For what grammar or logic is, how many kinds of questions there be, whatsoever of all these I know, 'tis in such manner in my memory, as that I have not merely taken in the image, and left out the thing.[20] So he has grammar and logic in his memory and not mere images of them. Yet when it comes to sounds, odors, or anything "felt by the body," the matter is different: "For surely the things themselves are not let into the memory, but the images of them only are with an admirable swiftness catched in, and in most wonderful cabinets stored up; whence they are as wonderfully fetched out again by the act of remembering." [21] Note that it is the *images* that are "fetched out" by the act of remembering. Does that mean that it is only the images that are remembered, and not the sounds or odors themselves? What does it mean to say that a sound is or is not in my memory, other than that I do or do not remember it?

Augustine says that *numbers* can be in my memory: "not their images but themselves." [22] He says that he can name the image of the sun and that image is in his memory. "Nor do I call to mind the image of that image, but the image itself; that is it which is present with me whenas I remember it." [23] But when he names a stone or names the sun, and they are not present to his senses, then what is in his memory are images of them.[24]

It appears that, for Augustine, what decides the question of whether something can be "in the memory" or not is whether it is in physical space. Presumably the precepts of grammar and logic, numbers, and mental images, are not in physical space; and so they can be in the memory. But odors, colors, mountains and rivers, are spread out in physical space, and cannot be "in" the memory.

19. Ibid.   20. Ibid., Ch. 9.   21. Ibid.   22. Ibid., Ch. 15.
23. Ibid.   24. Ibid.

They could be in the memory only if it was a physical receptacle, and it isn't.

It would seem that Augustine had lost sight of the huge variety of ways in which something, A, can be "in" something, B. My dog is *in* disgrace: but that doesn't mean that he is in a physical area named Disgrace. A man's career is *in* jeopardy: but Jeopardy is not a place where his career is. Sinatra is *in* a good humor: but that doesn't tell us where he is located. Rubinstein is *in* your will and last testament: but we don't know where he is.

To say that the ocean is "in my memory" (*in memoria mea*) should mean that I remember it; and if I remember it, this should mean that it is "in my memory." Since Augustine remembers the ocean, he should admit that the ocean is in his memory. If only an image of it is in his memory, this should mean that he remembers only an image of it. Augustine acknowledges that this is so. One of his examples of something he remembers is forgetfulness. He finds this to be a paradox he does not know how to resolve. For, on the one hand, if forgetfulness is present in his memory, how can he remember anything? On the other hand, it is certain that he remembers forgetfulness; and "Shall I say that that is not in my memory, which I remember?" He does not find it satisfactory to say that it is only the image of forgetfulness that is in his memory. "How can I say that the image of forgetfulness is kept in memory, and not forgetfulness itself, whenas I do remember it?" [25]

It is clear that if Augustine were treating the locution "*x* is in my memory" as merely equivalent to the locution "I remember *x*," then he would not be confronted with the seeming paradox of forgetfulness nor with the other confusions. He has a tendency to treat it in just that way. But also he has other conflicting tendencies. One of these is to think that if *x* is in my memory then I *have* or *am* *x*. According to this, if courage is in my memory I have courage; and if forgetfulness is in my memory I am forgetful. Another tendency already noted is to think that no physical thing can

---

25. Ibid., Ch. 16.

be in my memory, apparently for the supposed reason that a physical thing, A, can be *in* something, B, only if B is a physical area or receptacle. Since the memory is not a physical container, no physical thing can be in my memory but at most an image of it.

I will not dwell any longer on the sources of Augustine's confusions. A person can remember his deceased grandmother. He might have an image of her; but it would be wrong to say that he remembers the image and not her. Similarly, if Rome is in my thoughts, I am thinking of Rome and not of an image, facsimile, or surrogate. It is not impossible that one should remember a mental image; I remember a recurrent dream image that I had as a boy. But the objects of memory often are physical things (houses, streets, lakes, mountains). In remembering these things we frequently have memory images. But Augustine's remark that the physical things do not "enter the memory," but only their images, has no clear meaning other than the claim that we *do not remember* the physical things but only their images—which is false.

3.   There are some present-day philosophers who hold views of the following sorts: that we do not remember past events but only our *perceptions* of those past events; or that we do not remember events "taken simply" but only events "as experienced." Von Leyden, in his book *Remembering*, says that "though we claim to remember facts, events, or situations as they occurred objectively, what we actually remember is always past perceptions." [26] He gets started on this train of thought with the following assertion: "Everyone would agree that what we can remember is not just any past event or fact, but a certain kind of past events or facts, namely those that form part of one's own previous experience." [27] This claim is certainly not true. A fact I remember is that Jane Austen wrote *Emma;* but it would be hard to see any sense in saying that this fact formed a part of my previous experience, unless it merely meant that in order to remember it I must have previously learned

26. W. von Leyden, *Remembering* (London: Duckworth, 1961), p. 66.
27. Ibid., p. 60.

it. This is probably not what von Leyden meant, however, for in the next sentence he implies that "memory statements" refer only "to what one has personally witnessed in the past." [28] A. J. Ayer says something similar: "I remember that the Battle of Waterloo was fought in 1815, but I certainly do not remember the Battle of Waterloo. One very good reason why I do not remember it is that I was not alive at the time. . . . One speaks of remembering an event primarily in the case where one actually witnessed it; but in a derivative sense one can also be said to remember it if one witnessed some of its immediate effects." [29] It is not true, however, that the use of the verb "remember" restricts us to speaking of remembering only events that occur during our lifetime. After an extensive study of military history our instructor might give us a list of names of famous battles, asking us which of them we remember. The list might include Salamis, Marathon, Crecy, Austerlitz, and the First Battle of the Marne. One of us might say, "I don't remember Austerlitz, but I do remember the Battle of Crecy and how the English longbow won the day." In an appropriate context it is quite correct to speak of remembering an event that occurred centuries before one was born. There is a locution to which we resort sometimes when it is not clear to us whether an event that a person remembers is something he actually witnessed or is something he learned about through testimony or reading. If I say, "Oh, I certainly do remember the burning of the city hall," I might be asked, "Do you *personally* remember it?", and I might reply: "No. Because it burned down before I was born." I remember that dramatic event because my father was one of those who fought the fire and I heard him describe it many times. Von Leyden is wrong in his apparent assumption that one can remember an event only if one personally remembers it. [30]

28. Ibid.
29. A. J. Ayer, *The Problem of Knowledge* (London: Macmillan, 1956), pp. 159–160.
30. For a discussion of "personal memory" see my *Knowledge and Certainty*, pp. 214ff.

Von Leyden says that "we can never even attempt to recall any-thing but the way in which we happened to perceive an event in the past." [31] He allows that "in our ordinary use of language we talk about remembering as if it were about past events, not about our perceptions of past events. It is also true that our memories, veridical and non-veridical alike, always *appear* to be about some objective past event or fact, not about our past perceptions." [32]

This appearance and this way of talking are misleading, von Leyden thinks: "Our recollections concern our perceptions of past events, not these events themselves." [33]

This is a surprising view. The first thought that occurs is that a perception of a past event is itself a past event, and therefore if one remembers perceptions, *ipso facto* one remembers some past events—namely, those perceptions—and not merely perceptions of them, i.e., perceptions of perceptions. In the second place, as a matter of contingent fact, one does not always remember one's per-ception of a past event that one remembers. Suppose that I saw an airplane crash and burst into flames. Subsequently I remember not only the crashing of the plane against the earth and the flames shooting upward, but also the terror and nausea I felt. Would this be a case of my remembering "my perception" of a past event? But suppose that a few years later I still remember the crashing and burning of the plane, but I no longer remember the terror and nausea I felt. Do I still remember "my perception" of the past event? If so, the meaning of saying this is entirely obscure. I re-member the crumpling of the wings. Do I, therefore, remember *my perception* of the crumpling of the wings? What does this *mean*? Is there any *difference* between my remembering the crumpling of the wings and my remembering my perception of the crumpling of the wings? If in this philosophical use of language they are identical, then what is being said?

Earle has a view that is similar to von Leyden's. He says: "At first glance it might seem that what I remember is simple past

events, the building burning yesterday. . . . But it is equally clear
that in fact I am not simply related to a past burning building, but
rather to my past *experience* of the burning building, since if I did
not experience it in the past, I certainly could not now remember
it, that is, remember myself experiencing it." [34] Earle says it is a
"phenomenological fact" that "what I now remember, the event, is
not an event taken simply but an event as experienced." [35] It appears, however, that he tries to establish this "phenomenological
fact" by an a priori argument, and a bad one to boot. The argument lies in the first quoted remarks: What I remember is an event
as experienced, since if I had not experienced it I could not remember it. This is a non sequitur. The logical grammar of "remember" requires that if I remember *x* then previously I witnessed,
learned about, or (in a broad sense) experienced *x*. It does *not
follow* that to remember *x* is to remember learning about, witnessing or experiencing *x*. Earle thinks that in remembering a burning
building "I now remember (myself looking at) a burning building." [36] But this is not necessarily true, and more often than not it
is not true at all. If I remember the Battle of Salamis I may not
remember reading about it or being told about it. Similarly, if I
remember the burning of the plane I might not remember myself
looking at the burning plane. (I can remember taking a walk without remembering the motion of my legs, although my legs must
have been in motion if I took a walk). My attention will have been
fixed on the burning plane and not on myself; so it is to be expected that what I remember is the burning plane and not myself
looking at it.

Brian Smith says, "Certainly it is difficult to see what remembering an event could be other than remembering our perceiving that
event." [37] It is not clear what these philosophers think the difficulty is, or what they are trying to say. Suppose I remember a

34. William Earle, "Memory," *Review of Metaphysics*, 10 (September 1956), 10.
35. Ibid., p. 11.   36. Ibid.
37. Brian Smith, *Memory* (New York: Humanities Press, 1966), p. 89.

riot in Trafalgar Square. It took place thirty years ago, and various
things happened which I can describe. But I don't remember now
whether I witnessed the riot myself or heard about it at the time
from people who did witness it. I remember the riot; but I do not
remember seeing it or that I saw it. This would seem to be a plain
case in which I remember an event but do not remember my perceiving that event (if I did perceive it). Now a philosopher can re-
tort, "I should not say that you *remembered* the riot, unless you witnessed it and remembered witnessing it." Such a remark would,
however, merely register a discontentment with the actual use of
the word "remember," which is broader. The remark is not an insight but an expression of unease.

Von Leyden presents an argument to establish that what we
remember is only our past perceptions. He says, "The best way to
convince ourselves of the fact that our recollections concern our
perceptions of past events, not these events themselves, is to take
the case of a distorted or delusive perception of a certain past event
and ask ourselves in what sense, if any, any subsequent memory
purporting to have this event as its object is mistaken." [38] His own
example is more or less like this: Suppose that from my bus window I saw a lot of people milling about in Trafalgar Square and
also saw cameras being trained on them. I took it to be the filming
of a scene for a movie, whereas in fact it was a riot. Later on I say,
"I remember seeing the filming of a movie in Trafalgar Square."
This is not true. I did not see the filming of a movie and so I cannot "remember" seeing it. What I said was wrong; but, as von
Leyden remarks, "my memory in the case described cannot itself
be held responsible for the mistake." [39]

My statement that I remember so-and-so was incorrect; but there
was no mistake of memory. This is actually an interesting fact
about the grammar of the word "remember." It was sharply
brought to my attention by an example invented by Jaakko Hintikka: A boy is taught that Columbus discovered America in 1392.

38. Von Leyden, p. 61.   39. Ibid., p. 62.

Subsequently he says, "I remember that Columbus discovered America in 1392." But that is wrong; he cannot properly say that; yet his *memory* is not wrong!

Von Leyden draws an erroneous conclusion from this point of grammar. He says, "had I succeeded in remembering the scene in Trafalgar Square in its true character, my achievement in this case, as compared with my failure in the other, would have been the result of a correct past perception on my part rather than of a correct memory." [40]

The fact is that if I had remembered the scene "In its true character" (namely, as a riot) this would have been the result *both* of a correct past perception on my part *and* of a correct memory. Of course von Leyden's point is that *the difference* between the "achievement" and the "failure" would *not* be that in the one case my memory was correct and in the other case incorrect. Nevertheless, if I had observed the scene in Trafalgar and had known or believed that it was a riot, I could properly say later on, "I remember the riot in Trafalgar Square." This is contrary to von Leyden's thesis that we cannot ever remember scenes, incidents, or situations, "as they occurred objectively." [41]

Let us suppose that although one boy was taught that Columbus discovered America in 1392, another boy was taught that this occurred in 1492. Subsequently, the first one says, "I remember that Columbus discovered America in 1392," and the second one says, "I remember that it was in 1492." The first one's statement is unacceptable, the second one's is true; yet the first one *remembers what he was taught* just as well as does the second one. Von Leyden's claim that we do not remember past events or facts "in themselves," but only our past perceptions, is analogous to claiming that the second boy does not remember that Columbus discovered America in 1492, but remembers only that *he was taught* that Columbus discovered America in 1492. But this is wrong. Having been taught that the date was 1492, and this also being true, the second boy can

40. Ibid.   41. Ibid., p. 66.

rightly say, "I remember that Columbus discovered America in 1492." He might continue to remember this all his life, even though he no longer remembered having been taught it or that he had been taught it.

4. It is widely assumed by philosophers, psychologists, and neuropsychologists that remembering is a *causal process*. This assumption sometimes influences their conceptions of what the objects of memory are. The idea that remembering is a causal process often assumes the following rough schema: first, there is an "input" into the person or organism; second, the input creates a state of the organism of short or long duration; third, the proper stimulation of this state produces an "output" in the form of either a "conscious memory" or a behavioral "memory performance." There are different notions of what the nature of the "input" is. Some would think that it consists of sensations, or impressions, or perceptions, or experiences. Others would hold that it consists of stimulations of sensory receptors, or of nerve pulses or patterns of nerve pulses, or of patterns of energy at the sensory receptors, or of sensory "information" in the sense in which this latter word is used in the science of information theory.

The question of whether memory or remembering is rightly conceived of as a causal process will be taken up in Part Two. My concern here is with a tendency to assume that what is remembered, the object of memory, is identical with the supposed causal "input." If the input is assumed to be sensations, then it is supposed that what is remembered is sensations; if the input is experiences, then what is remembered is experiences; if the input is patterns of nerve pulses or "signals," then what is remembered is patterns of pulses or signals; if the input is "information," then "information" is what is remembered.

I want to warn against any such assumption. When we reflect on the use of the words "memory" and "remember" in actual language, we see that the range of the objects of memory is very great. We remember houses, mountains, rivers, dogs, faces, people. Can a mountain or a dog be an "input?" We remember sensations (e.g., of dizziness or depression); but this is only *one* kind of object of memory. We remember information, but only in the ordinary sense of "information," not in the sense of information theory. We neither perceive nor remember nerve pulses or patterns of nerve pulses. We can perceive, and remember, bonfires, horseraces, incidents, jokes, names; and none of those things are patterns of nerve pulses. We can remember experiences; but many things we remember (equations, facts, police regulations, poetry, how to change a tire, the road to Monterey, the capitol of Wyoming, his look when she told him the news) are not experiences.

We should be on guard against any inclination to assume that what we remember must be sensory impulses, or must be experiences, or must be "information," or must be anything else, regardless of whether this inclination springs from the conception of memory as a causal process or from some other source. A true conception of the objects of memory can be obtained only from reflection on the use of the words "memory" and "remember" in daily language. This reflection reveals that the objects of memory constitute a far richer variety than many memory theorists have supposed.

CHAPTER II

Memory As Direct
Awareness of the Past

1. The philosophy of memory has been largely dominated by
what could be called "the representative theory of memory." In
trying to give an account of "what goes on in one's mind" when one
remembers something, or of what "the mental content of remembering" consists, philosophers have usually insisted that there must
be some sort of mental image, picture, or copy of what is remembered. Aristotle said that when we remember there is something
"like an imprint or drawing." [1] William James thought that there
must be in the mind "an image or copy" of the original event; [2]
Russell said, "Memory demands an image." [3] In addition to the
image or copy, a variety of other mental phenomena have been
thought to be necessary. In order for a memory image to be distinguished from an expectation image, the former must be accompanied by "a feeling of pastness." One has confidence that the
image is of something that actually occurred because the image is
attended by "a feeling of familiarity." And in order that you may
be sure not merely that the past event occurred but that *you* witnessed it, your image of the event must be presented to you with a
feeling of "warmth and intimacy." When all the required phenom-

1. Aristotle, *De Memoria et Reminiscentia*, 450b.
2. William James, *The Principles of Psychology*, 2 vols. (New York: Henry Holt,
1890), I, 649.
3. Russell, *The Analysis of Mind* (New York: Humanities Press, 1921), p. 186.

thing in the present act of remembering." [10] Does this mean that
the past object puts in an appearance? The past act of mind, which
experienced that past object, *does* "persist into the present," says
Alexander, although "it persists as past." [11]

I cannot obtain a clear grasp of Alexander's view. It is my impression that Alexander was torn between conflicting inclinations.
He wanted to say two things, one being that, when I remember
something I previously experienced, that thing reappears to me, or
is "compresent," or "persists into the present," although when it is
thus present it bears the character of being past. The other thing
Alexander wanted to say was that, when I remember something
from my past, that past thing is in no sense present.

A more recent writer, William Earle, maintains that memory is a
"direct vision" of the past. Earle emphatically repudiates the notion
that in remembering there is a copy or representation: "When I
recall a past event, there is, I believe, no sense in which I can be
said to form an *image, copy,* or *representation* of anything." [12] He
adds: "What I remember, then, cannot appear to me, the remem-
berer, as a copy of the past, but must appear as the past event itself." [13] Earle holds that we do not remember objects or events
simpliciter, but only objects or events *as experienced.* [14] A person does
not just remember a burning building, but he remembers himself
looking at a burning building. I argued in Chapter I that this particular claim is wrong; but that is not the present issue. The important point for us here is not the view that the memory of past
events is always the memory of experiences. What concerns us is
the claim that in remembering a past experience we do not have a
representation of it but are "directly aware" of the past experience.
Earle says, "I am now directly aware not of a copy of the past experience with its object, but of that past experience itself." [15] Yet,
he rejects Alexander's conception that the object of memory bears
the mark of the past. "If we turn to the intrinsic character of what

10. Ibid., p. 127.   11. Ibid.   12. Earle, "Memory," p. 5.
13. Ibid.   14. Ibid., pp. 10–11.   15. Ibid., p. 11.

it is we are remembering," says Earle, "it is clear, I think, that it does not and can not contain within itself the predicate 'past' . . . nothing remembered can carry the predicate 'past' stamped on its face. . . . If we should suppose, for a moment, that the event recalled had as one of its internal properties the fact that it was past, we should find ourselves in the ludicrous position of remembering an event which is past with respect to itself." [16] Earle says, "Memory declares itself to be memory by its own intrinsic character of being precisely an immediate awareness of the past . . . an immediate vision upon the past." [17]

He rejects the view that since "the past does not exist now" it "has no being whatever" and therefore that what "exists for inspection" is only a present image and not the past experience itself.[18] He allows that "the past does not exist *now*," but he denies that it does not exist *at all*. He argues as follows: "As past, it is the subject of true propositions, and precisely what would such propositions be *about* if their subject matter had fallen back into pure nothingness. . . . The past must be what true propositions assert it to be; the past therefore has its own distinctive and determinate mode of being." [19]

If a man shaved off his beard last week, then, according to Earle's reasoning, that beard has a "mode of being" since it is true, for example, that it was a *red* beard. The trouble with this "argument" is that one doesn't know what it *means* to say that the beard the man formerly wore "*has* a mode of being" although it was destroyed last week. The only clue I have to the understanding of this odd locution lies in Earle's argument: to say that the no longer existing beard "*has* a mode of being" just means that various propositions about it *are* true, which in turn just means that the beard *had* various properties. On this interpretation, Earle's obscure claim turns out to be a redescription, misleadingly in the present tense ("has"), of the undisputed fact that the beard *was* red, shaggy, and so on.

16. Ibid., p. 12.   17. Ibid., p. 18.   18. Ibid., p. 22.
19. Ibid., p. 23.

3. To turn to the main point, I find it hard to make much sense out of the attempt to explicate memory as the "direct awareness" of a past event or object. As philosophers have used the expression "direct awareness" (also "immediate acquaintance," "direct apprehension," and so on), one thing they have tended to mean is that if a person, B, is "directly" aware of something, *x*, then B's knowledge of the existence of *x* is *not* based on any inference or any mediation by or through something other than *x*.[20] This part of the meaning of "direct awareness" *does* have an appropriate application to memory. To remember last week's bonfire is *not* to *infer* its past existence.

Another important feature of the customary usage given by philosophers to the expression "direct awareness" is that B is "directly" aware of *x* only if B's assertion that he is aware of *x* *could not be mistaken*. But no one ought to claim that memory comes up to this requirement of "direct awareness." It certainly is not a logical or conceptual truth that if anyone asserts that he remembers that *p*, or that he remembers *x*, he cannot be mistaken.

A third implication, I believe, of "direct awareness," in its philosophical use, is that if B is "directly" aware of *x*, then B and *x* *coexist*. Philosophers like to speak of "direct awareness" of pains and mental images; but this direct awareness is thought to apply to *present* pains and mental images. This implication makes hard sledding for any interpretation of memory as direct awareness. Although a person can be said to remember someone who is standing right before him, it is also true that we speak of remembering last week's bonfire or earth tremor. The bonfire is not now burning nor the earth now trembling. Furlong, for example, remarks that it seems "absurd to say that we can be acquainted with what is no longer present."[21] This remark illustrates the philosophical use (but not the ordinary use) of the expressions "acquaintance," "direct acquaintance," "immediate awareness," and so on.

20. See Section II of my essay "Direct Perception," in my *Knowledge and Certainty*.

21. E. J. Furlong, *A Study in Memory* (London: Nelson, 1951), p. 40.

Earle declares that memory is "an immediate awareness of the past." The implication, in philosophical language, would be that, if Robinson *now* remembers last week's earth tremor, then the tremor *now* exists. Earle explicitly repudiates this consequence ("the past does not exist now"). Yet he is pushed toward it by the idea of "immediate awareness." The result is a meaningless compromise. The earth tremor stopped; "It does not exist *now*; but still it *has* a mode of being."

It seems to me that the only intelligible part of the half-articulate notion that memory is a form of immediate acquaintance or direct awareness lies in its rejection of the conception, more commonly favored by philosophers, that when we remember some past object the remembering is done by means of a present image, copy, or representation of the object. This negative criticism is sound. The positive aspect of the notion, the striving to say that in remembering the object of memory is "compresent," or "persists into the present," or "has a mode of being," presents nothing more than vague pictures. I think it just to remark that the intelligibility of the direct awareness doctrine consists exclusively in its saying "No!" to the representative theory of memory.

Several proponents of the representative theory have thought the doctrine of direct awareness to be of sufficient interest to require a fairly painstaking rebuttal. Broad, for example, regards the remembering of events, places, persons, things, as closely analogous to sense perception—so much so that he calls it "perceptual memory." In his treatment of sense perception, Broad, as is well known, rejects the view, which he calls "naive realism," that the sensum, or sense-datum, of which we are "directly aware," is identical with the perceived physical object or with any part of it. Similarly, he undertakes an elaborate refutation of "naive realism" concerning memory, which is the view that the "mnemic datum" (as we might call it) or the "objective constituent of the memory-situation" (as Broad calls it), *that* which one is supposed to be directly aware of when one remembers a past event, is identical with all or part of the remembered past event.[22] Price, too, devotes careful attention to the view that the so-called "image" which, according to him, has to be present in "cognitive" remembering, and which is presumably an object of direct awareness, is identical with the remembered past event. Price finds formidable difficulties in that view, as would be expected.[23] Furlong devotes a chapter to the doctrine of "direct acquaintance with the past," and rejects the doctrine.[24]

4. I think it is possible to understand what it is that generates the controversy between the representative and the direct awareness theories of memory. First of all, we start with the assumption that when genuine remembering occurs, there is something that is variously called a "memory-act," "memory-event," "memory-process," or "the present occurrence in remembering." The next step is to ask, What is the *content* of this act, event, or process? It is as if we thought of the memory-act or memory-process as being a *container* (something like a box); and then we ask, What is *in* this container? What are its contents?

Now since the act or process is *remembering something*, it would be natural to suppose that a description of the contents of the container would be a description of what is remembered. We remember many kinds of things: events, persons, books, remarks, facts, situations, names, melodies, smiles, and so on. We are tempted to think of what is remembered as *present* in the "container" of the memory-act or memory-process. This way of thinking immediately gets us into trouble. For example, Robinson remembers his wife's putting her car keys in the kitchen drawer. We feel an absurdity in saying that this past incident is *present* in the act of remembering. We are tempted to say, in such a case, that what Robinson really remembers is the *fact* that his wife put the keys in

22. Broad, *Mind and Its Place in Nature*, Ch. 5.
23. H. H. Price, "Memory-Knowledge," *Proceedings of the Aristotelian Society*, Suppl. 15 (1936).
24. Furlong, Ch. 3.

that drawer; for the fact has no date, and therefore it does not seem *quite* so absurd to say that the fact is "present in Robinson's remembering." But in many cases the translation into a fact-locution is not plausible. Robinson remembers his father's smile: we do not want to render this as, Robinson remembers that his father smiled. Thus we feel driven to hold that what is present in this memory-act is not the thing that is remembered, his father's smile, but some substitute for it, an image or mental representation of his father's smile. Since we have "a craving for generality," we postulate that in *all* cases the "content" of remembering is a substitute for what is remembered. This solution leaves us dissatisfied, however, precisely because the substitute is *not* what is remembered. This dissatisfaction produces the protests against the representative theory.

In *The Blue Book* Wittgenstein gives a nice diagnosis of these conflicting inclinations. In the passage I am going to quote he is speaking, not of remembering, but of *wishing;* yet the diagnosis is appropriate for remembering as well. He is speaking of the inclination to feel that when we wish for something to happen, there must be, in our wish, a *shadow* (as he calls it) of what we wish for.

The idea that that which we wish to happen must be present as a shadow in our wish is deeply rooted in our forms of expression. But, in fact, we might say that it is only the next best absurdity to the one which we should really like to say. If it weren't too absurd we should say that the fact we wish for must be present in our wish. For how can we wish *just this* to happen if just this isn't present in our wish? It is quite true to say: The mere shadow won't do; for it stops short before the object; and we want the wish to contain the object itself.[25]

In an earlier passage Wittgenstein mentions a similar problem about *expecting.* We expect something that has not yet happened. If we compare *expecting* with *shooting* (and of course we realize that we cannot shoot something that isn't there), this gives rise to the question, How can we *expect* something that is not there? Wittgenstein remarks that, just as with wishing, "The way out of this difficulty

25. Wittgenstein, *The Blue and Brown Books* (London: Blackwell, 1958), p. 37.

seems to be: what we expect is not the fact, but a shadow of the fact; as it were, the next best thing to the fact." [26] And, he says, "The shadow, as we think of it, is some sort of picture; in fact, something very much like an image which comes before our mind's eye; and this again is something not unlike a painted representation in the ordinary sense." [27]

The motivation for insisting on the presence of a representation, in expecting, wishing, and indeed, in all *thinking*, is not difficult to grasp. We can think of a friend who is far away, or one who is no longer alive. It seems that our friend himself cannot be present in our thought of him. We feel forced to hold, as did Descartes, Locke, and Hume, that what is there in our thought is an *idea* of our friend; and we are strongly inclined to conceive of the *idea* as a picture or image of him. With regard to *belief* (for example, the belief that it was Jones who stole the money) we have an overwhelming inclination to suppose that the object, or the "immediate" object, or the "content" of the belief, or "what is believed," is not the *fact* that Jones stole the money, nor the *event* of his stealing it, but is a proposition. This is "the shadow" of the fact or event. In *The Analysis of Mind*, Russell says, in regard to his belief that Caesar crossed the Rubicon:

This event itself is not in my mind when I believe that it happened. It is not correct to say that I am believing the actual event; what I am believing is something now in my mind, something related to the event . . . but obviously not to be confounded with the event, since the event is not occurring now but the believing is. . . . What is believed, however true it may be, is not the actual fact that makes the belief true, but a present event related to the fact. This present event, which is what is believed, I shall call the "content" of the belief.[28]

Russell goes on to call the present event, which is the "content" of the belief, a "proposition." [29] In his paper of 1919, "On Propositions: What They Are And How They Mean," he divides propositions into two categories, those composed of images and those com-

---

26. Ibid., p. 36.   27. Ibid.
28. Russell, *The Analysis of Mind*, pp. 233–234.   29. Ibid., pp. 241–242.

posed of words. He regards propositions of the first kind as primary: "The primary phenomenon of belief consists of belief in images." [30] Image-propositions are more fundamental than word-propositions: "A word-proposition, apart from niceties, 'means' the corresponding image-proposition, and an image-proposition has an objective reference dependent upon the meanings of its constituent images." [31]

It is inevitable that we should be drawn to the same conceptions in regard to memory. We may recall how Augustine declared that it is by images that we remember the things perceived by sense: "For surely the things themselves are not let into the memory, but the images of them only are with an admirable swiftness catched in." [32] The feeling that since we cannot have the presence of the things themselves we do want to have "the next best thing" is wonderfully expressed by James Mill, in his saying that, when he remembers a previous sensation, there is present in him something that is not identical with the sensation, yet is "more like" it "than anything else can be." [33]

We noted Russell's view that when one believes that Caesar crossed the Rubicon, *what* one believes, or the *content* of one's belief, is not "the fact that makes the belief true," but is a *proposition*. In the most fundamental cases, according to Russell, the proposition is an image or a configuration of images. Russell held that one can have different "attitudes" toward one and the same propositional content—that is, one can expect it, or remember it, or want it, or believe it, or be afraid of it, or be in doubt about it, or just "entertain" it, and so on.[34] With regard to the "cognitive" attitudes of expectation, memory, and mere "assent," they may have exactly the same "content," and will differ only in the nature of the "belief-

30. Russell, "On Propositions: What They Are And How They Mean," in Russell, *Logic and Knowledge*, ed. R. C. Marsh (New York: Macmillan, 1956), p. 308.
31. Ibid., p. 309.   32. Augustine, *Confessions*, II, Bk. 10, Ch. 9.
33. James Mill, *An Analysis of the Phenomena of the Human Mind*, ed. J. S. Mill, 2 vols. (London: Longmans, Green, 1878), I, 51–52.
34. Russell, *The Analysis of Mind*, p. 243.

feelings" that are directed toward that content. Thus the expectation that it will rain, the memory that it did rain, and the belief or "mere assent" that it is raining may have the same propositional content, namely, a visual image of rain.[35] Or, to take Russell's favorite example, when I remember what I ate for breakfast this morning, "the process of remembering will consist of calling up images of my breakfast, which will come to me with a feeling of belief such as distinguishes memory-images from mere imagination-images." [36]

An interesting consequence of Russell's view that the "content" of an expectation and of a memory may be the same is that the "content," i.e., the proposition believed, contains no *tense.* This is an inevitable development of his theory that "in the most fundamental case" the content, or proposition, is just a complex image, since it is difficult to see how *tense* could be indicated by an image. Russell says that "it is clear that the images may be the same for a memory and an expectation, which are nevertheless different beliefs. . . . If this is so, difference of tense, in its psychologically earliest form, is no part of what is believed, but only of the way of believing it." [37] Future tense, or past tense, is supplied by the particular belief-feeling. If the image were of rain, the image-proposition might be expressed by the words "rain" or "raining." The particular kind of belief-feeling called "expectation" turns this into "It will rain"; memory belief-feeling turns it into "It did rain." Rain is expected, and rain is remembered; so *rain* or *raining* is the "content" of belief in both cases. Many different "propositional attitudes" may be directed upon the same content. Suppose, says Russell, that you have "a visual image of your breakfast-table. . . . You may expect it while you are dressing in the morning; remember it as you go to your work; feel doubt as to its correctness when questioned as to your powers of visualizing; merely entertain the image, without connecting it with anything external, when you

35. Ibid., p. 250.   36. Ibid., p. 175.
37. Russell, *Logic and Knowledge*, p. 308.

are going to sleep; desire it if you are hungry, or feel aversion for it if you are ill." [38]

Russell's position presents a feature that is distinctive in its boldness. This is the doctrine that what any propositional attitude is attached to is some occurrence in the mind of the person who has the attitude. What I remember or expect "is something now in my mind," "a present event." [39] What I remember is in all cases something that is simultaneous with the remembering; it is the content of the remembering. Thus the truism, affirmed by Reid, that when I remember today the fragrant flower that I smelled yesterday it is that flower and that odor I remember, and not an image or an idea—this truism is denied by Russell's view that what is remembered is "a present event." Aristotle was puzzled as to how we *can* remember an absent thing, if what we are aware of in remembering is only a present picture. Russell's response to this puzzle is to *deny* that we can remember an absent thing! What we remember *is* the present picture.

Russell is, however, not entirely single-minded on this point. He holds that an occurrence of genuine remembering contains the judgment "this occurred," and that the reference of the demonstrative "this" is neither clearly the past event nor clearly the present image, but is vaguely *both*. He declares that "if the word 'this' meant the image to the exclusion of everything else, the judgment 'this occurred' would be false." This statement is plainly opposed to his other doctrine that what we remember *is* the present image. In view of the absurdity of this doctrine it is not surprising that Russell himself should contradict it.

5.   We are faced with two conceptions of the nature of remembering. One conception is that memory is a direct awareness of what is remembered; the other is that we remember by means of a representation of what is remembered. These conceptions are opposed to one another, and neither seems satisfactory. I suggested that the

38. Russell, *The Analysis of Mind*, p. 243.   39. Ibid., pp. 233–234.

following imagery may influence us: We assume that in genuine remembering there is an act, experience, or event of remembering. We think of this act or event as having a *content*. When we try to say what this content *is*, we are forced to choose between two alternatives. Either the content of the memory-act or memory-event is the occurrence, situation, or thing that we observed or learned about in the past; or the content is an image, copy, or representation of the past occurrence, situation, or thing. We tend to think of the memory-act or memory-event as a container; and then we have the question, What is *in* the container?

I want to propose that there is an error in the initial assumption. It is wrong to think that there is a "memory-act" or "memory-event," in the meaning that philosophers have attached to those terms. If we resist this assumption then we shall not be confronted with the imagery of a container, nor with the problem of deciding what is *in* the container. Thus this motive for choosing between the two conceptions of memory would be removed.

If we go back to the example of Robinson's remembering his wife's leaving her car keys in the kitchen drawer and try to pick out the memory-act, or the memory-event, or the remembering, we are completely frustrated. In response to his wife's query, "Do you remember where I put my car keys?", the most relevant thing that may have occurred was Robinson's walking immediately to the kitchen drawer and fetching out the keys. The philosophers who assume the existence of an act or event of remembering, and then are worried as to what the *content* of it is, will *not* want to say that this action of Robinson's *was* the remembering, or the memory-event or memory-act, or even was an experience of "ostensible memory." Why don't they want to say that? Because an action of that sort is capable of having many different *meanings*. We can imagine an action of that description occurring in circumstances where it would not be an expression of Robinson's remembering that his wife put her keys in that drawer. Suppose that Robinson had, in response to his wife's query, shrugged his shoulders and said "I'm sorry," but then had walked over to the drawer, opened it (in order to get a tool) and, surprised at seeing the keys there, had handed them over to her. In the situation as originally described, Robinson's action was a manifestation of his remembering where his wife put the keys. In the second situation it was not. An action described as "Robinson's walking over to the kitchen drawer, taking out the car keys and handing them over to his wife," obviously can mean different things in different situations. We could say that such an action is *potentially* ambiguous. But the philosophical belief in a "memory-act" or "memory-event" or occurrence of "ostensible memory" is a belief in something that is thought of as being *intrinsically un*ambiguous. The act of memory, whatever it is, is supposed to be an act of memory *whenever* it occurs. It is a definite act with a definite, fixed nature. It differs from perception, imagination, decision, or anything else. As Thomas Reid says, "We may remember anything which we have seen, or heard, or known, or done, or suffered; but the remembrance of it is a particular act of the mind which now exists and of which we are conscious." [40] The conception is the same that Hume had when, in speaking of "the will," he said, "By the *will*, I mean nothing *but the internal impression we feel and are conscious of, when we knowingly give rise to any new motion of our body, or new perception of our mind.*" [41] The conception clearly is that when you do something "willingly," there is a definite phenomenon of willing it: whenever *that* phenomenon occurred you would be willing that same thing. Similarly, Reid assumes that when you remember today the odor of a rose smelled yesterday there is a particular act of the mind which, whenever it occurs, can be nothing other than *the memory* of that odor; it could not, for example, be *the anticipation* of it, or *the desire* for it.

6.   I think it is unquestionable that when philosophers try to describe "the experience of remembering," when they seek to find out "what exactly happens when we remember some past event," they

40. Reid, *Essays on the Intellectual Powers of Man* (Edinburgh: Bell and Robinson, 1785), Essay III, Ch. 1.

41. Hume, *Treatise of Human Nature*, Bk. II, P. III, Sec. 1.

assume that something must take place, which always and when-ever it occurred would be the remembering of that event. This is why memory theorists have striven so hard to give a fine, exact, ac-count of "what happens" in memory. As previously noted, William James thought that a necessary component of memory was "the re-vival in the mind of an image or copy of the original event." [42] He also thought that this resembling image is not nearly enough. For one thing, the image must be "referred to the past." This requires not only "a general feeling of the past direction in time," but also that we think of some name or symbol of the event, or else think of some contiguous events.[43] But, furthermore, in order for *me* to remember the event as occurring in *my* past, it must be attended with a feeling of "warmth and intimacy." No wonder that a memory-event is "a very complex representation." [44]

Russell spells out the composition of the memory-event in still greater detail. The first component is, of course, an image which is a copy of the past event. Then there is some component which makes us not only refer the image to the past, but also place the remembered event in a time ordering with other events. Russell is not sure *what* this component of the memory-event is, but he makes three conjectures. One is that there is a specific "feeling of pastness"; another conjecture is that there is a succession of images "in the same order as their prototypes"; a third suggestion (the most remarkable one!) is that there is a set of simultaneous images which gradually *fade*, and "by fading, acquire the mark of just-pastness in an increasing degree as they fade, and are thus placed in a series while all sensibly present." [45]

It is instructive to note how completely and explicitly *theoretical* is Russell's treatment of the problem of how we achieve the right temporal ordering of remembered events. He says the following about "memory-images":

They must have some characteristic which makes us regard them as refer-ring to more or less remote portions of the past. That is to say if we sup-

42. James, I, 649.   43. Ibid., p. 650.   44. Ibid., p. 651.
45. Russell, *The Analysis of Mind*, p. 162.

pose that A is the event remembered, B the remembering, and *t* the interval of time between A and B, there must be some characteristic of B which
is capable of degrees, and which, in accurately dated memories, varies as *t*
varies. It may increase as *t* increases, or diminish as *t* increases. The question which of these occurs is not of any importance for the theoretic ser-
viceability of the characteristic in question.[46]

Russell says both that the characteristic in question belongs to the
"memory-images" and that it belongs to "the remembering"—
which is confusing, since he does not want just to identify the two.
It is best to regard this alleged characteristic as simply one component of the total "memory-occurrence." Russell's remarks make it
completely clear that he is not giving an introspective report. He
doesn't even know what the "characteristic" is; but he thinks he
knows that it *has* to be there. Why? Obviously, because if it were
not there, then we should not be *able to do* something that we do
every day, namely, remember the temporal order of various events.

   In order to account for this same ability, James Mill produced
the most remarkable hypothesis in the whole literature of memory.
He employs the example of his remembering an occasion of George
III's addressing the two Houses of Parliament. Mill remembers not
only the person of the king but also the sound of his voice; and also
he remembers the audience. But there is combined with these "objects" the "idea" of himself both as having witnessed the scene and
as now remembering it. Mill says:

Now, in this last-mentioned part of the compound, it is easy to perceive
two important elements, *the idea of my present self*, the remembering self;
and *the idea of my past self*, the remembered or witnessing self. These two
ideas stand at the two ends of a portion of my being; that is, of a series of
my states of consciousness, intervening between the moment of perception, or the past moment, and the moment of memory, or the present
moment. What happens at the moment of memory? The mind runs back
from that moment to the moment of perception. That is to say, it runs
over the intervening states of consciousness, called up by association. But
"to run over a number of states of consciousness, called up by association,"

46. Ibid.

is but another mode of saying, that "we associate them;" and in this case we associate them so rapidly and closely, that they run, as it were, into a single point of consciousness, to which the name *Memory* is assigned.[47]

It is probable that Mill's belief in this high-speed mental process was motivated more by a desire to explain how one *could remember* any past event than by a desire to explain how we can remember its correct temporal order, although the hypothesis (if it were any good) would explain the latter as much as the former. Of course it is incredible that anyone should testify that he *recalls* having ever performed the feat that Mill thinks we must always go through when we remember anything. This theory would possess no plausibility whatever unless one supposed that this rapid transitting of states of consciousness is something that either "the mind" or the brain does for us without our being conscious of the process.

To return to Russell's account of the components of "the memory-event," an additional feature of its is a "feeling of familiarity" that accompanies the images and makes us "trust" them. Finally, there is yet another component of the total memory-experience, namely, a distinctive "feeling of belief," which is not present when one is merely imagining something; this belief-feeling is "the distinctive thing in memory." [48]

My aim is not to display Russell's ingenious inventions, but to point out that his intention, and that of most other memory theorists, is to assemble a package that *is and can be nothing other than the remembering* of some particular event. This is strikingly shown by the fact that Russell does not even require that what is remembered should have *occurred*. As G. E. Moore noted, Russell seems to assume that whether a person remembered something "depends only on what his state was at the moment, never at all on whether what he thought he remembered actually occurred." [49] This is one significance of Russell's famous "sceptical hypothesis" that the world might have been created five minutes ago "complete with

47. Mill, I, 330–331.   48. Russell, *The Analysis of Mind*, p. 176.
49. G. E. Moore, *Philosophical Papers* (New York: Macmillan, 1959), p. 217.

memories and records." [50] The point is that if a person had a visual image of dogs fighting, together with "a sense of pastness," "a feeling of familiarity," and "a feeling of belief," then he would be *remembering* a dog fight, regardless of what else was or had been the case, even if there had never been any dog fights nor any dogs!

7.   In reviewing these attempts by philosophers to describe the mental content of remembering, one should be impressed by the implausibility and even incredibility of their proposals. A still more important thing to be noted is the crucial assumption that of course there is a "memory-act" or "memory-event." What do I mean by calling this an "assumption"? Surely Robinson *remembered*, when asked, where the keys had been put. His remembering this was an event, a happening in the world. This is true. The assumption I am talking about is the assumption that whenever it is true that a person, A, remembered x, at time t, then at t A did something, or something took place in his mind, *which was the remembering*. This assumption may appear to be obviously true, but in fact it is profoundly false.

If we study the actual details of examples of memory, not viewing them through the veil of theory, not assuming that something or other *must* be the case, we shall come upon nothing whatever that has the property of being *the remembering*. What we do find is nothing other than various actions, gestures, utterances, images, and thoughts, which in some contexts are "manifestations" of remembering, but when placed in other contexts are not.

An idea that influences our thinking about the psychological concepts in general is the idea that when a person expects, wants, intends, or remembers x (and so on, through the whole range of psychological concepts) there is some event that in some vague sense is present "in" him, or there is some state *of* him, and the *intrinsic* nature of the event or state is such that whenever *it* is present in a

50. Russell, *An Outline of Philosophy* (London: Allen & Unwin, 1927), p. 7. I study this "hypothesis" in the first of "Three Lectures on Memory" in my *Knowledge and Certainty.*

person, that person expects, wants, intends, or remembers *x*. The full-blown conception at work here is that remembering where you parked your car is a distinct state of consciousness, and remembering your dental appointment is a different and equally distinct one; deciding to water the lawn is a unique conscious impression, and deciding to trim the rose bushes is another one; expecting Mike to visit you is a specific mental phenomenon, and expecting Nancy is a different but equally specific one. For every different particular thing that is wanted, hoped for, expected, regretted, believed, remembered (and so on), an absolutely specific and different mental content occurs.

My attempt to characterize this philosophical idea is rough; but it is adequate if the vague picture comes through. Indeed, the idea *is* nothing more than this vague picture.

8.   I believe that an even more fundamental picture forces itself on us when, as philosophers, psychologists, neuropsychologists, or psycholinguists, we want to learn more about thinking, intending, expecting, wanting, remembering, and the other psychological phenomena. We want to know what these phenomena *are*, what they *consist in*. Since the human organism has an inside and an outside, it is a natural idea that remembering, intending, and so on occur either inside or outside: they must be either something *inner* or something *outer*.[51] I think one tends to regard it as self-evident either that remembering, for example, consists in the outward manifestations of memory (e.g., the smile of recognition, the utterances, gestures, and actions that display correct remembering), or possibly in propensities and dispositions toward such outward manifestations; or, on the other hand, that remembering consists in some *inner* states or events. That remembering is either something inner or something outer seems to be an exhaustive disjunction.

When we explore these alternatives, however, we are frustrated and baffled. Consider a case in which you recognize someone

51. See my "Wittgenstein on the Nature of Mind," *American Philosophical Quarterly*, Monograph No. 4 (Oxford: Blackwell, 1970), pp. 17 ff.

whom you meet on the street. Let us suppose that you smile at him and say "Hi," and then you add, "You look very brown!" "Been at the seashore," he says. The two of you continue on your separate ways. Did the recognition "consist in" your smile and your utterance of "Hi"? Surely not. Some people greet absolute strangers in that way. A very friendly person may say to a complete stranger, "My, you look brown!"

A philosopher might hasten to propose that the recognition did not consist in any *actual* behavior, but in a propensity or disposition to say or do certain things. But one is hard put to make this plausible. A propensity or disposition to do *what?* To answer "Yes" to the question, "Do you know that man?"? The Apostle Peter, fearing for his life, had no propensity to acknowledge that he knew Jesus. His fear was a so-called "countervailing" condition. To accommodate this obvious kind of objection a philosopher may seek to define a complex set of conditions, such that if *all* of them were satisfied then recognition would have occurred. But these attempts are always unsatisfactory; either some circumstance has been neglected, thus providing for the possibility of a counterexample; or else the definition has become so complex that no one, perhaps not even the author, can understand it. A more fundamental consideration is that there is no definite set of *all* the conditions that would be relevant to the question of, say, whether a person A had recognized a person B. In a particular context of circumstances it may be absolutely clear that A recognized B when he smiled at him and greeted him. This does not imply, however, that there is a nontrivial description of those circumstances that *logically* entails that A recognized B. With a little inventiveness we can imagine some further logically possible circumstance, such that if it were added to the description of the context it would be wrong, or at least no longer clearly correct, to say that A recognized B. There is no point at which we could rightly say, "Given *this* set of conditions, nothing else whatever would have any bearing on whether A recognized B." Gottlob Frege held that a concept "must have a sharp boundary." "A concept that is not sharply defined is wrongly termed a concept." [52] This is not true of most of the concepts we employ in ordinary life. We are not taught to use them, and do not intend to use them, in conformity with some rigid set of necessary and sufficient conditions. As Wittgenstein remarks: "If someone were to draw a sharp boundary I could not acknowledge it as the one that I too always wanted to draw, or had drawn in my mind. For I did not want to draw one at all." [53]

9.   These reflections may make us turn away from the attempt to define recognition in terms of behavior or behavioral propensities, and to move to the other alternative, namely, to hold that recognition is an *inner* state or occurrence. The same for intending, believing, wanting, remembering, and so on. The difficulty here, of course, is to *specify* what the inner something is. In the case of memory we surveyed the variety of candidates that various authors have proposed: images; feelings of pastness, familiarity, fittingness; a belief-feeling that belongs uniquely to remembering; and so on. Some of these items are preposterous inventions; others are things that sometimes occur but often do not. And sometimes these latter occur in cases that are not examples of remembering.

Since attention to the phenomenology of remembering does not produce any specifiable item that will qualify as the remembering, we may feel inclined to make the most stultifying move of all, namely, to conclude that remembering something (e.g., a dental appointment) is an indescribable, unspecifiable, event or state. We feel that we *know* what it is, but we cannot *say* what it is. We are inclined to exclaim, with a special intonation, "It is just a *particular mental event!*" We feel that it *had* to be there, since we certainly did remember the dental appointment. We want to say that it was "a *definite, inner, occurrence.*" We can almost *see* it! [54]

52. *The Philosophical Writings of Gottlob Frege*, ed. P. Geach and M. Black (Oxford: Blackwell, 1960), p. 159.

53. Wittgenstein, *Philosophical Investigations*, ed. G. E. M. Anscombe and R. Rhees; trans. G. E. M. Anscombe (Oxford: Blackwell, 1953), para. 76. Occasionally I modify the translation.

54. Ibid., para. 305.

This desperate resort to an unspecifiable inner event evidences the strong grip of the metaphysical idea that when, at a particular time, a person remembers something the remembering is an occurrence *in* him at that time. This way of thinking results in a host of unanswerable questions. First of all, there would be a *multitude* of indescribable inner events, corresponding to the multitude of psychological concepts. How could one *learn* which of them is *remembering?* If one could not learn this, would one ever be *entitled* to say, "Oh, I have just remembered that I have a dental appointment"? Or suppose that a person did, in some way, come to know which particular inner event his remembering a dental appointment is, but also happened to have a bad memory, and consequently *mistook* some *other* inner event for it—but yet said, correctly, "Oh, I have a dental appointment today!" and showed up at the dentist's office at the right time! Here I am paraphrasing and adapting Wittgenstein's remark:

"Imagine a person whose memory could not retain *what* the word 'pain' meant—so that he constantly called different things by that name—but nevertheless used the word in agreement with the usual indications and presuppositions of pain"—in short he uses it as we all do. Here I should like to say: a wheel that can be turned though nothing else moves with it, is not part of the mechanism.[55]

I will not dwell here any further on the untenability of the idea that remembering something (or wanting it, expecting it, believing it, and so on) is an indescribable, unspecifiable, inner event.[56] Right here, I will only say that a philosopher who clings to this idea is, I believe, forced to hold of these privately known inner events that all of them *show* their nature to each of us in such a way

55. Ibid., para. 271.
56. I have studied this notion in several writings. Among them are the following: "Wittgenstein's *Philosophical Investigations*," in *Knowledge and Certainty;* "Behaviorism as a Philosophy of Psychology," in *Behaviorism and Phenomenology,* ed. T. W. Wann (Chicago: University of Chicago Press, 1964), pp. 148–149); "Wittgenstein on the Nature of Mind"; "Memory and Representation," *Noûs,* (1970); *Problems of Mind* (New York: Harper & Row, 1971).

that we do not have to, and indeed cannot, *learn* what they mean, nor can we *forget* what they mean; they have their meanings "written on their face"; they are events that *cannot* be misinterpreted. I will return to this idea in Chapter V.

10.   Those philosophers who have tried to identify and analyze "the act of remembering" or "the present mental occurrence in remembering" have been engaged in a hopeless enterprise. No image, feeling, thought, utterance, or action is, intrinsically and regardless of circumstances, the remembering of a dental appointment. There are gestures, utterances, and pieces of behavior that, in the human contexts in which they occur, are expressions of memory. A smile and a greeting would reveal *recognition* in one context, but just *friendliness* in another. Wittgenstein speaks of trying to remove the temptation to suppose that there *must* be a mental event of sudden understanding, or of hoping, or wanting, or believing, alongside or underneath the *expressions* of understanding, hope, belief, and so on.[57] He suggests the following "rule of thumb": "If you are puzzled about the nature of thought, belief, knowledge, and the like, substitute for the thought the expression of the thought, etc." When we reflect on the futile endeavors of the memory theorists, perhaps the best way to sum up the reason for their failure is that the memory-event or act they are trying to pinpoint is nothing that does or could exist. People remember things; but nothing that occurs, either inner or outer, *is* the remembering. The question, "In what does remembering consist?", should be answered in this way: It doesn't consist in anything!

11.   Now here we may think of an alternative. Why not identify the remembering, in each context, with the *expression* of memory that occurs in that context? Thus, in one case, Robinson's remembering where his wife put the keys would *consist* in his walking to the right drawer and taking them out; in another case, his remem-

---

57. Wittgenstein, *The Blue and Brown Books*, pp. 41–42.

bering this would *consist* in his uttering the words, "You left them in the kitchen drawer"; in still another case, it would *consist* in his having an image of his wife dropping the keys in that drawer; and so on.

Stanley Munsat endorses this suggestion. He fixes on the phenomenon of *suddenly* remembering something, and he addresses himself to the traditional question, *What happens when a person suddenly remembers something?* He discusses this matter with acuteness. He remarks:

> We know perfectly well what things or what sorts of things occur when someone suddenly remembers something. Sometimes, for example, the person who suddenly remembers something snaps his fingers and then charges off to do something, like taking the pot off the stove. And if these seem to be only "outward manifestations" of the *real* "suddenly remembering," perhaps we might mention such things as feelings of excitement, mental pictures, a sudden intake of breath. Have we now gotten to what is essential to suddenly remembering? Have we now penetrated the superficial "side effects" of suddenly remembering and gotten down to the real hard-core of the occurrence or process known as suddenly remembering? But none of these things can be what we are after either, for all of these might occur yet it be a case not of suddenly remembering, but, for example, suddenly realizing or suddenly figuring out that, or its suddenly occurring to one, or simply suddenly being struck by the fact that. . . . We are inclined to feel that a football, wherever it is and whatever is done to it, is a football; and, so too, a phenomenon which we point to as an example of suddenly remembering, wherever and whenever it should occur, is suddenly remembering. . . . But it is precisely because this is the sort of thing that we want to find that we will never find it. . . . And the reason why we will not settle on any one or combination of these as composing the essence of suddenly remembering is that none of these phenomena are in themselves or in combination either necessary or sufficient for the occurrence of the phenomenon of suddenly remembering.[58]

These remarks are perceptive and precisely right. Munsat then goes on to say something puzzling:

58. S. Munsat, *The Concept of Memory* (New York: Random House, 1967), pp. 41–43.

"Suddenly remembering" does indeed name a mental occurrence or episode. When I say "I just remembered . . . ," I am giving voice to something which just happened. What "just happened" *may* be, for instance, that I just had a mental image, and nothing else. I see no reason not to say that in such cases, the suddenly remembering consisted of the having of a mental image. However, it must be realized that this same image, occurring in a different context, could *not* be taken as a case of suddenly remembering.[59]

It seems to me that here some of the previous insight is lost. When I exclaim, "Oh, I just remembered that I have a dental appointment!", what "I am giving voice to" (to use Munsat's phrase) is not that I had an image of a dental chair (if I did have one). What I am giving voice to (if my memory is correct) is just this—that I suddenly remembered a dental appointment. It appears to me that Munsat was yielding here to the inclination to picture sudden remembering as something "inner" or "mental." Why else does he say that it is "a mental occurrence"? Is he thinking that one time it might be one mental occurrence and, another time, a different mental occurrence? The fact is, however, that there might be no mental occurrence *at all* in a case of sudden remembering, not even an experience of seeming to oneself to remember. For example, you and I are groping to recall the name of a mutual acquaintance: suddenly you exclaim "Prince!" and I say "Right!" Perhaps all that happened when you suddenly remembered the name was that you uttered the name. Was just that, by itself, a "mental" occurrence? I doubt that anyone will want to say so.

In addition to the mistaken claim that the expression "suddenly remembering" *names* "a mental occurrence," Munsat seems to me to be ill-advised in his apparent willingness to say that when, in suddenly remembering my dental appointment, if what happened was that I had an image of a dental chair, then the sudden remembering *consisted of* my having that image. If what happened was that I snapped my fingers and said "Dentist!", it would be equally per-

59. Ibid., p. 47.

missible to say that the sudden remembering consisted of *those* occurrences. Munsat is well aware that the meaning of such occurrences depends on their contexts. He is also aware that the typical
philosophical urge to uncover the nature of sudden remembering is
a desire to penetrate to some event or state that is *intrinsically* sudden remembering, a phenomenon such that "wherever and whenever it should occur" it would be sudden remembering. I think that
the cleanest way to react to this philosophical urge is to brand it as
an illusion, arising from a misconception about the concept of
memory and the other psychological concepts. It puts matters in
the clearest light to say that sudden remembering does *not consist in
anything*, rather than to say that one time it consists in a certain
expression of memory, another time in a different one, and so on.
At least this is how it appears to me.

12. Let me summarize the position I have been taking. There
have been two opposed views about the "content" of remembering.
One view is that in memory we are "directly aware" of the events
and objects that we witnessed in the past. The other view holds
that this cannot be, and that "the immediate given" of remembering is a present representation. The proponents of both positions
seem to have the idea that when a person remembers a certain
thing, x, something occurs that is "intrinsically" the remembering
of x. This occurrence is called the "experience," "act," or "event" of
remembering. The question that the two positions quarrel over is,
what is "contained" or "present" in the event of remembering? Is it
"the past event which we are *said* to be remembering," [60] or is it a
representation in the form of some "present mental occurrence"?
My own belief is that the assumption of an intrinsic memory-event,
when closely considered, simply fades away, no longer felt to be
intelligible. With its disappearance one is freed from the necessity
of choosing between these two rival "theories" as to what its *content*
is, and a fortiori from the necessity of thinking that since the past

60. Russell, *The Analysis of Mind*, p. 164. Emphasis added.

occurrence cannot be there in the memory-event, therefore what *is* there is a representation. In this way I try to remove *one* source of the assumption that there has to be a representation in remembering. More will be said about this assumption in Chapter V.

CHAPTER III

Genuine Memory Occurrences

1. We must take note of a philosophical idea that the actual grammar of the words "memory" and "remember" is seriously misleading. Some philosophers say that not everything that is *called* "memory" really is memory. They will say that memory "essentially" has certain properties, and that although we may call something "memory" that does not have those properties, it is not memory in the "strict" or "full" or "true" sense of the word. Suppose that a boy has been told to wipe his shoes on the mat before entering the house. Sometimes he does and sometimes he doesn't; when he does, it is said that he "remembered" to wipe his shoes, even though he may not have had the thought, "Now I must wipe my shoes," or may not even have realized that he had wiped his shoes. The philosophers referred to would say that this was not "genuine" memory.

Bergson gives an example of a contrast in two uses of "remember." Suppose that you decided to memorize a particular poem. You open the book and read the poem for the first time. You read it again and again until finally you succeed in memorizing it: this can be expressed by saying that now you "remember" it. You might also "remember" *that first occasion* of reading it. Bergson says that there is an important difference in the meaning of "remember" in these two cases. The remembering of the words of the poem is, he says, a "habit" acquired by repetition. To remember that particular occasion of reading the poem is not a habit. That particular occasion of reading it is an event with a date, and this event cannot be repeated. The memory of that "unique" event is a "representation" of it, whereas the other form of memory, "habit-memory," is not a representation but an "action." One can have the representation of the unique event "all at once," but remembering the words is "a series of movements spread out in time." Representational memories are "spontaneous," and they represent the past in images. (They also have effects on the body in the form of new dispositions to action.) Habit-memory, as said, does not *represent* the past. It is merely "an action of the body." The spontaneous representation of a particular past event is memory *par excellence*. Of habit-memory Bergson says, oddly, that it is memory "only because I remember that I acquired it." Habit-memory is "habit illuminated by memory rather than memory itself." [1]

2. We shall be examining a distinction that is commonly made by philosophers between memory as an *ability, power,* or *disposition,* and memory as an *occurrence*. It is often called a distinction between "dispositional" and "occurrent" memory. Roughly speaking, the idea is that there is a use of "remember" in which remembering is an *ability* to do something; and there is another use of "remember" in which remembering is *doing* it. It should be noted here that the "dispositional-occurrent" distinction does not coincide with Bergson's distinction between "true" memory (or memory *par excellence*) and "habit" memory. His "habit-memory" has dispositional and occurrent aspects. A man may remember a poem although he is not repeating it either aloud or to himself. One thing we may mean in saying that he "remembers" it is that he is *able* to repeat it from memory. Suppose we doubt that he remembers it; we ask him to repeat it, and to our gratification he does. We exclaim, "He remembered it!" (We wondered whether he was able to do something; and then he did it.) On the basis of his performance we could say both that he *remembers* it (meaning that he is able to repeat it) and that he *remembered* it (meaning that he did repeat it).

1. Henri Bergson, *Matière et Mémoire*, 6th ed. (Paris: Alcan, 1910), pp. 75–77.

In exactly the same way we can distinguish dispositional and occurrent aspects of the man's memory of his *first reading* of the poem. Suppose that we wonder whether he does remember the occasion; so we put him to the test. He then relates that he was leaning on a chair, and holding the book of poems in one hand and a glass of wine in the other; and that his friends, A and B, listened as he read aloud. This was the kind of account we were looking for, and on the basis of it we can say both that he *remembers* the occasion and that he *remembered* it.

3.   Russell wanted to adopt Bergson's distinction between "true" and "habit" memory; but he thought that even if the object of memory was a unique event it did not *follow* that remembering it was "true" memory; it might still be mere habit-memory. Russell says: "There is, for example, a habit of remembering a unique event. When we have once described the event, the words we have used easily become habitual. We may even have used words to describe it to ourselves while it was happening; in that case, the habit of these words may fulfill the function of Bergson's true memory, while in reality it is nothing but habit-memory." [2] He goes on to make the following interesting remarks:

In spite, however, of a difficulty in distinguishing the two forms of memory in practice, there can be no doubt that both forms exist. I can set to work now to remember things I never remembered before, such as what I had to eat for breakfast this morning, and it can hardly be wholly habit that enables me to do this. It is this sort of occurrence that constitutes the essence of memory. Until we have analyzed what happens in such a case as this, we have not succeeded in understanding memory. [3]

It is clear that Russell did not think of the distinction between "habit" memory and "true" memory as coinciding with the distinction between "dispositional" and "occurrent" remembering. If you asked me what I ate for breakfast two days ago, I might give an accurate account of it, from memory. This would be an instance of

2. Russell, *The Analysis of Mind*, p. 166.   3. Ibid., pp. 166–167.

"occurrent" remembering, as many philosophers use this term; but according to Russell it might not be "true" memory. For one thing, it would be "true" memory only if I had *images* of my breakfast. Russell says:

> Suppose you ask me what I ate for breakfast this morning. Suppose, further, that I have not thought about my breakfast in the meantime, and that I did not, while I was eating it, put into words what it consisted of. In this case my recollection will be true memory, not habit-memory. The process of remembering will consist of calling up images of my breakfast, which will come to me with a feeling of belief such as distinguishes memory-images from mere imagination-images.[4]

The belief that accompanies the images is a belief about the images, namely, the belief that what they picture or represent did occur. As Russell puts it, the "feeling of belief" that accompanies memory-images "may be expressed in the words 'this happened'." [5] But one does not have to believe that the images are *perfect* pictures or "copies" of what happened: "We may take it that memory-images, when they occur in true memory, are (a) known to be copies, (b) sometimes known to be imperfect copies." [6] Both Bergson and Russell agree that "true" memory requires *images*. "Memory *demands* an image," says Russell.[7]

4. This idea that remembering is not "true" or "genuine" remembering unless memory-images occur is very curious. Suppose that the following question is angrily put to me by a member of my family: "When you came home today did you enter by the back door or the front door?" Now Russell says, "What is the present occurrence when we remember?",[8] and Furlong asks, "What happens when we remember?" [9] The answer is that a number of different things could have happened. Let us consider a few of the possible cases:

    1) At first I don't know the answer to the question. Then I say

4. Ibid., p. 175.   5. Ibid., p. 176.   6. Ibid., p. 160.
7. Ibid., p. 186. Emphasis added.   8. Ibid., p. 173.
9. Furlong, *A Study in Memory*, p. 72.

aloud: "Let's see now. I rode home with Robinson. I got out in front of the house. I remember now that I walked down the driveway; so probably I came in the back door. Yes, I did. I remember wiping my shoes on the back porch and opening the screen door. But I didn't track in any mud, if that is what you are after." While saying these things I have no images, but I am looking with alarm at the angry face of the person I am addressing.

2) I say: "I seem to remember coming in the back door. Why do you ask?" To myself I am thinking with annoyance: "What is the purpose of this inquisition?"

3) I am at a loss. I do not say anything, and I try to picture what happened. Suddenly I see myself opening the back door, and I say with confidence: "I came in the back way. Did I do something wrong?"

4) I am repairing a light switch and am irritated by the intricacy of the mechanism. I answer abruptly, without imagery and without any silent thinking. "Back door. Now where does this blasted part go?"

5) I say: "I'm sorry. I forgot that we weren't supposed to use the back door. I hope I didn't step in the varnish?" I feel guilty, and I have an image of a footprint in wet varnish.

This is a tiny selection from the possible cases. Which of them are examples of "true" memory of my having come in by the back door? Would case 3 be the only one? But perhaps even 3 does not qualify, since my image was only of myself *opening* the back door and not of myself entering the back door. So was it "true" memory only in respect of the former and not the latter?

5. It is important to understand why memory-images bear such a critical weight in philosophical conceptions of "true" or "genuine" memory. For it is clear that they do not have *that* much significance in ordinary life and thought. Cases 1 through 5 would all be regarded in ordinary life as examples of remembering that one entered the back door. The question as to which of them was "true" or "genuine" remembering would scarcely be comprehended. Yet

philosophers have attributed the utmost importance to that distinction. Price once said:

It seems clear that we *could* not have memory-knowledge without some sort of image. What we might be tempted to describe as "imageless memory" is really memory in the purely practical sense of remembering how to *do* so and so. The doing might of course consist in uttering words; and the words might make up a sentence which did *de facto* correspond to a past situation; but we should not be remembering that situation (in the cognitive sense of "remember") though other people might think that we were.[10]

Thus if I am asked whether I came in the back door, and I answer without hesitation that I did, this would not be an example of remembering, in the "cognitive" sense, unless I had "some sort of image" of myself coming in the back door. There is also the implication that remembering in the "cognitive" sense is "true" memory, memory *par excellence*, the real McCoy. Why is the presence of an image so crucial? What does it do? Price gave an interesting answer to this question. In speaking of the "function" of a memory-image, he said: "Its function is *directive*. It gives a specific direction to our act of memory-knowing. It directs our attention upon just this part of the past as opposed to other parts." [11] What the image does, or what we do with it, is to pick out a particular chunk of the past. Price's remarks suggest this notion: that in having a memory-image the mind's attention is fixed upon some portion of the past, namely, the portion that the image pictures. If I said, "I came in the back door," without benefit of memory-image, then I should not be attending to that past event. It would not be an object before my mind, and therefore I should not really be referring to it or meaning it, when I uttered those words.

6.   Broad says that many things that are called "memory" in ordinary language "do not really deserve the name." [12] What are some of these forms of pseudo-memory? The first he describes as follows: "It is a fundamental fact about living organisms that, when

10. Price, "Memory-Knowledge," p. 25.   11. Ibid., pp. 32–33.
12. Broad, *Mind and Its Place in Nature*, p. 270.

they have performed a certain set of movements several times, they tend to acquire a more or less permanent power of repeating these movements with greater or less accuracy from time to time when suitably stimulated." [13] Broad says that this capacity should be called "retentiveness" rather than "memory." A second form of pseudo-memory, according to Broad, is the following: "We may acquire by practice the power of performing at will certain characteristic sets of bodily movements, such as those which are used in swimming. If we find that we can still swim when we get into the water after an interval, we should commonly say that we 're-member how to swim' or 'remember the movements of swimming.' *There is nothing cognitive about 'memory,' in this sense.*" [14] The third form of alleged pseudo-memory is a special instance of the second: "We may acquire by practice the power of uttering or writing at will a certain set of noises or marks, as a parrot or a monkey might do. There is no essential difference between this and the last case, if the noises or marks are meaningless to us." [15] Broad says of this third form, "Here too 'memory' is not a form of *cognition;* it is simply a kind of bodily action such as we perform when we find ourselves still able to swim after an interval." [16] The fourth example of pseudo-memory is described as follows:

One peculiar capacity which we may acquire by practice and retain is the power to call up an image which in fact resembles something that we have repeatedly seen or heard in the past. If we can do this, an external observer who knew of the fact would be inclined to say that we are remembering the thing which we have seen or heard in the past which the image in fact resembles. *But this would not be an accurate use of the word "memory" unless the image seems familiar to us and leads us to make memory-judgments.* Apart from this we have merely acquired and retained a peculiar kind of capacity; and "to remember," in this sense, is no more to perform a special kind of cognitive act than to swim is. [17]

Broad declares that "the four kinds of 'memory' which I have so far mentioned do not really deserve the name. In themselves they are

13. Ibid., pp. 268–269.   14. Ibid., p. 269. Emphasis added.   15. Ibid.
16. Ibid., p. 170. Emphasis added.   17. Ibid. Emphasis added.

modes of *behavior*, and not modes of *cognition*. . . . Such acquired
and retained modes of behavior may be necessary conditions of
genuine memory, but they are nothing more." [18]

We arrive at full-fledged cases of "genuine" memory only when
memory-judgments occur, i.e., when we judge that we made these
movements or heard these sounds before, or judge that we made
them or heard them on some particular occasion in the past. The
mere repetition of movements, sounds, or images is not memory:
but when we add the two features that, first, the movements and so
on feel familiar and, second, that the person judges that the movements or sounds occurred before, then we have "genuine" memory.
This is "a peculiar kind of cognition in which we seem to be in contact with a part of our own past history and with events which we
then experienced." [19] Broad offers the following explanation of
why the word "memory" is so frequently "misused":

I think that the name "memory" is often applied by external observers to
the first four cases (of pseudo-memory) because they unwittingly assume
that what is in fact a repetition of a past mode of behavior and is in fact
causally dependent on past behavior or past perception must be accompanied by a feeling of familiarity and a more or less determinate memory-
judgment about the past. A very little careful introspection will suffice to
show that this is a mistake. [20]

It may be doubted whether anyone other than a philosopher has
ever made the assumption that the movements of swimming, for
example, "must be accompanied by a feeling of familiarity and a
more or less determinate memory-judgment about the past," in
order to be "remembered." There could scarcely be a more implausible explanation of why we say in common language that a person
who learned the flutter-kick, and is still able to do it, "remembers"
the flutter-kick.

What I find of chief interest in Broad's discussion is the assumption that *genuine* memory, that which really deserves the name,
must include a feeling of familiarity and a judgment. What could

18. Ibid., pp. 270–271.   19. Ibid., p. 271.   20. Ibid.

be the justification for saying that only when those features are present do we have "memory" in the *proper* sense of the word? How is it to be decided what is the proper sense of the word other than by taking note of how the word is used? The actual use of the word is far from being as narrow as Broad thinks it should be—but what is the authority for his "should be"? Clearly there is none.

7.   Broad's view is interesting, not because it helps to reveal the true nature of memory, for it does not do that, but because it presents a philosophical "idealization" of remembering. An outstanding feature in this ideal conception is the requirement of *a judgment*. The function of "the feeling of familiarity" would seem to be subordinate to that of the judgment. I suspect that the feeling of familiarity is supposed to play a role similar to that which the image does in Price's view. Price said that the image "directs our attention." I believe Broad would say that the feeling of familiarity "guides our judgment." It enables us to make the judgment that we had seen or heard or done a particular thing in the past; the making of the judgment is a genuine "act of cognition." Broad says genuine remembering requires "a special kind of cognitive act." [21] Price says that remembering "in the cognitive sense" requires, or is, an "act of memory-knowing." Many philosophers have said that remembering is "a particular act of the mind." [22] It is pretty clear that the act of mind is thought to be an act of judging that x occurred or that x was previously witnessed or experienced.

This shows that, in this philosophical idealization, remembering is essentially *propositional*. A judgment is a *judgment that p*. In the case of memory the judgment is supposed to be about the past. So a "memory-judgment" must be the judgment that so-and-so occurred, or that so-and-so was witnessed by the judging subject.

Russell says that in "true" memory there is an image plus "a feeling of belief." The latter may be expressed in the words "This happened." Here the feeling of belief clearly embodies a judgment, an

21. Ibid., p. 270.   22. For example, Thomas Reid.

attitude of affirming a proposition. The function of the image, we may surmise, is *to provide a proposition*, something which can be asserted. The image furnishes a *content* for the judgment. Without an image the judgment would be *empty:* one would not be asserting anything.

The idea that the memory-image provides the proposition to which the memory-judgment is applied is made quite explicit by Stout. In speaking of the role of images in memory he says that an image "more or less resembles" a previous impression or sensation: it is "conceived as being a modified recurrence or reinstatement of the original sensation." [23] The part played by the image in "the act of remembering" is to provide an object for our thought. Stout says:

It is the existential presence and the nature of the image which determines for thought the occurrence of a certain past impression as its special object. The image is the specifying content of the thought, determining it as the *idea* of a specific impression. Apart from the image or something discharging an equivalent function, this thought would be empty—indeterminate or directionless; apart from thought the image would be blind—without reference to anything beyond itself, and, therefore, without reference even to itself. [24]

It is far from clear what Stout means by "thought" here. But it is plausible to suppose that he means the same propositional attitude that Russell called "belief" and Broad called "judgment." The object or content of thought is a proposition—that so-and-so is the case; or, perhaps better, so-and-so's *being* the case. The proposition is presented for judgment embedded, so to speak, in an image. Without a memory-image there would be nothing for a memory-judgment to affirm or deny. If no judgment occurred there would be no "act of cognition" and, therefore, no remembering "in the cognitive sense." In this philosophical idealization of memory, remembering is or involves a "particular act of the mind." This act is

23. G. F. Stout, *Studies in Philosophy and Psychology* (London: Macmillan, 1930), p. 366.
24. Ibid., p. 367.

the act of judging that a proposition is true or false. Now if (as is likely) the small boy who "remembers" to wipe his shoes on the mat does not formulate and affirm in his mind the proposition, "I have been told to do this," then a philosopher whose thinking is captured by the idealized conception of memory will say that the boy's remembering to wipe his shoes was not "true" or "genuine" remembering. This philosopher will feel further constrained to say, on reflection, that many or even most other applications of "remember," in ordinary language, are not "accurate" uses of the word.

8.   It will be useful to look again at the proposals that have been made as to what "the mental process of remembering" is, or how remembering "works." Various complex mental processes have been suggested. We must note, however, that these theories are put forward as accounts of "occurrent" remembering and not of remembering in the sense of an ability or disposition. This distinction was mentioned previously, but it should be discussed more fully. We said that the rough idea of the distinction is that there is a use of "remember" in which remembering is an *ability* to do something; and there is another use of "remember" in which remembering is *doing* it. Philosophers often designate this contrast (misleadingly, as will be seen) as a distinction between "dispositional" memory and "occurrent" or "episodic" memory.

Broad says that there is a difference between "memory-powers" and "memory-acts." He says: " 'To remember' is an ambiguous word, which covers both an act and a power. When I say that I remember so-and-so I may be referring either to the power or to a particular present exercise of the power. When I say that I *am* remembering so-and-so I am understood to be referring to a particular present exercise of the power, and not merely to the power itself." [25] We ought to be struck by the oddity of Broad's use of the continuous present, "I am remembering." Do we say, "I am re-

---

25. Broad, p. 223.

membering that he fell in the mud," or rather, "I remember that he fell in the mud"? If someone asked, "Do you remember what you did with the suitcase?", I would answer, "I remember putting it under the bed," not "I am remembering putting it under the bed."

I do not claim that the continuous present or past of "remember" is never used. Suppose several people are chatting together and a friend approaches and asks what they are talking about. One of them might reply: "We are remembering the dances we used to have in the village." I would take this to mean that they were *recalling* those dances, or *reminiscing* about them. To my ear the word "remembering" seems somewhat inappropriate, strained, here; but perhaps it is not. In any case, it appears that the continuous forms of "remember" are equivalent to "recalling" or "reminiscing" or "reliving in memory." "Recalling" is "calling to mind." You can say that a dog remembered where he hid his bone, but it would sound funny to say that he "recalled" where he hid it. This is because there is no clear sense in saying that a dog calls things to mind. Watching a person's face you might think, "He is remembering the embarrassment he felt on that occasion." [26] You mean that he is recalling his embarrassment, reliving it, dwelling on it in memory. You would expect him to be having images and sensations connected with that humiliating scene.

9.   It would seem that, in Broad's distinction between "memory-acts" and "memory-powers," a memory-act is *recalling* something, i.e., calling it to mind. This suggests to me that a memory-act is thought of by Broad as "genuine" remembering just because it is calling something *to mind*. In further elaboration of his distinction, Broad remarks that if someone asked him, "Do you remember Jones?",

I might quite truly answer "Yes" even though I were not at the time performing any memory-act at all. So long as I believe that I *could* remember [him] *if* I tried I should be justified in saying that I do remember [him]. If,

26. I owe this example to Robert Shope.

on the other hand, he had said to me: "Are you remembering Jones?" I should not be justified in saying: "Yes" unless I were at the time actually the subject of a memory-situation with Jones as its epistemological object.[27]

Broad's technical terminology is forbidding. Ignoring it, the natural meaning of "Are you remembering Jones?" would be to ask whether one was "dwelling in memory" on how Jones looked, smiled, frowned, or on some of the strange, or typical, things he used to do or say. If a "memory-act" is recalling something or dwelling on it in memory, then in a great many cases when we remember things there is *no* memory-act. Suppose that when Robinson comes home from work he usually lays down his car keys in different places and then often forgets, the following day, where he left them. This particular morning we are interested in observing whether Robinson will remember the whereabouts of the keys. Before leaving the house, and while absorbed in a conversation with us, he walks to the basket in which he dropped the keys yesterday, takes them, and then departs. We say to each other, "He remembered this time!" It need not have been the case that he *visualized* the keys or the basket, or that he *recalled* putting them there (if one means by this, *calling to mind* his putting them there), or that he *relived* or *dwelt in his mind on* the event of his putting them there the previous day. The case, as I describe it, is not an instance of Bergson's or Russell's "habit-memory" or Broad's "retained mode of behavior," since my hypothesis is that Robinson did not often put the keys in that basket—indeed might have never done so before. Nor did Robinson search about in many places until he found the keys, but instead went smoothly and directly to the basket. Nor had he spotted them there just before, since the basket was placed behind a chair where he would not have seen it. And so on. This was as genuine an example of remembering as one could have, and yet there was no "memory-act" in the sense of Broad, nor any "memory-judgment," nor was it "genuine" memory in Bergson's or Russell's tendentious sense of this expression.

27. Broad, p. 222.

10. Broad's conception of a distinction between powers and acts is what many philosophers would subscribe to as a distinction between "dispositions" and "occurrences"; and they would say that an expression of the form "I remember x" may mean either a disposition or an occurrence. For example, Wrinch says that there is an ambiguity in the sentence, "I remember the face of the girl I saw yesterday":

> I may mean that a definite phenomenon is occurring which may be called "a memory of the face of the girl I saw yesterday". On the other hand, I may mean that I could produce a phenomenon of this kind. . . . A memory of the second kind can be called a dispositional memory and one of the first kind a memory act. A dispositional memory, then, can be said to be a possibility of memory acts.[28]

In some previous writing of mine on memory I distinguished something that I called "perceptual memory," stipulating that "perceptual memory," as I used the expression, *required* memory images.[29] I still believe (although other philosophers have disagreed) that when we say "I remember x," sometimes we *mean* "I have an image of x," and that when we say "I don't remember x," sometimes we *mean* "I don't have an image of x," or "I don't picture x," or "I don't see (hear) x in my mind." For example, if I were asked, "Do you remember a student named Grabowski who took a course with you several years ago?", I might reply, "I do remember that I had a student of that name; I seem to recall that he wrote good essays; but at the moment I don't remember him." After some striving I might say, "*Now* I remember him; he was blond and smiled a lot." I believe that there is a use of the expression "Now I remember him!" in which I would not say that *unless* I had *visualized* him.

I suspect that this is the sort of phenomenon that Wrinch has in mind when she speaks of having "a memory of the face of the girl I saw yesterday." If this is correct, then Wrinch is holding that "memory acts" are cases of perceptual memory, and that all, or at

---

28. D. Wrinch, "On the Nature of Memory," *Mind*, 29 (1920), 46.
29. See my *Knowledge and Certainty*, pp. 204 ff.

least the most fundamental, occurrences of remembering are instances of perceptual memory. I believe this view to be mistaken.[30]
It is possible that there should be, and perhaps are, people who
have no capacity for visual, auditory, or other imagery, and who,
therefore, have no capacity for perceptual memory, and yet who
function quite well at remembering appointments, where they left
their keys, the recipe for lentil soup, what Smith said yesterday,
and so on. There is a genuine concept of perceptual memory, but it
does not hold a position of central or crucial importance in the family of concepts of memory.

11.   The question whether we should accept a distinction between
"dispositional" and "occurrent" memory and, if so, how we should
understand the distinction, is puzzling. Certain linguistic facts
seem to force the distinction on us. At the same time the distinction tends to commit us to a false view of the concept of memory.
Let us consider the kind of linguistic fact that supports the distinction. There is a characteristic difference in meaning between the
sentences, "He remembers the Greek alphabet," and "He remembered the Greek alphabet." The first sentence might be said in
response to the question, "Does he still remember the Greek alphabet, after all these years?" The question asks whether the person
referred to *can* do something, e.g., can say the alphabet from memory or can identify the letters of the alphabet. The reply, "Yes, he
remembers it," says that he does have the ability (or abilities). The
reply does not imply that there has been a recent manifestation of
the ability. It works like the remark, "Yes, he speaks German,"
when this is an answer to the question, "Is he able to speak German?" Of course, "He speaks German," may also mean that the
person referred to speaks German habitually, or often, or most of
the time. I doubt that the sentence, "He remembers the Greek
alphabet," has a comparable use. In any case, I wish to pick out a
use of the sentence in which it attributes an *ability* to the person re-

30. Ibid., pp. 210–212.

ferred to. This is what Broad calls a "memory-power." It is inaccurate to call it a "disposition," since the latter implies a tendency or inclination. ("He has an irritable disposition.") Thus the first term of the "dispositional-occurrent" distinction is a misnomer. The second term, "occurrent," is, as we shall see, seriously misleading.

Ryle calls attention to "two widely different ways in which the verb 'to remember' is commonly used." [31] He goes on to say:

By far the most important and the least discussed use of the verb is that use in which remembering something means having learned something and not forgotten it. This is the sense in which we speak of remembering the Greek alphabet, or the way from the gravel-pit to the bathing-place, or the proof of a theorem, or how to bicycle, or that the next meeting of the Board will be in the last week of July. To say that a person has not forgotten something is not to say that he is now doing or undergoing anything, or even that he regularly or occasionally does or undergoes anything. It is to say that he *can* do certain things, such as go through the Greek alphabet, direct a stranger back from the bathing-place to the gravel-pit and correct someone who says that the next meeting of the Board is in the second week in July. [32]

Without taking sides on Ryle's assertion that the most important use of "remember" is one in which remembering something means having learned and not forgotten it, we can see that he is calling attention to the fact that there is a use of "He remembers so-and-so" which means that the person referred to has an *ability* to do something and, although it is the present tense of the verb, does not mean that this person "is now doing or undergoing anything." Ryle describes the second use of the verb as follows:

Quite different from this is the use of the verb 'to remember' in which a person is said to have remembered, or been recollecting something at a particular moment, or is said to be now recalling, reviewing or dwelling on some episode of his own past. In this use, remembering is an occurrence; it is something which a person may try successfully, or in vain, to do; it oc-

31. G. Ryle, *The Concept of Mind* (New York: Hutchinson University Library, 1949), p. 272.
32. Ibid.

cupies his attention for a time and he may do it with pleasure or distress and with ease or effort.[33]

There is indeed a use of "remember" in which someone can be said to have remembered something at a particular moment. Suppose, for example, a man came out of a room after a meeting and, noticing that he did not have his topcoat, thought to himself, "Where did I leave it?" Then, as he started down the stairs, he suddenly remembered. This sudden remembering is surely an occurrence "at a particular moment"; it could have been clocked on a watch.

This example of sudden remembering could also be called "sudden recollection" or "sudden recalling." But it is *not* an example of "reviewing or dwelling on some episode" in the past. Thus, when Ryle says, "In this use, remembering is an occurrence," he is actually referring to a number of different types of remembering—that is, to a number of different uses of the word "remembering." The sudden remembering (of my example) was an occurrence at an instant of time, but not an occurrence having *duration*—that is, not an occurrence of which it would make sense to ask, "How long did it go on?" (I am thinking of such a contrast as that between the flight of a thrown ball through the air, and the ball's striking a wall. The flight of the ball has duration but its striking the wall does not.) Whereas, reliving or dwelling in memory on some episode might occupy half an hour or a whole afternoon. If we are to speak of "occurrences" of remembering, and I see no reason why we should not, some of these occurrences will have duration and some will not.

12.   In saying that someone "remembers" x (present tense) we are usually referring to an ability or power; and in saying that someone "remembered" x (past tense) we are usually referring to an occurrence. Yet I think that the "ability-occurrence" or "disposition-occurrence" distinction is, or can be, seriously misleading when applied to remembering. Why do I think this? Because of what I

33. Ibid., p. 273.

said in Chapter II in criticism of the philosophical idea of a "memory-act" or "memory-event." When a person remembers something, nothing takes place which can be specified as *being the remembering*. Let me illustrate this again with the example of the man who suddenly remembered where he had left his topcoat. Let us suppose that as he came out of the meeting-room he realized that he did not have his coat, and he said with some anxiety to his companion, "Where could I have put my coat?" A moment later, as he started down the steps, he suddenly remembered. Now what might have happened at that moment? Different things, of course. Let us consider just one case: he snapped his fingers and exclaimed with glad relief, "I put my coat in Tom's car!" These were the only events, occurring at that moment, which were relevant to his remembering where he left his coat. Yet no single one of those events, nor any combination of them, was *identical* with the remembering. Those very same events could have occurred when it was *not* an instance of his remembering where he had left his coat. Suppose that in fact he had not put the coat in Tom's car; or that he was rehearsing the lines of a play as he started down the steps, and did not know a Tom, and had not left his topcoat anywhere but was wearing it; or that he was Chinese and knew no English, and had been drilled in the memorization and pronunciation of that one English sentence, without having any idea what it meant. The phenomena of the snapping of the fingers or the feeling of relief or the exclamation can be expressions of remembering only within a special setting. This setting would have to include a variety of facts, such as that the speaker knows English, he has a topcoat, he has noticed its absence, he had left it in Tom's car. Given such a setting, the occurrence of those phenomena will provide us with a situation of which it is right to say, "He suddenly remembered." Those phenomena do not in themselves ("intrinsically") provide us with that situation. Yet they are what *occurred* at that moment.

Here I have been referring to sudden remembering, which is durationless. But the same point is true of durational remembering, such as reliving, reviewing, or dwelling in memory on some scene č

or event. Those very images, those very feelings of pleasure or horror, those very same remarks (e.g., "I can see him now, standing there on the roof!"), could occur when one was not remembering a lived through experience but, instead, portraying a scene in imagination, or enacting (with realism) a part in a play.

13.   So we have the seeming paradox: at time *t* a person, S, remembered that *p*—yet nothing occurred at *t* which is identical with S's remembering that *p*. Of course one can say that it is trivially true that something did occur at *t* which was identical with S's remembering that *p*, namely, S's remembering that *p!* But my point is that the description, "at *t* S remembered that *p*," is true only because of the circumstances in which the phenomena of snapping the fingers, the sudden feeling of relief, and so on, occurred—and that those circumstances include things that did not occur at *t*, as well as things that did not occur at all. This apparent paradox creates uneasiness about the appropriateness of applying the ability-occurrence distinction to remembering. The justification for this uneasiness can be shown by considering other cases in which we should apply the ability-occurrence distinction without hesitation. For instance, we ask of someone, "Can he play the piano?" In different contexts this means different things. In one context it may mean, "Is he permitted to play the piano?" In another it may mean, "Is he well enough to play it?" One thing it often means is, "Has he learned to play the piano?" An affirmative answer, when the latter meaning was intended, takes the form "Yes, he plays the piano." Here the simple present tense is used to report that he is able (i.e., has learned, knows how) to play it, but not to report a manifestation or exercise of the ability. To make this last report we use either the continuous present ("He is playing the piano right now") or the simple past ("He played the piano yesterday").

The ability-occurrence distinction is genuinely presented by such grammatical contrasts as "plays the piano—is playing the piano," or "juggles three balls at once—is juggling three balls at once," or "does push-ups—is doing push-ups," or "speaks German—is speaking German." Playing the piano, juggling, doing push-ups, speaking German, are not dependent on a setting, on circumstances, in the way in which remembering is. This person is doing push-ups: perhaps he never did them before or will never do them again; but indisputably he is right now doing push-ups. This other person is unquestionably speaking German: perhaps it is a miracle ("speaking with tongues"); perhaps he never had any training in German, perhaps he doesn't understand anything he is saying; nevertheless those are German sounds and sentences he is producing right now. Whereas, whether a person now *remembers* that so-and-so, or now *understands* the orders he received, or now *intends* to do x is in part determined by past and future circumstances, not just by what is going on *now*.

"He remembers the way to the quarry" attributes an ability to him. A manifestation of that ability would be, for example, his leading us through the woods to the quarry. What he did on this occasion was not, however, *intrinsically* a manifestation of remembering the way to the quarry: perhaps he had just a confident and successful hunch as to how to get there. I said that the ability-occurrence distinction is misleadingly applied to remembering. But it does not *have* to be misleading. I see no objection to speaking of memory abilities and memory occurrences, *provided* this does not mislead one into confusedly assuming that an occurrence of remembering is intrinsically an occurrence of remembering.

14. Munsat has perceived the misleading nature of the ability-occurrence distinction when applied to memory. He is opposed to thinking of remembering "as an experience, phenomenon or occurrence." [34] He says: "There is, then, a use of remember in which I am claiming to be able to do something, and a use of remember in which I am doing it. But when I am doing it, I am not remembering (since there is nothing called remembering which is anything I

34. Munsat, *The Concept of Memory*, p. 62.

could be doing)." [35] Now this is wrong, for there is something one can be doing which is called "remembering," namely, reliving, recalling, dwelling in memory on some past incident. I think, however, that Munsat has simply expressed himself badly here, and that what he wanted to say was that remembering does not consist of present events that are intrinsically remembering.

Yet Munsat does espouse a general view as to what it is to remember. His view is that "to remember is either to be able to or actually to make memory *claims.*" [36] He thinks that the *doing* which is a manifestation of a memory ability is always *making a statement*, or, as he puts it, *claiming* that such-and-such is the case. More exactly, his view seems to be that the most *basic* form of remembering consists of making claims. He says:

It is the central thesis of this book that "remembering that" statements are the basic sort of memory statements, that "remember that" statements are either claims to be *able* to "get certain things right on the basis of past knowledge" (third person), or simply claims about what things are the case, while claiming to have authority to make these claims (this authority being previous knowledge). The upshot of this is that memory is essentially neither an occurrence nor an episode. "Remember" covers, among other things, "dispositions" in Ryle's very broad technical sense of "disposition." *To remember is to be able to do certain things, specifically to relate what one previously knew.* [37]

This is a one-sided view. One's memory of where one left one's coat could be manifested in just walking over to Tom's car to fetch it, just as the memory of a tune can be manifested in humming it, and just as one's remembering that oatmeal should be cooked in salted water can appear in the action of salting the water.

Such actions or bits of behavior are not statements or claims, and often they would not belong to claim-making contexts, yet it is possible for them to occur in such contexts. For example, A and B have disagreed as to how a certain tune goes: B says, "It goes like this," and then hums a tune. Here the humming would be part of

35. Ibid., pp. 66–67.   36. Ibid., p. 73.
37. Ibid., pp. 83–84. Final sentence not emphasized in the original.

an assertion, claim, or judgment. This should be compared with the case in which A and B are waxing floors, and have not talked about tunes, and then B begins to hum a tune while he works. Here there is no judgment or claim; yet B's memory of the tune is manifested in his humming. Similarly, one's memory of how to use a sextant may be revealed in one's actually using it, and also in one's telling someone how to use it. But there is no justification for thinking that the latter is a more *basic* form of memory-*doing* than is the former.

Munsat's view is a subtle example of the characteristic philosophical tendency to "overintellectualize" memory. This is the tendency to think that memory "in the true sense of the word," or "memory in the fullest sense," or "genuine" or "cognitive" memory involves the judgment or claim, "This occurred." I criticized this notion previously. The words "memory" and "remember," as they are actually used, range over a huge spectrum of cases. In some of these cases there are memory-images; in some there are claims or judgments; in some there is a "reliving" of the past; in some there is "trying" to remember, in some there is just confident behavior. Philosophers feel tempted to concentrate on a portion of the total range and fix on it as "memory in the fullest sense" or as "genuine" memory. But these stipulations are unjustified.

CHAPTER IV

Exercises in Futility

1. We have noted how various philosophers have drawn a contrast between "genuine" or "true" memory on the one hand, and "habit-memory" or "a repeated mode of behavior" on the other. Also, they have been at pains to distinguish memory occurrences from memory abilities. The interest of philosophers has been largely centered on genuine memory occurrences rather than on abilities, powers, or habits. They have wanted to give an account of what happens, or what *must* happen, when a genuine occurrence of remembering takes place. What is the process of remembering? What are its essential components?

We have seen that the various features that philosophers have postulated as requirements of genuine occurrences of remembering range from fantastic inventions to real but rare phenomena. In surveying the theories of memory one may feel that they have an aspect of "wildness" which is almost embarrassing. Perhaps more than any other concept, memory seems to provoke outlandish ideas, strange mythologies, far removed from daily realities. A well-known remark by Wittgenstein has an especially appropriate application to the philosophy of memory: "When we do philosophy we are like savages, primitive people who hear the expressions of civilized men, put a false interpretation on them, and then draw the queerest conclusions from it." [1]

A good many philosophers, however, will not be moved by criti-

---

1. Wittgenstein, *Investigations*, para. 194.

cism that declares the postulated features of memory either nonexistent or very rare. This criticism has too much of an *empirical* cast. The various mental mechanisms have been put forward as *requirements* of genuine occurrent remembering. Their philosophical exponents can take the position that genuine occurrent remembering *is* a comparatively rare phenomenon. More likely, however, they will feel inclined to think that since these features *must* be present in our daily remembering they *are* there, and it is merely prejudice or careless introspection on the part of the critic that leads him to reject them. In this chapter a different tack will be tried. An attempt will be made to show, first, that the various mental mechanisms do not solve the problems they were devised to solve, that they do not fulfill their *raison d'être;* and, second, that they are inherently paradoxical in that they are inconsistent with the concept they are supposed to explain.

Previously we noted how the various features of the mental mechanisms were put forward in order to solve what were felt to be theoretical problems about memory. They were thought to *explain* various aspects of memory. My present aim will be to show that even if the various feelings and flavors commonly ascribed to "the present mental content of remembering" really did exist, they would still have no explanatory value. It will be convenient to concentrate once more on the details of the theory of memory proposed by Russell in *The Analysis of Mind*.

2.   The first item in Russell's analysis, of course, is the image. He holds Hume's view that when we remember there occur in our minds *copies* of previous impressions or sensations.[2] Let us move to a second point in Russell's analysis. He says: "If we are to know—as it is supposed we do—that images are copies, accurate or inaccurate, of past events, something more than the mere occurrence of images must go to constitute this knowledge. For their mere occurrence, by itself, would not suggest any connection with anything that had happened before." [3] It is easy to understand

2. Russell, *The Analysis of Mind*, pp. 158–159.   3. Ibid., p. 160.

Russell's thinking here. Suppose I have an image of a man climbing a tree. Whether it is a "stationary" image (i.e., an image without movement in it) or whether it is a "moving" image (i.e., an image in which climbing movements occur in succession), it would seem that nothing in the purely visual aspect of the image "suggests any connection" with a past, a present, or a future event. If the image were translated into a painting on canvas, this could as easily be a picture of how a man *will* look when he climbs a tree, as it could be a picture of how a man *did* look. We could express this by saying that nothing in the visual aspect of a picture will represent the *tense* of the picture. Russell's view, as I understand him, is that nothing in the visual, auditory, or, generally, the sensible aspect of an image represents tense. Reference to tense is contained solely in a "belief-feeling": he says, "the tense in the belief that 'this occurred' is provided by the nature of the belief-feeling involved in memory." [4] He thinks there are "three different kinds of belief-feeling." They are "memory, expectation and bare assent." [5] The latter contains no temporal reference; expectation refers to the future; memory refers to the past. Russell says:

When I have seen a flash of lightning and am waiting for the thunder, I have a belief-feeling analogous to memory, except that it refers to the future: I have an image of thunder, combined with a feeling which may be expressed in the words: "this will happen." So, in memory, the pastness lies, not in the content of what is believed, but in the nature of the belief-feeling. I might have just the same images and expect their realization; I might entertain them without any belief, as in reading a novel; or I might entertain them together with a time-determination, and give bare assent, as in reading history. [6]

Russell thinks that in genuine remembering, the *content* is the image; just as in expectation, the content is the image. Since images are tenseless in their sensible aspect, there is a problem as to how time reference gets into memory. I have, for example, an image of a man climbing a tree. This image will be a component of a memory only if there is also aroused in me a "belief-feeling" which can

4. Ibid., p. 185.   5. Ibid., p. 176.   6. Ibid., pp. 176–177.

be expressed in the words "This occurred." I can then be said to *remember* a man's having climbed a tree, or that a man climbed a tree. The image does not in itself refer to past, present, or future; but when the memory belief-feeling occurs this makes the image "point to," or mean," a *past* event. As Russell puts it: "The memory-belief confers upon the memory-image something which we may call meaning; it makes us feel that the image points to an object which existed in the past." [7]

It will be helpful at this point to try to obtain a general view of the problem that Russell thinks an analysis of memory must solve. We make statements on the basis of memory. We say, for example, "I remember a man climbing a tree at the picnic." Russell's problem is this: What *leads me to think* that I remember a man climbing a tree? Or it could be put this way: What is my *basis* for thinking that I remember a man climbing a tree? Or like this: How do I *tell* that I remember a man climbing a tree? For one thing, why do I speak of a man climbing a tree instead of, say, a dog digging a hole? For another thing, why do I speak of *remembering* instead of *imagining* or *expecting?*

Russell has an answer for both parts of this apparent problem. I speak of remembering a "man climbing a tree" because I have an *image* of a man climbing a tree. It should be noted that this view has the consequence that, if what I remember is Lyndon Johnson (and not just some man or other) climbing a tree, there will have to be a difference in the image. Since the image is the *content* of what is believed in remembering, to remember some man or other climbing a tree and to remember Lyndon Johnson climbing a tree would seem to require somewhat different images. In one case the image would be of some man or other, and in the other case it would be of Lyndon Johnson. One can see a difficulty for the theory emerging here. There is, of course, a difference between remembering that some man or other climbed a tree, and remembering that this or that particular man climbed a tree. If an image provides the con-

7. Ibid., p. 179.

tent of a memory-belief, how will this difference appear in the image? How will the image of some man or other differ from the image of a particular man? Could an image of Lyndon Johnson serve as an image of some man or other? I do not find that Russell's theory provides an answer for this problem. I will not, however, treat it as a major criticism, since some property of the image might be "cooked up" to handle this point.

We have noted how Russell says that there is no *tense* in the image and that tense is provided by the belief-feeling. But there are different kinds of belief-feelings, one kind having future tense, another kind having past tense, one kind having no tense, and (presumably) another kind having present tense. Why is it that one of these belief-feelings rather than another is aroused in me? If we think of the various belief-feelings as containing *judgments* which have tense ("This will occur," "This is occurring," "This occurred"), then the question may be put: How do I tell which judgment to make?

Russell's answer, as we know, is that the judgment "This occurred" is based on, or provoked by, some "characteristic of the image.[8] It may be a bit misleading for Russell to speak this way, since the "characteristic" is nothing that belongs to the sensible aspect of any single image. We might say that it is an "external" rather than an "internal" property of the image. It will be recalled that Russell's three conjectures as to what this property might be are, first, a "feeling of pastness"; second, the appearance of the image in a series of successive images that occur "in the same order as their prototypes"; third, the appearance of the image in a set of simultaneous images that differ in their degree of being "faded."[9] One or another of these devices will make us regard the image "as referring to more or less remote portions of the past."[10]

3. This would be a good point at which to raise a question that may seem naive but is not really so. It is a question that has an

8. Ibid., pp. 162–163.   9. Ibid., p. 162.   10. Ibid.

application to all of the various features of the mental mechanisms that are postulated for memory. The question is: Why does "a feeling of pastness," for example, lead me to judge, or to believe, that the image which it accompanies is an image of something that *occurred?* Or if an image, B, is preceded by another image, A, and followed by a third image, C, why should this lead me to believe that the event of which B is an image occurred *between* events A and C? Or if an image, B, is more "faded" than an image, C, why should I think that event B occurred *before* event C?

Obviously an answer Russell cannot give is to say that it is a matter of induction—that people have learned by experience that an image accompanied by a feeling of pastness is an image of an event that occurred. And the same for the other conjectured devices. Such an answer is not available because the device or devices that lead one to believe that the event represented by one's image *occurred*, and lead one to "assign a place to it in the time-order," are supposed to operate in *all* cases of "true" memory. As Russell says, "memory forms an indispensable part of our knowledge of the past." [11] We cannot obtain some knowledge of the past, without relying at *any* stage on memory, and then make correlations between what we have learned about the past in this way and the various features of the assumed memory mechanism, such as feelings of pastness or familiarity. The accumulating of experience, whether this takes the form of testimony, written records, or knowledge of natural laws, will necessarily involve memory, both on the part of those who collect the information and those who subsequently make use of it. We cannot have a kind of knowledge of the past that is free of all employment of memory, both in its generation and application, against which we can measure the postulated memory indicators, and come to have reliance on them by induction or association.

Russell explicitly rejects the suggestion that we might have "a way of knowing the past which is independent of images, by means

11. Ibid., p. 165.

of which we can criticize image-memories." [12] He means to say that "true" memory, with its complex apparatus of images and feelings, cannot *in general* be checked against information that does not make use of "true" memory. Furthermore, he implies that our acceptance of the signs and indicators of "pastness," "time-order," and "accuracy" in our images, cannot be derivative from any form of experience, whether this is association, conditioning, or induction. Russell says, "our confidence or lack of confidence in the accuracy of a memory-image must, in fundamental cases, be based upon a characteristic of the image itself." [13] (The "characteristic" in this instance is the external property that the image has of "feeling familiar.")

Broad has the same view as does Russell, and states it more emphatically. When a person either remembers something or thinks he remembers it, Broad calls this "a memory-situation." He says that a "memory-situation" has an "objective constituent," and he regards this as parallel to the "objective constituent" of a "perceptual-situation." A "perceptual-situation" would be an instance of sense perception. Broad holds that in sense perception there is a "sensum" or "sense-datum." He thinks that "the memory of particular events, places, persons or things," [14] which he calls "perceptual memory," is like sense perception, at least in the respect that something occurs in perceptual memory which plays a role similar to the one that the "sensum" or "sense-datum" is supposed to play in perception. Thus the objective constituent of a memory-situation might be thought of as a "memory-datum." Broad's view is that a memory-judgment or memory-belief is, in some sense, *based on* the memory-datum ("the objective constituent") just as a perceptual judgment or belief is, in some sense, based on the sensum. The memory-datum would presumably consist of imagery and/or feelings of "familiarity" or "fittingness."

Broad is very clear on the point that a memory-judgment or belief is *not* derived by induction from some feature of "the objec-

12. Ibid., p. 161.   13. Ibid.
14. Broad, *Mind and Its Place in Nature*, p. 222.

tive constituent," nor indeed by an *inference* at all, either inductive or deductive. He says:

Memory-beliefs, like perceptual beliefs, not only *are* not reached by inference from the objective constituent of the situation but *cannot* be supported by such inference without logical circularity. When I remember the tie which my friend wore yesterday I do not first notice an image of a certain characteristic shape, colour, etc.; then recollect the general principle that the power to have an image always originates in a past perceptual experience whose objective constituent resembles the image; and then infer from these two premises that there must have existed a certain tie and that I must have seen it. And, if I did profess to reach my memory-judgments by an inference of this kind, the validity of my argument would be open to the following attack. How do I come to know the general principle that all images are copies of past sensa, which is an essential premise of the supposed inference? If we say that the general principle is established inductively, we must suppose that there are *some* cases in which we can remember a past sensum, compare it with a present image, and notice that the latter resembles the former. Now these instances will be useless for establishing the general principle unless, in *these* cases at any rate, we can remember the past sensum *without* using the general principle and making an inference from it. It would therefore be impossible to establish the general principle inductively unless there be *some* non-inferential memory judgments about past sensa. The only way of avoiding this objection would be to take the desperate step of saying that we know *a priori* that every image must be a copy of a past sensum, and that the power to call up an image must have originated through the sensing of this sensum. It seems to me quite plain that this principle is not *a priori;* and I do not know that anyone has ever asserted that it is so.[15]

Broad goes on to say: "Of course I am not maintaining that particular memory-judgments, like particular perceptual judgments, may not be supported or refuted by arguments. They certainly can be. But the arguments always presuppose other memory-judgments which must simply be accepted on their own merits." [16] This was probably the point that Russell had in mind when he said that "in fundamental cases" one's confidence in the "accuracy" of an image must "be based upon a characteristic of the image itself."

15. Ibid., pp. 233–234.   16. Ibid., p. 234.

4. The position stated by Broad and Russell is, and should be, representative of all theories that postulate a mental mechanism of remembering. Broad and Russell understand clearly enough that there is not, and cannot be, any explanation of why the working of the mental mechanism results in such-and-such memory beliefs. They see that to such a question as "Why does 'a feeling of pastness' lead one to believe that one's image is an image of something that occurred?" *there is no answer.* And if we ask, "Why does 'a feeling of familiarity' make me confident that my image is accurate?" there is no answer. And likewise, there is no answer to the question, "When an image, B, occurs after an image, A, and before an image, C, why does this make one believe that the *event*, B, occurred *between* the events A and C?"

Broad puts the point very nicely. In speaking of the characteristic of "familiarity," he says that *"we are so constituted"* that when the objective constituent of a memory-situation "manifests the characteristic of familiarity, *we inevitably apply the concept of pastness."* [17] Familiarity *means* pastness "to such beings as we are." This "meaning" is "primitive and unacquired." [18]

Broad is saying that it is just a brute fact about people that when we have an image of, let us say, a man climbing a tree, and the image is familiar, then we believe that a man climbed a tree. We do not do this because of previous learning or experience. We just do it! This is our natural response to the familiarity of an image.

Actually, this is false. When I was a child I had a recurrent dream in which I fell from a cliff and soared across a wide green meadow. In later years I often had that image; so I can say that it is a *familiar* image. But I have never *believed* that I fell from a cliff and soared across a green meadow. Furthermore, in most of the cases in which I have memory-images, the images are *not* familiar in the sense in which the image of a soaring flight over a meadow is, for me, a familiar image. The philosophers who espouse an image with the property of familiarity as a part of the mechanism of memory

17. Ibid., p. 266. Emphasis added.   18. Ibid., pp. 266–267.

will say, of course, that they do not mean "familiarity" in the sense in which that recurrent image is familiar to me. But then it remains entirely obscure what they do mean by the "familiarity" that is supposed to be a constant property of memory images.

5. This criticism is, however, a digression. My main purpose at present is to call attention to the way in which these attempts to explain memory come to an abrupt *end*. A memory theorist puts such a question as this to himself: "How can a person recount, with such a high degree of accuracy and confidence, something he did?" The answer is as follows: "He is guided by an image that feels familiar." This answer provokes the further question: "Why does an image that feels familiar make it possible for the person to give an accurate and confident report?" The answer of the memory theorist is: "It just does! This is a primitive fact!"

Now why are we not satisfied with answering the *first* question in the same way? Why should we not be content with holding that when a person is able to give a confident and fairly accurate report of something he witnessed, without relying on the testimony of others, or on any inferences, tips, or clues, but is able to give the report "purely on the basis of memory" (as we say)—why are we not content to hold that a person's ability to give such a report is a primitive fact about people? Why are we not willing to allow that this is a natural human power?

6. Two children might play the following game: One is the "leader" and the other the "follower." From a starting position the leader makes some sequence of movements and returns to the starting position. The follower is then supposed to imitate the movements he has just observed. There might be a referee who judges whether the imitation is accurate. Now we know that a normal child of, say, ten years of age will be able to imitate simple movements with perfect accuracy. We also know that as the complexity of the leader's movements increases there will be more and more failures on the part of the follower to repeat the exact movements.

Let us consider a sample movement: the leader raises an arm and lowers it again to his side; the follower then does the same. Is the follower's performance more intelligible to us if we assume that he had a mental image (that "felt familiar") of the leader's movement? Will his ability to "get it right" seem mysterious to us unless we interpolate an image that feels familiar? Why should this be so? Do we think that the image *tells* him what to do? So that without an image he would not *know* what to do? And if he got it right this would be pure luck?

There are three things wrong with such ideas. First, this is not an ordinary conception of either "mysteriousness" or "luck." If the follower were *blindfolded*, then his getting it right *once* would be "luck" and his getting it right *frequently* would be "mysterious." This is how these words would ordinarily be applied. But if the follower *saw* the movements, we would not apply those words to his performance. What is coming into play, therefore, is a *philosophical* use of the words "luck" and "mystery." Second, if we are trying to explain how the follower *knows* what to do, then why don't we ask how he knows that the image he has is a *correct* image? Shall we demand a second image with which he is to compare the first one? And a third one with which to compare the second? And so on? [19] Third, isn't it mysterious that the follower should learn what movement he is to make *from an image?* Has he been taught any rules for translating an image into action? Suppose he has an

19. This point is not the same as, but is related to, the point made by Wittgenstein in the following remarks: "Supposing I teach someone the use of the word 'yellow' by repeatedly pointing to a yellow patch and pronouncing the word. On another occasion I make him apply what he has learnt by giving him the order, 'choose a yellow ball out of this bag'. What was it that happened when he obeyed my order? I say 'possibly just this: he heard my words and took a yellow ball from the bag'. Now you may be inclined to think that this couldn't possibly have been all; and the *kind* of thing that you would suggest is that he imagined something yellow when he *understood* the order, and then chose a ball according to his image. To see that this is not *necessary* remember that I could have given him the order, 'Imagine a yellow patch'. Would you still be inclined to assume that he first imagines a yellow patch, just *understanding* my order, and then imagines a yellow patch to match the first?" (*The Blue and Brown Books*, pp. 11–12).

image of a raised arm: is it obvious that he should take this as meaning that he is to raise his arm? Why should he not take it as a *warning against* raising his arm? Or why should he ascribe *any* meaning to the image?

We have a tendency to be startled by the ordinary phenomena of memory when we think of them philosophically. For example, the leader makes a gesture and a few moments (or an hour) later the follower repeats that gesture. Or the leader utters a sentence and the follower repeats that sentence. Or one person shows another person a bolt of cloth of a certain color and asks him to fetch another bolt of the same color from the next room, and he does so. Or a sequence of letters is shown on a screen, and a few minutes later a subject is asked to say what letters were shown, and he does so with accuracy. These are a few of the countless different kinds of manifestations of memory.

When we consider such examples, we feel the necessity for some intermediary step.[20] We think that otherwise the performances would be "mysterious," "inexplicable." We do not understand how the subject could *know* what to say or do. The favorite intermediary is of course an image accompanied by various feelings ("familiarity," "pastness," "fittingness"). If the man who went into the next room to fetch a bolt of cloth to match the color of one he had just seen carried in his mind an image of that color, then (we think) he would know which color to fetch, and there would be no mystery about his getting it right. This "explanation" falls apart, however, as soon as we ask some questions. How does the man know that if he has an image of green color, say, he should fetch a bolt of green color? Why not a yellow bolt, or a blue bolt, or a bolt that is yellow *and* blue?

There seems to be a knowledge-gap between the man's looking at the first bolt and his subsequent response of selecting in the next room another bolt of the *right* color. We felt the need to fill this gap with an image (attended with certain feelings) that he consulted as

20. Cf. ibid., p. 130.

he selected the second bolt. But when we think about this intermediary, we realize that it, too, presents us with a gap. For why does
an image that feels familiar *guide* the man's action? How does *it* inform him which cloth is of the right color? Surely we have another
gap here that needs to be filled by a secondary intermediary whose
function will be to inform the man how to interpret the first intermediary. But exactly the same sort of question can be raised about
the second intermediary. What tells the man how to interpret *it?*
Thus we are confronted with still another gap, which requires still
another intermediary. *And so on!*

7.   The philosophy of memory is replete with intermediary steps
that are thought to be the components of the "process of remembering." They are what I have called "the mental mechanisms" of
remembering. Their function is to *direct, guide, inform.* They *tell* us
whether what we are doing is remembering, imagining, or expecting. They *inform* us that some event, B, *occurred;* and also that it occurred *after* event A and *before* event C. These mechanisms explain
how we are able to make the *right* responses so easily and accurately: how we can imitate gestures and movements we have observed; repeat sequences of words, letters, or numerals we have
heard or seen; fetch the right bolt of cloth; give an account of some
happening we witnessed; tell someone the way to the gravel pit;
know where we left the hammer. But each intermediary step
presents us with the same kind of problem that, in the first place,
started us along the road of inventing intermediary steps.

    The lesson to be learned is that the intellectual perplexity about
memory that set us off in search of intermediary steps *cannot be removed* by the interpolating of any number of intermediate steps.
This insight might have been suggested by the abrupt way in
which Russell and Broad terminate their search for intermediaries.
Of "familiarity" Russell says the following: "In an image of a well-
known face, for example, some parts may feel more familiar than
others; when this happens, we have more belief in the accuracy of

the familiar parts than in that of the unfamiliar parts." [21] Russell does not attempt to explain *why* "we have more belief in the accuracy of the familiar parts." His idea is that *we just do*. He does not try to devise another intermediary to intervene between the familiarity of an image and one's belief in the image, and to explain why familiarity gives rise to belief. He is ready to stop at the supposed brute fact that familiarity does give rise to belief. It is the same with Broad. He says that "we are so constituted" that when an image or other item of mental content exhibits the character of familiarity then "we inevitably apply the concept of pastness." [22] Broad is willing to accept this as a fact without further explanation. He says that "to such beings as we are" familiarity means pastness. It just does! Broad does not seek a further intermediary step to explain how the characteristic of familiarity in an image makes us think that it is an image of something that previously existed.

A philosopher's uneasiness about the mysteriousness of memory cannot be quieted, if he thinks deeply enough, by the postulating of an intermediary step "in the mind." Each intermediary that is conjured up to fill a gap in explanation *creates its own gap*. Every piece of mental mechanism (image, feeling of warmth and intimacy, sense of pastness, feeling of fittingness, feeling of familiarity) that is supposed to direct or guide our memory responses gives rise to the same question: How does it guide us? How does *it* tell us what to do? The conclusion that should be drawn is that the thinking up of possible features of mental content will bring us no nearer to the goal of understanding memory. No hypothesis about what goes on in our minds when we remember, as to how remembering *works*, will remove our puzzlement.

8.   Wittgenstein explains this general point in the simplest possible terms. First of all, he imagines a "language-game" in which a builder, A, is building a structure with building stones consisting

21. Russell, *The Analysis of Mind*, p. 161.   22. Broad, p. 266.

of slabs, pillars, blocks and beams. His helper, B, brings the stones to A as A calls for them. A and B have a language consisting solely of the words "slab," "pillar," "block," and "beam." A calls out one or another of these words; B brings the stone which he has learned to bring at such-and-such a call.[23]

Wittgenstein was not using this example for the purpose of discussing memory. But it can easily be given this application, since the helper's response is a manifestation of memory. A philosopher who demands a mental mechanism of remembering will feel that the fact that B hears A call out "slab," together with the fact that B has had a certain training, is not a sufficient explanation of the fact that B knows which kind of stone to fetch. He will want to hold that there must be, in addition, some *connection* or *association* "in B's mind" between the word "slab" and that kind of stone.

Let us consider what such a connection might be. We will suppose that when B hears A say "slab!" he sees in his mind a diagram in which the words are correlated with the stones. In B's mental picture the four names are in one column and the four stones in an opposite column. There is an inclination to say: "Now we understand why B brings a slab when A says 'slab.' He is guided by the diagram he sees in his mind. The diagram shows him which kind of stone goes with which word."

Wittgenstein reminds us, however, that there can be more than one way of reading a diagram, just as there can be more than one way of interpreting a signpost. We tend to see this more clearly if we substitute a table or diagram drawn on paper for the mental image of a table.[24] Let us imagine, therefore, a "language-game" similar to the previous one except that the helper, B, makes use of a table drawn on paper. Instead of calling out the words, the builder, A, hands B a piece of paper on which one of the words is written. B then consults the written table.

23. Wittgenstein, *Investigations*, para. 2.

24. The device of substituting a physical model or counterpart for a mental image (e.g., a piece of red paper in place of an image of a red patch) is employed by Wittgenstein, and is recommended by him as helpful in avoiding the "occult" aspect of mental processes. E.g., *The Blue and Brown Books*, p. 4; *Investigations*, para. 141.

Wittgenstein gives the following account of how such a "game" might be played:

B has a table; in the first column are the signs used in the game, in the second pictures of the building stones. A shows B such a written sign; B looks it up in the table, looks at the picture opposite, and so on. So the table is a rule which he follows in executing orders.—One learns to look the picture up in the table by receiving a training, and part of this training consists perhaps in the pupil's learning to pass with his finger horizontally from left to right; and so, as it were, to draw a series of horizontal lines on the table.

Suppose different ways of reading a table were now introduced; one time, as above, according to the schema:

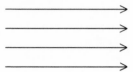

another time like this:

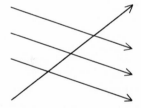

or in some other way.—Such a schema is supplied with the table as the rule for its use.

Can we not now imagine further rules to explain *this* one? And, on the other hand, was that first table incomplete without the schema of arrows? And are other tables incomplete without their schemata? [25]

The point I wish to bring out is the following: in regard to any physically drawn table or chart, there could, logically speaking, be a question of how to interpret it (how to read it). The intended in-

25. Wittgenstein, *Investigations*, para. 86. Cf. *The Blue and Brown Books*, pp. 90–91.

terpretation of the table could itself be presented on the same piece of paper on which the table is drawn, as a schema for reading the table. We see at once that there could, logically speaking, be a question of how to interpret *this schema*. We can imagine that a second schema should be drawn below the first one, the second being the interpretation of the first. If there was a problem of interpreting the *second* schema, then a third one might be added. But still a fourth one might be required; and so on. This point is clearly expressed in the following remarks by Wittgenstein:

> We give someone an order to walk in a certain direction by pointing or by drawing an arrow which points in that direction. Suppose drawing arrows is the language in which generally we give such an order, couldn't such an order be interpreted to mean that the man who gets it is to walk in the direction opposite to that of the arrow? This could obviously be done by adding to our arrow some symbols which we might call "an *interpretation*". It is easy to imagine a case in which, say to deceive someone, we might make an arrangement that an order should be carried out in the sense opposite to its normal one. The symbol which adds the interpretation to our original arrow could, for instance, be another arrow. Whenever we interpret a symbol in one way or another, the interpretation is a new symbol added to the old one.[26]

With any symbol or sign, there *can* be a question of what the interpretation of it is, of how we should read it or take it. Memory theorists have displayed ingenuity in thinking up mental signs that will inform and guide our responses to past experience. The mental signs (images and various feelings) *must* be there, it is thought, because otherwise we should not be able to describe what we witnessed, or to fetch the right bolt of cloth, or to direct a person to the gravel pit. The fact of my having been to the gravel pit several times in the past cannot, it is felt, be an *adequate explanation* of my ability to lead someone to it now. "How do I know which way to go? I must have an image, or something like it, that guides me."

Thinking in this way, we insist on the necessity of a mental image or mental plan or schema. But we should not stop there. We

26. Wittgenstein, *The Blue and Brown Books*, p. 33.

should ask: How does *it* tell us which way to go? If we consider it as comparable to a map drawn on paper, we immediately realize that one may not understand a map, not know how to interpret it, not even know that it is a map. From the fact that a person is looking at a map it does not follow that he knows how to use it. But the same thing holds for any supplementary schema (e.g., arrows indicating the directions) which might be attached to the map. There could be a question of how to interpret *it*. (Such supplementary schemata are exactly parallel to the various feelings that supposedly accompany a memory image.) Any schema added to the map as an explanation of the map will simply be another sign, which might in turn need to be explained by still another sign. "How does one explain to a man how he should carry out the order, 'Go *this* way!' (pointing with an arrow the way he should go)? Couldn't this mean going in the direction which we should call the opposite of that of the arrow? Isn't every explanation of how he should follow the arrow in the position of another arrow?" [27] Of course our philosophical conclusion should not be that it is impossible to explain to anyone how to carry out an order. Rather it should be this: if we feel that there is a *gap* between an explanation in physical signs and the behavior appropriate to executing the order, then our desire for a smooth, gap-free explanation cannot be satisfied by a *mental* intermediary occurring between the physical sign and the appropriate behavior: for the mental intermediary will carry a gap with it just as much as will the physical sign. A mental image of an arrow might not tell me where to go any better than does a physical arrow. If we think that a mental arrow can have its meaning *intrinsic* to it, whereas a physical arrow cannot, we are assigning to the "mental" an occult, mysterious aspect. If I have a mental image of an arrow pointing to the left, and even if I say to myself "I should go left," it *might* happen that I was still in doubt as to which way to go. Just as this might happen if I saw a physical arrow pointing to the left, or if someone said to me, "You should go left."

27. Ibid., p. 97.

On the other hand, it might also happen that once I had a mental image of an arrow pointing to the left I knew immediately that I was to go to the left, and I executed the order correctly and confidently. I did not require a further intermediary to fill "the gap" between the mental arrow and the appropriate action. But it is also the case that it might happen (and *does* happen—indeed, it is the normal case) that upon being told "Go *this* way," and being given a pointing gesture, I know which way to go: I do the right thing and with confidence; I require no intermediary thing, no further explanation, no additional guidance. The words and gesture are adequate. If one thinks, on a priori grounds, that they *cannot* be adequate, then one is forced, in consistency, into the self-defeating position of holding that *nothing* can be adequate, not even any mental intermediary, no matter how complex or subtle.

9.   The application of these thoughts to our topic of memory should be clear enough. A great deal of human behavior consists of what we might call "memory responses." We imitate gestures we saw; we repeat words we heard; we describe events we witnessed; we sing and play music we have studied; we carry out orders given to us previously; and so on. When we philosophize about memory we begin to wonder what it is that guides the memory responses, what it is that tells us what to do or say. The past events, the previous orders, the training we received, are all "dead and gone." We "cannot evoke the past bodily," Russell says.[28] There must be something *right now*, in "the present mental content of remembering," that is the basis for our confidence that we saw a man climb a tree, or that we should fetch a green bolt of cloth and not a blue one, or that the melody goes like *this*, and so on. How can my *past* experience guide me in the *present?* How can I *know* what to do or say, unless there is something, here and now, that *informs* me? The memory theorists have felt that there must be a "mnemic datum," some content of "immediate awareness," a "present experience,"

28. Russell, *The Analysis of Mind*, p. 161.

that is *"directive."* This is what explains why the correct memory response occurs: why we say (with confidence) that a man (not a woman) climbed a tree; why we bring back the green cloth (not the blue); why we whistle the melody like *this* (not like *that*); how we know that the bursting of the water pipes occurred *before* the hurricane (and not *after*).

We noted that some of the proposed constituents of the mnemic datum are entirely fanciful, and others are actual but infrequent occurrences. The motive for insisting on a mnemic datum is to explain *how we remember*. This is deemed to be an explanation of how we are able to make accurate memory responses so frequently, and also of how we are able to make them so *confidently* (why we have memory-*beliefs*). The memory theorist is worried by the "awkward gulf" between the past experience and the present response. This "temporal gap" creates, he feels an "explanatory gap" which must be filled. The worry about the awkward temporal gap is allayed by imagining that there are various images and feelings temporally contiguous with the memory responses. It is conceived that memory responses are guided by something in the present instead of something in the past. The temporal gulf between the past event and the present remembering remains: but it is no longer an obstacle to the understanding of how we remember.

What I have been trying to make clear in this chapter is that the memory theorists' strategy for bypassing the temporal gap does not succeed in bridging the *explanatory* gap. Once this is realized there should no longer be any philosophical motivation for believing in the necessity of a mnemic datum. The memory theorists have invented various items of present mental content in order to explain the occurrence of normal memory responses. These inventions have, of course, yielded nothing more than "brute fact" explanations. That is the way the memory theorists want it. They do not want the items of consciousness that constitute the mnemic datum to be *definable* in terms of memory. For example, the sense in which an image is claimed to be "familiar" must not be the ordinary sense in which a room is familiar: for when we say this of a room we

mean we remember it. Thus the memory theorists cannot invoke
the familiar sense of "familiarity" to explain how we remember, for
this would involve circularity. Similar things could be said of "the
sense of pastness" or "the feeling of fitting." Nor can the functioning of the items of present consciousness in accounting for our
memory responses be explicable in terms of some inference from
past experience. Thus Broad says that memory-judgments are not
derived from features of the mnemic datum by *any* inference, "deductive or inductive." [29] He and Russell and the others hold that it
is just a brute fact that we respond in such-and-such ways to the
items of the mnemic datum: "we are so constituted."

10.   I do not wish to claim that brute-fact explanations are never
acceptable. Far from it. What is objectionable is a maneuver that,
in seeking to avoid a brute-fact explanation of memory responses,
invents a mythology of mental items belonging to "the present occurrence of remembering," and then accepts a brute-fact account
of the relation between those fancied items and our memory responses. If the memory theorists permit an appeal, as they do and
must, to what our nature is, to how we are constituted, then it would
seem that they have no adequate rationale for generating their
philosophies of memory in the first place. Why should they not be
content with accepting at face value the connections between past
experience and our memory responses, that are verified by daily
experience? Why not admit that if a normal person is shown a
green object and ordered to bring another of the same color from
the next room, he is able to comply *without* the assistance of a mental mechanism? Why not accept, simply as a fact, that some people
are gifted with a memory for music and others are not, without
trying to explain this difference by holding that the former must be
guided in their playing or singing by auditory imagery which the
latter lack? Why not concede that the influence of past training and
experience is frequently *direct*, in the sense that it does *not* work its

29. Broad, p. 233.

effect by producing in us an apparatus of images and feelings, which in turn controls our responses? The philosophers have been unable to believe what is before their eyes—that, for example, a person who witnessed an event can later give an account of what he saw. "There must be more to it than that," they think. They cannot accept, as a brute fact, that a person who has witnessed an event is subsequently able to describe it. They feel that there must be a memory-process which *explains* this ability. But the memory-process, consisting of some complex of imagery and feelings, which they interpose between the original perception and the memory response, does not make the ability any more intelligible than it was before.

The memory theorist makes a useless movement. He invents a memory-process to fill what he thinks is an explanatory gap; but his own explanation creates its own explanatory gap. He is deceived in thinking that some progress in explanation has been achieved. A gap offended him; a gap remains. It is as if a man did not like to have paint on a wall, so he tried to get rid of it by *painting* over it.

Wittgenstein speaks of a "general disease of thinking which always looks for (and finds) what would be called a mental state from which all our acts spring as from a reservoir." [30] An illustration of this is our philosophical tendency to think that we call different shades of red by the same name ("red") because we see what is common to them; [31] another is our tendency to think that we speak of mental "strain" and physical "strain" (that is, we use the word "strain" in both cases) because we *perceive a similarity* between mental strain and physical strain.[32] The postulated perception of a similarity or of a common feature is the reservoir from which flows the particular acts of naming. But we find that we cannot indicate what is common to different shades of red; nor can we say what the similarity is between the strain of holding up a weight with one's outstretched leg and the strain of trying to decide a move in chess.

30. Wittgenstein, *The Blue and Brown Books*, p. 143.
31. Ibid., pp. 130–131.   32. Ibid., pp. 129–133.

The "seeing what is common" or the "perception of similarity" is supposed to be the mental state from which flows our application of the same name. Since we cannot, however, specify the common element in different shades of red (other than to say that they are all *red*) nor the similarity between the different cases in which we speak of "strain," this explanatory movement is futile.

Philosophical thinking is replete with such illusions of explanation. The "analysis of memory" is a superb illustration. Fanciful or even fantastic mental states or processes are conjured up to explain the everyday phenomena of memory. In regard to many of these mental items we are either involved in circularity or else we have no criteria for their occurrence: for example, for the "feeling of familiarity" that is attached to *all* memory images, and "the constant feeling *sui generis* of pastness" to which *every* experience "falls prey." And with each of the features of the supposed process of remembering we are brought up short when we ask, How does *it* work? How does *it* guide our memory responses? It is evident, and should have been evident from the beginning, that these intermediary memory-processes will present the same explanatory problem that was originally felt to be a problem. It is no exaggeration to call the intellectual striving that persists in erecting these self-defeating structures a "disease" of thinking.

11. Memory, in some forms, is knowledge. If I say, "I remember that Man o' War won the third race", I imply that I know that Man o' War won the third race. If we say of someone, "He remembers where he left the tickets," we imply that he knows where he left the tickets. If a man remembers the way to Grantchester, then he knows the way to Grantchester. On the other hand, we say that a boy remembered to wipe his feet on the door mat; but we cannot say that he "knew to" wipe his feet on the mat. Presumably he knew *how to* do it: but this is not the same as what we said he remembered. We cannot in all cases deduce a statement of the form "He knew *x*" from a statement of the form "He remembered *x*."

Also there is correct and incorrect memory. Suppose you recited a poem from memory, getting the first two lines exactly right but getting two words wrong in the third line. What we say here is that you remembered the first two lines correctly, and with respect to the third line that "You didn't remember it correctly," or "Your memory of it was incorrect," or "You remembered it incorrectly." If you remembered the third line incorrectly, it follows that you did not know it perfectly; it doesn't follow that you didn't know it at all; instead it follows that you did know it, but imperfectly.

If a person remembered that p, we will, normally, want to say that he knew that p, and that if he did not know that p, then he did not remember that p. But one can imagine cases in which we would be hard put to know what to say. Suppose that a person had some strange, weird, improbable adventure as a child. In later life he comes to believe that the adventure was a fantasy; he believes that those events never took place, but yet he "remembers" them very well. He remembers that p, that q, that r, and so on: but he does not *believe* that p, that q, that r. Should we say that he *knows* that p, that q, that r? This would be a strain on the word "know". Feeling the unsuitability of applying "know" here, would we be reluctant to say that he really *remembers* that p, q, r? Perhaps so; perhaps not. In the normal case one who remembers that p believes that p. In the abnormal case we have imagined, it is hard to know what to say. Our difficulty does not prove that there is no strong connection in the language between remembering that p and knowing that p. Quite the contrary; it arises from the fact that there is such a connection. We cannot go so far as to say that in all cases remembering that p is knowing that p; nevertheless this is normally so.

12.   Let us concentrate on the normal cases in which remembering is knowing. It is tempting to assume that whenever we *know* something our knowledge rests on some evidence, reasons, or grounds. Indeed, when philosophers try to *define* the word "knowledge" they typically make this a requirement of the definition—mistakenly, in my opinion. Previously we noted how some philosophers have said that much of what is *called* "memory" does not "deserve" the name.

Only when it is "cognitive"—that is to say, when it is *knowledge*,—does it really deserve that title. We have an inclination to think in something like the following way: Genuine knowledge is not mere guessing, or getting it right by luck. Guessing and luck are *blind;* but knowledge is not blind. When a person acts and judges from knowledge, he knows *why* he acts and judges as he does. He is aware of grounds or reasons; they *inform* him, they *guide* him.

It is inevitable that this thinking should be applied to memory. "Cognitive" or "genuine" memory, being knowledge, must have reasons or grounds of some sort. This assumption makes it easy to believe in a mental mechanism of memory. The images and various feelings that compose "the present occurrence when we remember" are the grounds or basis for our memory responses and judgments.

When we stop thinking so abstractly, however, and try to give concrete applications to these ideas, we realize that they are completely wrong. Thomas Reid says: "A past event may be known by reasoning; but that is not remembering it. When I remember a thing distinctly, I disdain equally to hear reasons for it or against it. And so I think does every man in his senses." [33] I wish to defend Reid's point. Let us suppose that a man knew that, in a town where he formerly dwelt, the church was next door to the railroad station. How did he know this? Let us say that he consulted a map of his old home town, and the map clearly indicated that the church was next to the station. If his knowledge was based *solely* on his current study of the map, then his knowledge was not *memory.*

To take another example, let us suppose that a man had long ago witnessed a naval engagement. Subsequently he is questioned as to what transpired: How many vessels were involved? What were their relative positions at the beginning of the battle? Which ones were sunk? In order to answer these questions he refers to a diagram of the battle which he found in a volume of naval history. If his answers are derived exclusively from features of the diagram,

33. Thomas Reid, *Essays on the Intellectual Powers*, Essay VI, Ch. 5.

this implies that his knowledge of what transpired is not memory. Why does it imply this? Because it implies that his knowledge of the battle would have been the same *had he never witnessed it!*

The town map and the naval diagram were both *representations;* one showing the arrangements of streets and buildings, the other displaying the dispositions of the fleets and the number and losses of vessels. Now it is clear that there is a strong inclination to think that when we truly remember something there must be a *representation* of it in the mind. One philosophical motive for stuffing "the present occurrence when we remember" with a complex of images and feelings is to provide a representation that will be our *source of information* as to what the past thing or event was that we witnessed. But the point that is so obvious in regard to the physical representations applies with equal force in regard to the mental representations. Insofar as a representation is the entire source of one's information, one's knowledge is not memory, regardless of whether the representation is a mental something or a physical something. The man whose information about the naval battle derived solely from the diagram had *no* memory of the battle. The same would be true if he derived his information entirely from an image together with some peculiar feelings such as "familiarity" or "pastness."

Ryle rejects the view that memory is a *source* of knowledge and also that remembering is one way of "coming to know things." [34] I should say that he is half right and half wrong. Remembering can be a way of coming to know something: for example, at first I did not know where I had put my watch and then later I did know— that is, I remembered. I came to know something in remembering it, and in this sense memory is a source of knowledge. But the memory theorists have had a conception of memory as a source of knowledge that is more exciting than this. They have supposed that when we remember there is a memory-process of some complexity, consisting of features that go to make up a representation, *on the basis of which we learn* what the past event was. Ryle rightly

34. Ryle, *The Concept of Mind*, pp. 273–274.

declares that remembering is no sort of "learning, discovering, or establishing." [35] This implies that, if a representation occurs when I remember where I put my watch, I do not learn or discover from the representation where I put my watch.

The memory theorists have partly realized this but partly they have not. Russell says that some knowledge of past events is "obtained by inference." Memory, however, is not like that: "it is immediate, not inferred." [36] It will be recalled that Broad, too, declares that "memory-judgments" are not arrived at "by inference" from "the nature and existence" of the image, or the feeling of fittingness that is, supposedly, a component of "the memory-situation." [37] Thus those theorists hold that the knowledge we have when we remember is not obtained by inference from the mental items which compose "the present occurrence in remembering." Yet they also want to hold that those mental items are in *some* sense the basis of our memory-knowledge. When we have an image together with a feeling of familiarity and a sense of pastness, we do not *infer* that what is pictured in the image occurred. We simply respond with the judgment "This occurred," because we are so constituted—or, as Thomas Reid would say, "by a principle of our nature." The items of mental content serve, as it were, as *natural signs* to which we respond by a kind of instinct. Russell says that memory-images are not "noticed in themselves, but merely used as signs of the past event." [38] Perhaps he would say the same of the feelings of familiarity and pastness. Our response to these signs would not be due to any training or education. We have not *learned* to be guided by them; nevertheless, they guide us. Thus the theorists agree with Reid's point that learning about a past event by reasoning from some datum is not *remembering* it; yet they want to insist on the presence of natural signs in the mental content of remembering as the basis for our memory-knowledge.

35. Ibid., p. 274.   36. Russell, *The Analysis of Mind*, pp. 172–173.
37. Broad, p. 235.   38. Russell, *The Analysis of Mind*, p. 185.

13. The memory theorists (some of them at least) realize that it is imcompatible with the concept of memory to hold that remembering an event is *learning of* or *inferring* its occurrence from anything whatever, including the supposed items of mental content. Yet they cannot tolerate the idea that the knowledge one has when one remembers something has *no basis at all*. So their thinking moves in the direction of postulating natural signs which will guide the memory responses, these signs being elements in the *process* of remembering. Russell says that the images, and presumably the other signs, are *not* "noticed in themselves." This is significant. If I do not notice the signs, then I cannot refer to them as *my reasons* for making the memory-judgments which I do make. Russell's remark suggests that the mental signs play the role of *causing* the memory responses rather than of providing reasons, grounds, or evidence for them. The idea of *being guided* can be retained; but now it is to be understood more in the sense in which I might guide a person's hand by grasping and moving it with my own hand, rather than in the sense in which in walking with a person I might guide his path by advising and cautioning him about features of the terrain. In the latter case he would have reasons for walking in this or that direction, namely, my advice and warnings. In the other case he does *not* have reasons for the movements of his hand, although the movements are guided.

It appears that there is an ambiguity in Russell's conception of how the various features of mental content "explain" our memory-judgments. He is concerned to give an account of how "the present occurrence in remembering" can yield *knowledge* of the past. He says, "We shall have to find, if we can, such an account of the present occurrence in remembering as will make it not impossible for remembering to give us knowledge of the past." [39] One would expect that his account will tell us how "the present occurrence in remembering" provides us with *grounds* for our memory-judg-

39. Ibid., pp. 173–174.

ments, grounds which would justify us in claiming that we *know* that Man o' War won the third race, and that we *know* where we left the tickets. Yet we find Russell holding not only that memory-judgments are not inferred from anything, but also that the features of mental content are not "noticed." But if we do not notice them we cannot appeal to them in *justification* of our claim to knowledge of the past. The conclusion for Russell ought to be that no one *has* any justification for such claims and that memory is not a form of knowledge; there is no "memory-knowledge." His "analysis of memory" has failed in its ostensible purpose.

Russell's analysis would thus seem to gravitate toward a different kind of explanation of memory-judgments, namely, a *causal* explanation of their occurrence rather than a justification of them as claims to knowledge. The various aspects of a memory-judgment are *caused* by the various mental components of the "memory-process." There is, for example, some feature of the memory-images "which *makes* us regard them as referring to more or less remote portions of the past." [40] And when an image "feels familiar," the *effect* on us is that we believe in the accuracy of the image. Russell's statement that some parts of an image "may feel more familiar" than other parts, and that "when this happens, we have more belief in the accuracy of the familiar parts than in that of the unfamiliar parts," [41] would seem now to be open to an interpretation in terms of the causation instead of the rational justification of memory-beliefs.

14.   This shift in interpretation will not, however, make the position of a memory theorist any more tenable. This can be seen from the following imaginary case. Let us suppose there is a tribe of people who respond *instinctively* to arrow-signs by going in the direction the arrow points. They have not been trained or conditioned to do this; they just do it. Let us further suppose that they are dependent on such signs, in the sense that if the signs are not

40. Ibid., p. 162. Emphasis added.   41. Ibid., p. 161.

present then in proceeding along paths or roads which they have traversed frequently, toward familiar destinations, they become confused at intersections, not knowing in which direction to go; or else they make incorrect turns as frequently as correct ones. When the signs are present and visible, they proceed confidently and correctly; when the signs are absent or not visible, they are bewildered and lost. A correct description of this state of affairs would be to say that these people have "*no memory* for roads and paths."

It might be objected that perhaps the signs serve as *reminders*— that when these people see the signs they then *remember* which way to turn. But this is not correct. A reminder evokes memory, and the latter normally goes beyond the reminder. If a person is reminded of some matter, there will occur to him additional information about that matter, information not contained in the reminder. This is not true of the people I am imagining. They have no knowledge of which turnings to take in order to get to the next village, a place they have visited frequently. They respond to the signs automatically, and are lost without them. The signs do not evoke knowledge they already have, and so are not reminders.

The dependence of these people on the signs could be easily tested and demonstrated. For example, if the sign pointing to the next village were reversed, these people would go off confidently in the wrong direction.

It is assumed, as said, that their behavior is not influenced by the signs unless they *see* the signs. We can imagine, however, that these people do not *notice* the signs, in the sense that they do not *look for* such signs and, furthermore, they are not *aware* that they are influenced by the signs: they would never say that they made a turn to the right, instead of the left, *because* a sign pointed to the right. When one of them makes a right turn at an intersection, the presence of a sign is not his reason or his justification for that choice, although his choice was caused by his seeing the sign. It may be thought that these people "associate" the arrow-signs with right turns and left turns. One *can* say this: but all it comes to in their case is that seeing the signs *causes* them to make the corresponding

turns. They do not think of the signs as *rules* for how they should
go. They do not think of an arrow pointing to the right as *meaning*
that they should go to the right. They will not say to one another,
"If an arrow points to the right, you should go to the right." In
fact, one of them cannot tell another what route to take, except in
the sense of leading him along the correct path when the signs are
present and visible.

These people may strike one as monstrously strange, as indeed
they are. I am assuming, however, that in most respects they have
normal human memory powers. And even among us there are
striking differences in the sorts of things that people can remember,
some having astonishing memory for music, poetry, or mathematical formulae, whereas others have almost none.

This imaginary example is presented as a parallel to the causal
interpretation of the functioning of the various features of the alleged "memory-process" in guiding our memory-judgments and
responses. The only significant difference intended is that in the
imagined example the signs are physical signposts, whereas the
conception of the philosophers is that the signs which cause our
memory responses are mental in nature. The imagined example
provides a case in which it is indisputable that the people do *not*
remember the paths and turns, do not remember the way to the
store, do not remember that at this intersection they should turn
right. Their not remembering is *entailed by* their absolute dependence on signs for guidance.

One may feel an inclination to think that this entailment holds
only when the signs are *physical*. It is entirely inexplicable, however, that the mere difference between mental and physical signs
should make this logical difference. An absolute dependence on
signs for finding one's way to the store is incompatible with remembering the way to the store, regardless of the nature of the
signs.

It will help to see this if we modify our imaginary example by
substituting sensations for physical signs. Let us suppose that the
people of the tribe are so constituted that they turn to the right

when they have a throbbing sensation in the right ear, and to the left when they have the same sensation in the left ear. They have not been taught or conditioned to do this. Nor have they taken any notice of this regularity. They do not think of the sensations as reasons for turning, nor as indicators of the correct route. But a throbbing sensation in the right ear does in fact cause them to take a right fork. If they have no ear-sensations at an intersection, they are bewildered as to which way to turn. This is true no matter how frequently they have come through that intersection on the way to the given destination. We have to say of these people, just as we did of those in the previous example, that they have *no memory* for paths and roads. They cannot *remember* the way to the store. Whether they get to the store and back is a matter of their having a fortuitous sequence of sensations. The explanation of their having made the correct turns is not that they remembered the way.

The general point these fanciful examples are meant to elicit is the following: If a response is determined solely by the perception of some contemporaneous thing, then it is not a *memory* response. This is so whether the contemporaneous thing is physical or mental.

15.   Of course the perception of something often serves as a *reminder;* hearing the word "oven" in a conversation may remind one to buy a loaf of bread, or a pain in the knee may remind one of an appointment with a dentist.

Here I will undertake a digression into the puzzling role of imagery in memory. Sensory imagery frequently occurs in remembering and is often an aid to memory. People will testify that some imagery helped them to remember something, or that they would not have (or even *could not* have) remembered the thing without that imagery. A man might tell us that he would not have remembered that the 9 P.M. train does not run on Thursdays if he had not seen the timetable in his mind. Now how did the image aid him? How was it related to his remembering? Can such an example as this be reconciled with my assertion that remembering cannot be derived solely from a representation of what is remembered?

It will be helpful to obtain a clearer conception of what a memory-image is. It is not merely an image that *accompanies* remembering. It has to be an image *of* some remembered thing. But even this is not enough. A man might remember, from his reading, that Hannibal crossed the Alps with an army. When he remembered this, he might have had an image of Hannibal leading his troops through the Alps. He remembered that Hannibal crossed the Alps and had an image of Hannibal doing it; yet we should not want to say that he had a memory-image of Hannibal crossing the Alps. In order for someone's image to be a memory-image, it must be an image of something that he himself perceived and remembers.

Let us try to deal now with the question of what the relationship is between memory-images and remembering. Is this a causal relationship? Do memory-images cause remembering? I believe there is a respect in which this is false, and another respect in which it is true. I will explain.

We said that a memory-image must be an image of something previously perceived and remembered. Furthermore, memory is incorporated into, contained in the memory-image. A memory-image is itself an exemplification, an embodiment, of remembering. Suppose that a person has a mental image which he describes to us. I mean that he gives that kind of description which consists in saying what it is an image *of*. If it is a memory-image, his description of his image will display some *correct remembering*. In specifying the subject of his memory-image, he must exhibit some correct memory of that subject. If he says that his image is of the Eiffel Tower, and then adds that it barks and wags its tail, then what he has is, to that extent, not a *memory-image* of the Eiffel Tower, although it could be that he does have a memory-image of the tower, to which has been added a play of imaginative fancy. If it is just an image of a barking, tail-wagging creature, then no memory of the Eiffel Tower is incorporated into that image.

A description of a memory-image of *x* necessarily manifests *some* correct memory of *x*. And since the description describes the memory-image, the memory-image itself embodies some correct remembering. Some correct remembering is logically internal to a memory-image. Correct remembering enters into the constitution of a memory-image.

If this is so, we can see the respect in which it is false that a memory-image is a *cause* of remembering. It cannot cause the remembering that is embodied in the image. Perhaps we can say that the memory-image portrays the remembering that is embodied in the image.

That a memory-image is itself an embodiment of remembering seems true enough. But this does not adequately explain the *usefulness* of memory-images. Can they be aids to memory in some way other than by being portrayals of remembering? Yes. We can see how a memory-image can be a *cause* of remembering. It cannot cause the remembering that it itself embodies and portrays, but it can cause *other* remembering related to the subject of the image.

Consider an example. S was in a room with a number of people when a man was shot in that room. The police question S in order to learn the exact location of everyone in that room when the shot was fired. S remembers that A and B were talking in one corner. He does not remember where C was. He then calls up a memory-image of the room. He sees in his mind the corner where A and B were, an adjacent wall with a bookcase, a fireplace, and a curtained doorway. As soon as he has an image of the doorway, he remembers that C was standing *there* when the shot was fired. His memory-image of the doorway *reminded* him of C's location.

A double relationship between memory-images and remembering comes out clearly in this example. S's image of the room did not remind him that the room had a bookcase, fireplace, and curtained doorway; his memory of those items was internal to his image. But the image did remind him of C's location.

If, instead of forming an image of the room, S had produced from memory a pencil sketch of the room, the same double relationship to remembering could hold. As S draws the curtained doorway (this action being itself an embodiment of remembering), he suddenly remembers that C was standing in that doorway, and he tells us that the act of sketching the doorway had reminded him of this. The sketch was both an embodiment of remembering and a reminder. I see no difference between the mental image and the pencil drawing in these respects. We can imagine people who did not have memory-images but who had the practice of rapidly sketching on paper scenes and incidents they were recalling. Sketches and memory-images can both be embodiments of remembering and causal aids to remembering.

H. H. Price employs the same analogy; but his remarks show, I believe, a mistaken conception. He says, "We use visual images rather as we use maps or sketch-plans to find our way about a piece of hilly and wooded country; and when someone else asks us the way to Little Puddlecombe, we refer to this mental map and read off the answer." [42] By the "mental map" in his example, Price means a memory-image. In saying that we "read off" the information from the image, Price implies that the information is *in* the image and also that we *obtain* the information *from* the image. But these two conditions cannot be mutually satisfied in respect to the same piece of information. The only sense in which the information could be *in* the memory-image would be that the image *embodied* our memory of the way to Little Puddlecombe, in which case we could not be *obtaining* this information from that image. On the other hand, if a memory-image is not itself an embodiment or portrayal of certain information, still the image may *cause* us to remember that information. This would be no more surprising than the fact that overhearing the word "oven" caused me to remember that I was told to buy bread. Just as seeing an acquaintance passing by on the street may cause me to remember a number of things about him, so also seeing him in my mind may produce a flood of remembered information about him. My image of him *reminds* me

42. H. H. Price, *Thinking and Experience* (New York: Hutchinson University Library, 1953), pp. 235–236.

of facts about him in just the same way as does my seeing him on the street.

I suspect that the idea that memory-images enable us to remember facts by allowing us to *read off* the facts from the images results from confusing that property of memory-images which consists in their being *embodiments* of remembering with that other property of memory-images which consists in their being *causes* of remembering. This confusion leads us to think that a certain piece of information is already *in* the image and that yet we *obtain* it *from* the image. Both things cannot be true.

16. My argument has been that a response that is determined solely by the perception or awareness of some present thing is not a memory response, whether that thing is a physical map or sign, or whether it is some sensation or image. But, as said, the perception or awareness of some present thing can be a *reminder*. A reminder is that which evokes *memory*. A present perception is not a reminder and the response it elicits is not a memory response unless the occurrence of that response is due in part to the influence of some *past* experience, perception, or training. You remember to buy a loaf of bread because you were previously told to do so, even though you would not have remembered to do so had you not overheard someone speaking of an "oven." It is a conceptual truth that the influence of the past enters into the explanation of memory responses.

The thrust of many theories of memory, however, is to deny this. They postulate some mental mechanism of memory in an attempt to give an adequate explanation of occurrences of remembering *without* any appeal to the influence of past perception or experience. The explanation will be solely in terms of the "present mental contents" of the supposed "memory-process." This aim, and the motive for it, is exhibited very clearly in these well-known remarks by Russell:

Everything constituting a memory-belief is happening *now*, not in that past time to which the belief is said to refer. It is not logically necessary to the existence of a memory-belief that the event remembered should have occurred, or even that the past should have existed at all. There is no logical impossibility in the hypothesis that the world sprang into being five minutes ago, exactly as it then was, with a population that "remembered" a wholly unreal past. There is no logically necessary connection between events at different times; therefore nothing that is happening now or will happen in the future can disprove the hypothesis that the world began five minutes ago. Hence the occurrences which are *called* knowledge of the past are logically independent of the past; they are wholly analysable into present contents, which might, theoretically, be just what they are even if no past had existed.[43]

I have tried to show elsewhere that the idea of its being logically possible that the world began five minutes ago "complete with memories and records" is incoherent.[44] Here I will briefly make three points.

First, when Russell says, "It is not logically necessary to the existence of a memory-belief that the event remembered should have occurred," he is using the expression "a memory-belief" ambiguously. We speak of remembering in many locutions: for example, "S remembers that *p*," "S suddenly remembered that *p*," "As S remembers it, *p*," "This is how S remembers it, namely, that *p*," "According to S's memory of the occasion, *p*," "S believes he remembers that *p*," "It seems to S that he remembers that *p*." Now if the first two locutions on this list are descriptions of what Russell means by "a memory-belief," then he is certainly wrong in claiming that it is not necessary to the existence of a memory-belief that what is remembered should have occurred. Those two locutions are so used in actual language that, if *p* is false, then it is not true that S remembers that *p*, nor that S suddenly remembered that *p*. None of the other locutions on this list, however, carry this entailment. Therefore Russell's claim is correct only if "a memory-belief" is something that is properly described by those latter locutions or similar ones.

Second, even if we restrict the expression "memory-belief" to

---

43. Russell, *The Analysis of Mind*, pp. 159–160.
44. See my *Knowledge and Certainty*, pp. 187–202.

cover only such things as fall under these latter descriptions (e.g., "It seems to S that he remembers that p," or "S believes he remembers that p"), I think it is impossible that *all* memory-beliefs could be false. We can see this if we reflect on the ways in which memory-beliefs are expressed. Many memory-beliefs are expressed in words, particularly in past-tense sentences such as "I put the screwdriver in the garage." If S said that to me, and I believed he was being truthful, but I was uncertain whether his memory was correct, I could make the following comment: "S believes he remembers putting the screwdriver in the garage." If I did this I would be attributing to S a "memory-belief." I would make this attribution on the basis of S's words to me only if I believed that S knew how to use those words to make a report about the past and was so using them. Many memory-beliefs are attributed to people on the basis of their own reports of past actions and events, but of course only on the assumption that they know how to use language to make such reports. And here is the important point: we would never attribute this know-how to any person unless we supposed that a good many of those utterances of his, which were presumed to be reports of past actions and happenings, had been *true*. Suppose that a child who is learning to speak has begun to use present-tense language correctly to report some of his own actions and perceptions. Next he begins to make utterances that have past-tense grammatical form, but if we interpreted them as reports of past happenings they would all be false, whereas if we took them as reports of present events they would be true. What should we think? Of course what we would think is that this child is using past-tense grammatical forms to report and describe present events. Certainly we would not attribute to him a lot of *false memory-beliefs*. Everything would be against the supposition that he had learned how to use language to make reports about past occurrences. My argument is that one of our principal criteria for attributing memory-beliefs to people (namely, their own reports of past occurrences) requires that many of those memory-beliefs should be true. Therefore, Russell's idea that all memory-beliefs, as normally expressed, could be false is not a logical possibility, since it is not a coherent idea.

A third idea which tempts philosophers to try to account for memory solely in terms of "the present mental content of remembering" is the feeling that, because of the "awkward gulf" between the present and the past,[45] the latter is *inaccessible* and so should be kept out of an analysis of memory. The "inaccessibility of the past" is a muddle. We *hear* the sound of the police siren *growing louder;* this logically implies a comparision of something present with something past; so what does it mean to say that past events are "inaccessible"? And what would it be like for them to be "accessible"? Perhaps there floats before our minds some hazy, self-contradictory, idea of past and present events occurring simultaneously. Insofar as it *makes sense* for past events to be "accessible," they are often, but not always, accessible.

17.   Various tempting but erroneous ideas drive Russell and other philosophers to try to formulate an "analysis of memory" that will treat memory responses as "logically independent of the past." That this position is self-contradictory is clearly seen from the fact that Russell also wants to regard memory as a form of *knowledge.* "There can be no doubt," he says, "that memory forms an indispensable part of our knowledge of the past." [46] But *knowledge* of the past is not logically independent of the past: if someone *knows* that it rained last week, it logically follows that it rained last week. Russell's uneasiness about the concept of memory leads him to vacillate on the question of whether memory is knowledge. When he says that occurrences of remembering are *"called* knowledge of the past," he is insinuating that this may be a common error.

I have been trying to show that Russell's analysis is also self-contradictory in a different way. In trying to analyze memory-judgments and responses solely in terms of various alleged features of "the present mental occurrence in remembering," he is denying the

45. Russell, *The Analysis of Mind*, p. 164.   46. Ibid., p. 165.

requirement of the concept of memory that a piece of behavior, or a belief, or a judgment is a manifestation of memory only if its occurrence is due, in part at least, to some past learning, perception, or experience. It is ironic that the ingenious mental apparatus invented by Russell to account for remembering, should be, in its very nature, inconsistent with the concept of remembering.

CHAPTER V

The Picture Theory
of Memory

1. A prominent feature of philosophical views about memory, as we have seen, is the notion that genuine memory occurrences involve a *representation* of what is remembered. Sometimes this is the very word that is used, as when Bergson says that "genuine" memory (as contrasted with "habit-memory") is a "representation." Martin and Deutscher say that "nobody actually remembers anything until he comes to the point of representing in some way what he has observed or experienced." [1] James says that memory involves a "complex representation." [2] And he quotes Ladd, who says the following about memory: "It is a fact of consciousness on which all possibility of connected experience and of recorded and cumulative human knowledge is dependent that certain phases or products of consciousness appear with a claim to stand for (to represent) past experiences to which they are regarded as in some respect similar." [3] Many philosophers who have claimed that "genuine" or "cognitive" memory requires an image have thought of the latter as being a "representation" of what is remembered. James Mill says that when you remember something you must have an "Idea" of it. If what you remember is a sensation, the "Idea" of it is

1. C. B. Martin and M. Deutscher, "Remembering," *Philosophical Review*, 75 (1966), 172.

2. James, *Principles of Psychology*, I, 651.

3. C. T. Ladd, *Physiological Psychology*, Pt. II, Ch. X, Sec. 23. Quoted by James, I, 688.

not a sensation but is "more like the sensation, than anything else can be; so like, that I call it a copy, an image of the sensation; sometimes, a representation, or trace of the sensation." [4] Mill is prepared to label the memory-idea, quite indifferently, as an "image" or "representation" or "copy" of what is remembered.

Philosophers have typically thought of the memory-representation as being *like* what is remembered, or as being *similar,* or as being a *copy* or *picture* of it. Aristotle says that remembering involves an "image" which is "like a sort of picture" or "like an imprint or drawing in us." We perceive the image as a "sort of copy" of the remembered thing.[5]

As we know, some philosophers want to say that the memory-image is only part of the total memory-representation. James thinks that in remembering there is "an image or copy" of the remembered event; but in addition there must be "a feeling of the past direction in time," and also a feeling of "warmth and intimacy." These features taken together compose a "representation." [6] In the whole representation there is not only a feature corresponding to the past event, but also a feature corresponding to its being a *past* event, and also a feature corresponding to its being an event "in *my* past."

What all of these philosophers have thought is that when one remembers something a "memory-event" occurs, and that it has a *structure* which contains a detail corresponding to each detail of what is remembered. This view is set forth in some remarks by Harrod. He imagines a man who remembers having walked along a certain street. Harrod says that this memory ("memory-event") is "a whole of parts with a complex structure." [7] There does not have to be an element in the "memory-event" corresponding to each property of the street that the man walked along, since he will not have observed every property of the street, and also he may have forgotten something of what he did observe. But there will be in

4. Mill, *An Analysis of the Phenomena of the Human Mind,* I, 51–52.
5. Aristotle, *De Memoria et Reminiscentia,* 449b–451a.   6. James, I, 649–651.
7. R. F. Harrod, "Memory," *Mind,* 51 (1942), 48.

the memory-event an element for each *remembered* property of the street. Harrod says:

> The material of the houses may be remembered but not the number of storeys, and so on. *The memory event must then be as complex as what is said to be remembered, which is a selection of a total experience, for how otherwise can we say how much of it is remembered?* And these must be properly disposed in relation to one another. It will not do if the paving stones are on the roofs and the slates in the street. *In fact, the memory must be in some sense a copy of the thing remembered.* This does not involve the alleged fallacy in the copying theory of truth, because that theory postulates that the mind is aware of a copy rather than a reality, and so introduces an otiose *tertium quid*. In this account the memory event is merely said to constitute or contain a copy of what is supposed to be remembered. Finally, to postulate that the structure as a whole is a copy does not prejudge the question whether each element has any sensory similarity to the remembered elements.[8]

Harrod's "memory event" is, of course, the same as Russell's "present mental content of remembering." The memory-event has to be a "copy" of what is remembered, not a copy of the actual street which the man remembers, but a copy of the street *as he remembers it*. It is in this sense that the memory-event must be "as complex as what is said to be remembered."

Harrod's reason for thinking this must be so is extremely interesting. He asks the rhetorical question, "For how otherwise can we say how much of it is remembered?" By "we" he would seem to mean anyone who remembers anything, and by "say" he may mean "tell" or "judge" or "know." Harrod's view might be that unless the memory-event were as "complex" as the thing one remembers (*as* one remembers it) one would not *know* whether one did, or did not, remember any particular feature of the thing. The man who walked along that street will not, for example, know that he remembers seeing a fire hydrant unless there is, in his memory-event, an element that corresponds to, and stands for, a fire hydrant. Or perhaps Harrod's view is not that the man will not *know* that he remembers seeing a fire hydrant, but rather that he will not

---

8. Ibid., pp. 49–50. Emphasis added.

remember seeing a fire hydrant. He will not even *think* "fire hydrant," if there is no part of his memory-event that means "fire hydrant."

Harrod is stating a case for a mental apparatus of remembering. On his view remembering works in the following way: you observed or experienced something, A, that had features x, y and z. Subsequently the question is put to you whether you remember feature x of A. You have a memory-event that corresponds to A (or, perhaps, to your "experience" of A). This memory-event is a more or less accurate "copy" or "picture" of A. If there is in your memory picture of A an element that corresponds to feature x of A, this means that you remember A *as* having feature x. (Whether A did actually have feature x is a different matter.) If in your memory picture there is no element that corresponds to x, this may mean that you do not remember A as having feature x. Or it may mean that you remember A as not having feature x. I will not try to decide in which of these two ways the absence of an element from the memory picture is to be taken, but will assume that at least the weaker sense is intended: namely, that the absence of an element corresponding to x would entail that you do not remember A as having x.

Stout states a view that seems to come to the same as Harrod's. He says, first of all, that "While we are remembering, the remembering is an actual experience." [9] "The appeal to memory," he says, "is an appeal to what we are now actually experiencing. . . ." [10] Stout is holding that remembering something involves a "memory-experience." This is the same as Harrod's "memory-event." Now how do we "appeal to" a memory-experience: what part does it play in remembering? Stout says the following:

In remembering past experience as such we are cognizant of it as past relatively to our own actual present in the moment of remembering it. Our total object is a complex unity which includes present and past in relation to each other. We are aware of the actual present as continued back into a

9. Stout, *Studies in Philosophy and Psychology*, p. 166.   10. Ibid.

certain past specially connected with it; and of this past as prolonged forward into the actual present. But this seems possible only on one condition. Since the past itself is not actually experienced there is no clue to it, unless the actual present is stamped with a character due to the fact that the result of past experience is continued into it. Further, this character must be specifically different according to the specific nature of the past which is remembered. I do not, of course, mean that reminiscence consists in apprehending this character of the actual present. On the contrary, this character by its intrinsic nature is so essentially relative and incomplete that it cannot be apprehended at all without apprehending what is required to complete it, i.e. the past experience which is remembered. This view seems to me to be fully borne out by introspection. If I ask myself how and why I am justified in asserting on the evidence of memory that I have had this or that past experience I find only one answer, and this seems sufficient—my actual present would not be such as it is if it had not behind it a certain actual past. Hence I maintain that in relying on memory we are relying on immediate present experience. We can have one leg in the past only because the other has a foothold in the present.

If this is denied, the only alternative seems to be clairvoyance or absolutely *a priori* knowledge of matters of fact. But we no longer believe in miracles.[11]

Stout's view seems to be the following: when we remember a past event we do not experience over again the past event itself. What we have is a present memory-experience. This memory-experience is "essentially relative," in the sense (I believe) that we are aware of it only as a picture or copy of the past event. And this memory-experience "must be specifically different according to the specific nature of the past which is remembered." That is to say, every variation in our present memory-experience entails a variation in the way we remember the past event. We would have "no clue" as to the nature of the past event if the present memory-experience did not have a certain definite character. In remembering something we must "rely" on our memory-experience. Otherwise, memory would be miraculous.

It should be noted that Stout says that "in remembering past events, we have a knowledge which is immediate in the sense that

11. Ibid., pp. 175–176.

it is not inferential or representative in any ordinary or natural meaning of these terms." [12] In saying that memory is not "inferential," he is agreeing with Reid, Russell, Broad, and many others, that one does not infer some feature of the past event from some character of the present memory-event. I find it a bit puzzling, however, that Stout should deny that in remembering we have "a knowledge" which is *"representative."* I understand his view to be that in remembering a past event we have an "experience" or "memory-event" which *is* a representation of the past event. When Stout says that our "knowledge" is not "representative," I take him to mean no more than that it is not based on some process of inference, and not to mean that in remembering there is no representation.

It is pretty evident that these various attempts to say what is essential to remembering are inspired by the same conception. This conception is the following: At some time in the past we perceived some thing or event—a face, a river, a footrace. The footrace (it is supposed) had a *structure;* but also our perception (or "experience") of it had a structure. Subsequently we "remembered" the footrace. What does this mean? It means that there occurred or, perhaps, that we produced, something that had more or less the *same* structure as did our perception of the footrace. If the second structure was exactly the same as the first one, then our memory of the footrace, as we perceived it, was exactly correct. To say that we had "forgotten" some details of the footrace, would mean that for some elements or relations in our perception of the footrace there were not corresponding elements or relations in the "memory-event." There would always be, however, an *exact* correspondence between the "memory-event" and the footrace, *as we remember the latter.* This is really a tautology: for it means that we remember the footrace *as* we remember it.

2. The important point to notice is that, on this conception, remembering requires *a one-to-one correspondence* between the elements

12. Ibid., p. 166.

and relations of two numerically different structures. The fact that the "memory-event" is thought to stand in a one-to-one correspondence with the past reality, as remembered, is what leads philosophers to say that in remembering there must be a "copy" of what is remembered. Harrod, for example, remarks that the "memory-event" can be said "to constitute or contain a copy of what is supposed to be remembered." The idea of a one-to-one correspondence is also what lies behind the notion that memory involves a "picture" of what is remembered, or involves a "presentation" that "resembles" or is "like" or is "similar" to what is remembered.

The surprisingly widespread insistence by philosophers that remembering requires *images* may also, I believe, be attributed to this assumption of a one-to-one correspondence between the "memory-event" and what is remembered. It is interesting to note how philosophers are often willing to substitute other words for the word "image." James says that memory involves "an image or copy of the original event." James Mill says that we remember something by means of an "Idea," and the latter he calls, indifferently, an "image," a "copy," a "representation." Stout says that when we remember something an image is "the specifying content of the thought"; and he adds, "Apart from the image or *something discharging an equivalent function*, this thought would be empty." [13] So what does this job does not have to be exactly an *image*. Something other than an image will suffice, provided it has the right sort of structure.

Woozley claims that "the plain man" has the following conception of memory:

   (a)   the event remembered is not what is immediately before the
           mind in remembering;
   (b)   what is immediately before the mind in remembering is an
           image;

13. Ibid., p. 367. Emphasis added.

(c) the image in some way represents or symbolizes the event of which it is an image.[14]

What Woozley has expounded is a full-blown philosophical theory of memory (held by Aristotle and others) rather than a conception to be attributed to "the plain man," although it is true that almost anyone, in a philosophical moment, can be enticed into accepting this theory. But I am more interested in what Woozley goes on to say. He asks why "we" accept proposition (b) above. His answer is that "what we mean in general by 'image' is that an image is the sort of thing that we have before our minds when we remember." [15] I do not take this to be anything like an accurate account of how in fact the word "image" is commonly used since, as previously noted, we are often ready to say that a person "remembered" something regardless of whether he had an image of it. The significance of Woozley's statement is that it indicates a philosophical inclination to *call* that mental thing which, it is thought, *must* be present when we remember, an "image," regardless of what it is, just so long as it performs the service of "representing" the past event.

There is a curious vagueness in the way philosophers have spoken of the requirement of an image. When we remember something, there must be "some sort of image," "something like an image," "some sort of image, copy or representation." It would appear that the persistent philosophical claim that "Memory demands an image" (Russell) is not an insistence on what is *literally* an image, but rather an insistence on the presence of a "complex structure" which will provide a representation by virtue of having a one-to-one correlation with what is remembered. The structure is called a "copy," a "picture," an "image." This would explain why the traditional view of philosophers that memory requires an image is not refuted by the commonplace observation that very frequently when

14. A. D. Woozley, *Theory of Knowledge* (London: Hutchinson University Library, 1949), p. 39.
15. Ibid., p. 40.

we remember something there is no image. The word "image," or "copy," or "picture" is something a philosopher seizes on, perhaps with some embarrassment, for lack of a better word, to indicate the representing structure that is thought to be present in the "memory-event" as a matter of a priori necessity.

3. Let us examine more closely the notion that in remembering something one must "represent" it or produce a "representation" of it. Suppose that you called on a friend and then later the two of you left his house together. You saw him lock the front door, and later you remembered that he locked it. Philosophers typically ask, "What happened when you remembered?" Now a variety of different things could have happened, as may be seen from the following imaginary cases:

1) He asks you, "Did I lock the front door?" You promptly reply, "Yes," without any effort to remember or any imagery. Your attention is concentrated on driving your car over an icy road.

2) He says nervously, "I wonder if I locked the front door." You say sternly, and with emphasis, *"Yes, you locked the front door."* Since this friend frequently has this worry, what you think to yourself is, "Are we going to have another outbreak of anxiety over whether the door is locked?"

3) He says, "Do you recall whether I locked the door?" At first you can't remember. You say, "Let's see now." You have a feeling of tension. You try to picture his departure from the house. You have an image of him bending over the doorknob. Suddenly you say, with a feeling of relief, "Yes, you locked it."

4) There has been a police investigation and the police officer says to you: "I want you to act out for me the movements your friend made in leaving the house." You comply by first walking to the bedroom and picking up your friend's briefcase. Then you go to the closet and take his coat off the hanger. You walk out the front door and lock it. You walk down the porch steps to the garage. While carrying out this performance you are nervous and

anxious. You think to yourself, "Will he be cleared?" In your mind's eye you see your friend's pale face behind bars.

5) The police officer says: "I am going to relate the sequence of his movements on leaving the house as I believe they occurred. If I mention something you do *not* remember, please hold up your hand." The officer then relates a sequence of events, including the locking of the door. You listen carefully, with some feeling of tension, and with your eyes fixed on the officer, but without any other notable sensations, thoughts, or images. When the officer says, "He paused on the porch to put on his coat," you raise your hand.

6) As you are driving together, an hour after leaving the house, you say to your friend, "I notice that you locked your front door. Are you afraid of burglars?"

4. All these are cases in which you remembered that your friend locked the door. And, of course, an indefinitely large number of other cases are possible. In regard to which of our examples would it be natural to say that you "represented" his locking the front door, or had or gave a "representation" of it? Surely not in the first case, in which you merely said "Yes." Surely not in the fifth case, in which you did not raise your hand when the officer said, "Then he locked the door." In the third case you had an image of him bending over the doorknob, not an image of him locking the door.

It seems that only in the fourth case, where you *acted out* the sequence of your friend's actions, would there be any naturalness in speaking of a "representation." And what you represented, or gave a representation of, was *the sequence of his actions* in leaving the house. It does not seem right to say that you represented or gave a representation of any *single* action, such as his picking up his briefcase, or his locking the door. It is true that if there was something eccentric or distinctive in the way he locked the door, and you proceeded to *imitate* the particular way in which he went about locking it, then we might say that you represented *the way* he locked it or gave a representation of *his way* of locking it. Even then it would not be natural, or even good English, to say that you represented *that* he locked it or gave a representation of *the fact* that he locked it.

Martin and Deutscher do not hold, as so many philosophers have, that the representation must take the form of mental imagery. For them a memory-representation might take the form of physical action. They give the example of a man who had witnessed another person swimming with a peculiar kind of stroke. Later he cannot name or describe it, or even visualize it; but he can imitate it. "He gets into the water, experimenting a little until suddenly he gets it right and exclaims, 'Aha, that's it!' " [16]

In the circumstances as described, swimming with that stroke would indeed be a manifestation of memory, and it would also be a representation of how the person swam. On Russell's theory the representation would have to be an image. Martin and Deutscher are right in holding that a memory-representation might be a sequence of physical behavior. Russell's view is that remembering consists of a representation plus the judgment "This occurred." In Martin and Deutscher's example there is a striking parallel: there is a representation plus the exclamation "Aha, that's it!" Another example of a memory-representation given by them is a man's painting, on a canvas, a detailed picture of a farmyard scene that he witnessed as a boy. (In this example there is no "Aha, that's it!", since the painter is supposed to believe that he is painting a purely imaginery scene.)

I agree that swimming in a certain way might be a representation of how someone swam and that painting something might be a representation of a past scene, and also that both might be forms of remembering. But this is a long way from accepting the universal claim that remembering necessarily involves a representation. Martin and Deutscher say, "Somebody may have observed an event, but unless he is recounting it to himself, telling others or in some other way representing it, then, roughly speaking, he is not remembering that event." [17] These remarks imply that to recount

16. Martin and Deutscher, pp. 161–162.   17. Ibid., p. 172.

something is to represent it. I think this is true, because to recount what happened is to *tell in detail* what happened. This is possible only if there are *details*, a number of items or aspects, which can be set forth more or less accurately. Recounting is analogous to imitating a sequence of movements or to painting a detailed scene. These are all "representations." A representation can be *more or less* accurate. So can one's recounting or relating an episode, or one's imitation of someone's speech or movements, or one's painting a real scene.

It is wrong, however, to suppose that in all cases of remembering something there is a representation. Martin and Deutscher say the following: "On anyone's account of memory, it is not enough that someone should have observed or experienced something in the past. He must do something in the present. 'What sort of thing must he do in the present, in order to be said to remember?' is a difficult and very general question." [18] In our case 5 the police officer related a sequence of events, and when the officer said, "Then he locked the front door," you did *not* raise your hand; nor did you say to yourself, "That's right, he locked the front door," nor did you see, in your mind's eye, your friend locking it. The officer correctly took the fact that you did not raise your hand as signifying that you remembered that your friend locked the door. But what did you *do* "in order to be said to remember"? Was *not-*raising-your-hand what you did? But your "not-raising-your-hand" cannot be said to be "a more or less accurate representation" of the locking of the door. It is not a representation at all. By not raising your hand you indicated that you remembered that your friend locked the door: but you did not give a representation of his locking it, nor a representation of how (or the way) he locked it; nor did you "represent the fact" that he locked it.

5. The point of the preceding reflections is to show that when philosophers insist that memory requires a representation they are

18. Ibid.

not following the actual use in the language of the words "represent" and "representation." When Martin and Deutscher declare that "nobody actually remembers anything until he comes to the point of representing in some way what he has observed or experienced," they intend, of course, to be stating a conceptual truth and not an empirical generalization. The verbs "remember" and "represent" are not, however, bound together in this strict way in their ordinary use. This conceptual connection does not lie in the language, but instead in Martin and Deutscher's view of the nature of memory. They do not understand what remembering is or how it works *unless* it involves "a representation." But if they broadened their base of examples of remembering and paid closer attention to the language, they would begin to feel, I believe, that "represent" and "representation" are not entirely happy words for indicating that necessary thing which, on their view, must be present in all remembering. Like the philosophers who have insisted on *imagery* as a necessary condition for genuine memory, so Martin and Deutscher too might want to qualify their requirement of a *representation* by saying that what is required for memory is "some kind of representation," or "something like a representation," or "some sort of representation or picture" of what is remembered. "Representation" is not quite the right word, any more than "image" is. Martin and Deutscher say that the question of what a person must do in order to remember something is "a difficult and very general question." By "very general" they imply that there is some sort of act or event that is present in all cases of remembering; and by saying it is a "difficult" question they imply that it is hard to say exactly what that act or event is.

6.   I think that in Wittgenstein's *Tractatus* we find the most elegant statement of the viewpoint that dominates the philosophers who believe that whenever one remembers something a "memory-event" must occur or be produced, which is an *image, copy, picture,* or *representation* or what is remembered. Wittgenstein's book makes no

reference to memory. It deals in the most general terms with the nature of saying and thinking. Remembering, and saying what one remembers, would be special cases falling under the general theory of the book.

The central idea of the *Tractatus* is that a sentence (*Satz*) that has sense (*Sinn*) is a *picture* of reality. The meanings of individual words have to be explained to us, but when we know the meaning of the words that compose a sentence, the sense of the sentence does not have to be explained to us. "A sentence *shows* it sense" (4.022).[19] A sentence shows its sense in just the way, Wittgenstein supposed, that a picture shows what it is a picture of. "A sentence is a picture of reality: for if I understand a sentence, I know the situation it presents. And I understand the sentence without having had its sense explained to me" (4.021). A sentence shows how things are in the world if it is true (4.022). And this is just what a picture does. An unfamiliar sentence composed of familiar words is able to communicate a new state of affairs only because it is a *picture* of the state of affairs. "A sentence says something only in so far as it is a picture" (4.03).

The *Tractatus* contains a precise conception of what a "picture" is and how it must be related to what it depicts. A picture is composed of elements that are related to one another in a definite way (2.14). A state of affairs in the world is composed of things that are related to one another in a definite way. In order for something to be a picture of a certain state of affairs or situation (*Sachlage*) there must be, according to the *Tractatus*, a one-to-one correspondence between the elements of the picture and the things in the state of affairs. "The fact that the elements of a picture are related to one another in a determinate way represents that the things are related to one another in the same way" (2.15). The particular connection

---

19. Wittgenstein, *Tractatus Logico-Philosophicus*, trans. D. F. Pears and B. F. McGuinness (London: Routledge & Kegan Paul, 1961). First published in 1921. Occasionally I modify the translation.

of its elements is the *structure* of the picture, and the *possibility* of this structure Wittgenstein calls "the pictorial form of the picture" or its "form of representation." He also characterizes pictoral *form* as the *possibility* that the things in reality to which the elements of the picture correspond are related to one another in the same way as are the elements of the picture (2.151). In other words, the pictorial form or form of representation is the *possibility* that the picture-elements and the corresponding reality-elements should each be arranged in an identical structure. If this possibility is realized the picture is *true,* and if not it is *false.* If it were *not possible* for the combination of picture-elements and the combination of reality-elements to have the same structure, the picture could not be a picture, either true or false. "There must be something identical in a picture and what it depicts, to enable the one to be a picture of the other at all" (2.161). A picture and the reality that it depicts must have in common the same *form* of representation (2.17). That is to say, they must have in common the possibility of exemplifying the same structure.

The *Tractatus* remarks that it may not *seem* that a *sentence* is a picture; but when we reflect on what is required in order to be able to say something, its character as a picture becomes evident:

At first sight a sentence—one set out on the printed page, for example—does not seem to be a picture of the reality with which it is concerned. But no more does musical notation at first sight seem to be a picture of music, nor our phonetic notation (the alphabet) to be a picture of our speech. And yet these sign-languages prove to be pictures, even in the ordinary sense, of what they represent (4.011).

In order for a sentence to have sense—that is, to say something—that is, to be a picture—it must contain as many elements as does the state of affairs it portrays. "In a sentence there must be as much to be distinguished as in the situation it represents. The two must possess the same logical (mathematical) multiplicity" (4.04). A sentence is connected by rules of projection to the situation it depicts. When we consider the role of these rules of projection, the pictorial character of the sentence becomes manifest.

There is a general rule by means of which the musician can obtain the symphony from the score, and which makes it possible to derive the symphony from the groove on the gramophone record, and, using the first rule, to derive the score again. That is what constitutes the inner similarity between these structures which seem to be so entirely different. And that rule is the law of projection which projects the symphony into the language of musical notation. It is the rule for translating this language into the language of gramophone records (4.0141).

So does a picture, too, have an "inner similarity" with what it depicts. This similarity is due to the presence, *in* the picture, of the picturing (pictorial) relationship (*die abbildende Beziehung*). The picturing relationship, which makes something into a picture, *belongs* to the picture (2.1513). This picturing relationship "consists of the correlations of the picture's elements with things" (2.1514). These correlations are not something we find ready made, but something that we create when we turn a group of elements into a picture. "We make for ourselves pictures of facts" (2.1). A picture is connected with reality by virtue of the correlations that we have established. "These correlations are, as it were, the feelers of the picture's elements, with which the picture touches reality" (2.1515). We lay the picture "against reality, like a ruler" (2.1512). If something is to serve me as a picture, I must connect the picture-elements with reality-elements.

The same thing holds for *sentences* as for pictures. Suppose we are presented with a spoken or written sentence: i.e., a "sentence-sign" (*Satzzeichen*). We *use* this perceptible sign "as a projection of a possible situation" (3.11). Wittgenstein says that "the method of projection is the thinking of the sense of the sentence" (3.11). We think of a possible situation by correlating elements of the sentence-sign with elements of reality, according to some rule of projection.

Wittgenstein says that "a sentence (*Satz*) is a sentence-sign (*Satzzeichen*) in its projective relation to the world" (3.12). It is the *Satz* which is a picture, not the *Satzzeichen*. We create a *Satz* by imposing a projection on the *Satzzeichen*. Thus a *Satz* is a picture because it includes the projection imposed on the string of words or sounds.

There is no problem of "interpreting" a *Satz* because it already *contains* its interpretation. This is how a *Satz* can show its sense. Bruce Goldberg describes the *Tractatus* view as follows:

> How is it that a picture is able to represent reality? How is it that it is able to represent the reality it does? Wittgenstein's answer is that the picture "includes the pictorial relationship, which makes it into a picture" (2.1513). In possessing the picture I know what reality it represents. There is no further problem of interpreting it. The lines of projection are already there, in the picture. The picture *shows* what reality it represents. This is what Wittgenstein means by saying that "a proposition *shows* its sense" (4.022).[20]

Let us consider now what a *thought* is. Wittgenstein says: "A thought is a sentence (*Satz*) that has sense" (4). To speak of "a *Satz* that has sense" is somewhat redundant, since "a *Satz* is a *Satzzeichen* in its projective relation to the world" (3.12). Strictly speaking, a *Satz* cannot be without sense. "An applied, thought out, *Satzzeichen* is a thought" (3.5). An applied, thought out, *Satzzeichen* is also a *Satz*. So a *Satz* is a thought, and a thought is a *Satz*. And a *Satz* is a picture; so a thought is a picture. "A logical picture of facts is a thought." (3).

It is at least misleading, however, to say that a physical sentence (*Satz*) is a thought. A written or spoken sentence is not a thought unless it is being *used* to project a possible situation. But an identification of sentences and thoughts may be more than misleading: it may be an erroneous interpretation of the *Tractatus*. Shortly after Wittgenstein had finished writing the *Tractatus*, he was asked by Russell, in a letter, "Does a thought (*Gedanke*) consist of words?" The reply was: "No! But of psychical constituents that have the same sort of relation to reality as words. What those constituents are I don't know." [21] In the same letter Wittgenstein says, "I don't know *what* the constituents of a thought are but I know *that* it must

20. Bruce Goldberg, "The Correspondence Hypothesis," *Philosophical Review*, 77 (1968), 449. I am indebted to this article, and still more to many discussions with Goldberg, for a better understanding of the *Tractatus*.

21. Wittgenstein, *Notebooks 1914–1916*, trans. G. E. M. Anscombe, (Oxford: Blackwell, 1961), p. 130.

have such constituents which correspond to the words of Language." [22]

It appears, therefore, that Wittgenstein's conception of what a thought is was not set forth very clearly in the *Tractatus*. A thought is not to be identified with an uttered sentence—not even with a sentence that "has sense." A thought cannot be identified with a sentence-sign "in its projective relation to the world." A thought and a physical sentence are two different things, with corresponding constituents of different natures. *Each* of these two things is a picture. In a notebook entry of 1916, when the *Tractatus* was being written, Wittgenstein says: "Now it is becoming clear why I thought that thinking and language were the same. For thinking is a kind of language. For a thought too is, of course, a logical picture of a proposition and therefore it just is a kind of proposition." [23] Wittgenstein's view appears to have been the following: When you think a thought, there is a "psychical" structure. To express the thought in language is to project that same structure into the words of a physical sentence. The physical sentence *becomes* a picture by the virtue of the fact that the psychical picture is projected into it. If the picture is true there are *three* things that have the same structure but different natures: the psychical picture, the physical sentence, the state of affairs in the world.

Thus a spoken sentence *derives* its pictorial character from a psychical picture: but the psychical picture does not derive *its* pictorial nature from anything! As Goldberg puts it: "A picture is an ordered *psychical* structure. The sentences we utter have the meaning they do because of the relationship in which they stand to these psychical structures." [24] The same word-sentence can mean dif-

22. Ibid., p. 129.   23. Ibid., p. 82.

24. Goldberg, p. 450. David Favrholdt, in his book on the *Tractatus*, argues convincingly, that a *Tractatus* thought, that which is composed of psychical (mental) constituents, is radically unlike a sentence composed of physical signs, in that the physical sentence will require a method of projection or a "key of interpretation," in order to have a sense; whereas the thought, the mental structure, not only does not need a key of interpretation but even cannot have one. An essential feature of the picture theory is that there has to be something that *shows* its sense, and this should

ferent things on different occasions of utterance, depending on which psychical picture is projected into it.

The *Tractatus* says, "A proposition is a picture of a situation only in so far as it is logically articulated" (4.032). A meaningful sentence is not a jumble of words, but an articulated structure (3.141). When this articulation is achieved, the proposition is divided into its simple components, called names," each of which stands for a simple object. A proposition pictures a situation in the world only when the proposition is completely divided into names. A particular combination of names will necessarily depict one and only one possible situation in the world—that is, one and only one combination of the corresponding simple objects. "A proposition communicates a situation to us; therefore it must be *essentially* connected with the situation" (4.03).

But where does this complete articulation occur that turns a sentence into an unambiguous depiction of uniquely one situation? Where is it achieved? Apparently not in an ordinary physical sentence, such as "The window is to the left of the fireplace." For this

---

mean that its sense does not derive from a key of interpretation but is, so to speak, *intrinsic*. But it is completely implausible to suppose that any physical picture or sentence could have such a remarkable property. But with *thoughts* ("mental" structures) the situation seems to be totally different. As Favrholdt somewhat naively puts it: "Whenever we think or have a thought, we inevitably know what the thought pictures or describes. We never have to think of a key of interpretation which indicates how the thought is to be 'read' " (D. Favrholdt, *An Interpretation and Critique of Wittgenstein's Tractatus*, [Copenhagen; Munksgaard, 1967], p. 84). Favrholdt makes the more sharply compelling point that if a key of interpretation had to be added to a thought in order to turn the latter into a picture, then the picture theory would be involved in an infinite regress: for a key of interpretation would itself be a thought, which would not picture anything until a key of interpretation was in turn applied to it, and so on (ibid.). The picture theory, in order to avoid this incoherence, has to assume the existence of something that is a picture, and *not* by virtue of the application to it of a method of projection or key of interpretation. A thought, consisting of a configuration of mental elements, is on this view intrinsically a picture. It can, however, be made perceptible to the senses; it can be expressed in physical language. As Favrholdt says: "The expression of the thought is carried out by replacing the elements of the thought by the elements of the propositional sign. Thus the propositional sign suddenly becomes a picture, a projection of a possible state of affairs" (ibid., p. 88).

sentence certainly does not have a unique sense on all occasions of utterance. The complete articulation does not occur in the physical pattern of sounds or marks. Where does it occur?

The only possible answer, from the viewpoint of the *Tractatus*, is that it takes place in our *thinking* or *meaning*. Wittgenstein wrote in his notebook the following remark: "It seems clear that what we *Mean* must always be 'sharp'." [25] One could express the same idea by saying that what we *think* is always sharp, or that our *thoughts* are always sharp, always unambiguous. The physical sentences, however, in which our thoughts are clothed are not "sharp." The *Tractatus* says: "Language disguises thought. So much so, that from the outward form of the clothing it is impossible to infer the form of the clothed thoughts" (4.002). On the face of it this seems to contradict another assertion of the *Tractatus*, to wit: "All the propositions of our everyday language are actually, just as they are, in perfect logical order" (5.5563). If language badly disguises thought, how can our "propositions" be in perfect order? It seems that Wittgenstein was here identifying "propositions" with *"thoughts"*—not with physical sentences, not with *Satzzeichen*. According to this conception thoughts are clear and perfectly ordered, just as they are. Their clarity is not impaired by the vagueness and ambiguity of their physical embodiment, their "clothing."

7. If I am giving a correct reading of the *Tractatus*, then some of the descriptions of wrong ways of philosophical thinking that Wittgenstein subsequently provided in *The Blue Book* can be seen to apply to his own previous viewpoint. In the *Tractatus*, as I summarized it, a physical sentence derives its meaning from a thought. The physical sentence *could* mean this or *could* mean that: it is capable of different interpretations. But the thought which, on a particular occasion, is projected into the physical sentence cannot itself be open to different interpretations. It is *the meaning* of the sentence. It is to *it* that a correct interpretation of the sentence leads.

25. Wittgenstein, *Notebooks*, p. 68.

To understand the meaning of a physical sentence is to come into the possession of something (*not* the sentence) the meaning of which *shows* itself—something the meaning of which is transparent, self-revealing, unambiguous. It is something that not only does not require interpretation but *cannot* be interpreted. It is where interpretation ends. In Goldberg's phrase, it is a "meaning terminus." [26] In *The Blue Book* this idea is described as follows: "What one wishes to say is: 'Every sign is capable of interpretation; but the meaning mustn't be capable of interpretation. It is the last interpretation.' " [27]

The *Tractatus* says that a *Satz shows* its sense (4.022). But as we are now reading the *Tractatus* no arrangement of spoken sounds or written marks can "show its sense." No structure of physical signs can be a meaning terminus. It is only a *mental* state or process, a psychical structure, that can have this remarkable feature. And thus, only *it* can be truly a *picture.* Our physical sentences obtain all of their life and meaning from the psychical pictures that are projected into them. In *The Blue Book* Wittgenstein describes this idea as follows:

It seems that there are *certain definite* mental processes bound up with the working of language, processes through which alone language can function. I mean the processes of understanding and meaning. The signs of our language seem dead without these mental processes; and it might seem that the only function of the signs is to induce such processes, and that these are the things we ought really to be interested in. . . . We are tempted to think that the action of language consists of two parts; an inorganic part, the handling of signs, and an organic part, which we may call understanding these signs, meaning them, interpreting them, thinking. These latter activities seem to take place in a queer kind of medium, the mind; and the mechanism of the mind, the nature of which, it seems, we don't quite understand, can bring about effects which no material mechanism could. [28]

I take these remarks to be a correct characterization of Wittgenstein's own thinking when he wrote the *Tractatus*. The "organic"

26. Goldberg, p. 446.   27. Wittgenstein, *The Blue and Brown Books*, p. 34.
28. Ibid., p. 3.

part, which gives "life" to language, is a mental state or process, composed of "psychical constituents." It is because of the presence of the organic part that the physical sentences of language *say* something about the world.

Viewed in this light the *Tractatus* belongs to a traditional conception of the relation between language and mind. *Tractatus* "thoughts" (composed of psychical constituents) do the job of Locke's "ideas." Locke says that man was so fashioned by God that he was able "to frame articulate sounds, which we call words." But, he adds, "this was not enough to produce language; for parrots, and several other birds, will be taught to make articulate sounds distinct enough, which yet by no means are capable of language." [29] In order for there to be genuine language the words a man utters must connect with "ideas within the mind." Locke continues, "Besides articulate sounds, therefore, it was further necessary that he should be able to use these sounds as signs for internal conceptions; and to make them stand as marks for the ideas within his own mind, whereby they might be made known to others, and the thoughts of men's minds be conveyed from one to another." [30] Signs take on meaning, and become language, by virtue of being connected with "internal conceptions." The latter give life to the signs, just as do the *Tractatus* "thoughts," which are composed of psychical constituents that correspond to the words of language.

8. To return to the topic of memory, the conception that a thought is a picture has the immediate implication that to *remember* something is to picture it. This will hold of course only for "occurrent" remembering, and only for it when it is "cognitive" or "genuine." It is to be noted that the *Tractatus* conceives thought to be always propositional in form; a thought is a *Satz*, and the general form of a *Satz* is: "This is how things stand" (4.5). Now one might think that the result of this view for the topic of memory would be that propositional or "factual" remembering (remembering *that* so

29. Locke, *Essay Concerning Human Understanding*, Bk. III, Ch. 1, Sec. 1.
30. Ibid., Bk. III, Ch. 2, Sec. 2.

and so) would be pictorial, but that it would not be the case that remembering an event, such as a collision, or remembering a thing or object, such as a face, or a room, or a river, would require a picture. But on the view of the *Tractatus* the perception of any complex object or event is propositional in form. "To perceive a complex means to perceive that its constituents are related to one another in such and such a way" (5.5423). If the perception of something is propositional, then presumably remembering what one had perceived would also be propositional.

It is worth reminding ourselves here of the tendency in the philosophy of memory to think that factual memory is the "essential" or "core" ingredient of all forms of memory. The memory of events or objects, remembering *how*, remembering *when*, remembering *where*, and so on—all these involve remembering *that*, plus specific features of their own.[31] The belief in the centrality of factual memory fits hand in glove with the picture theory of thinking. From the union of these two ideas there would emerge the conclusion that remembering is necessarily picturing or representing.

We have observed the striking tendency, exhibited during many centuries of philosophical thought, to insist that when we remember something there must be a "memory-event," which is a copy, picture, image, imprint, or some sort of representation of what we remember. This is supposed to be a requirement for "genuine" remembering, as contrasted with "habit" or "dispositional" memory. I suggest that one source of this prevalent view are the following two ideas: First, in "genuine" or "cognitive" remembering one must *think of* what one remembers. Aristotle remarks that "whenever someone is actively engaged in remembering, he always says in his soul . . . that he heard, or perceived, or thought this before." [32] Second, to think of something *is* to represent it, to portray it, to form a picture or copy of it in a certain medium.

---

31. For such a view see E. M. Zemach, "A Definition of Memory," *Mind*, 77 (1968), 530. Also see footnote 9 of Chapter I.

32. Aristotle, *De Memoria*, 449a.

9. There would seem to be a provocative parallel between Aristotle's doctrine that "the soul never thinks without an image," [33] and the view of the *Tractatus* that a thought is a picture. Although I am not competent to have confident opinions about Aristotle, I have a hunch that there is in Aristotle a strong anticipation of the picture theory of *Tractatus*. Aristotle asserts in *De Anima* what might seem to be a surprising view, namely, that "actual knowledge is identical with its object" (431a). In "actual" as contrasted with "potential" knowledge the mind is actively thinking of the object of knowledge. Now, says Aristotle, "the mind which is actively thinking is the objects which it thinks" (431b). But in what way is the mind *identical* with the objects which it thinks? If I think of a stone, does my mind become a stone? No. When I think of a stone, my mind receives the "form" of the stone: "It is not the stone which is present in the soul but its form" (431b). I may be taking in a wrong sense what Aristotle means by the "form" of the stone, but his remark does *suggest* to me (perhaps incorrectly) that he had a view similar to Wittgenstein's in the *Tractatus*, namely this: when I think of something, my thought has, or is, a structure (a "psychical structure"), and if my thought is true or accurate, then the thought-structure and the structure (i.e., Aristotle's "form") of the object of thought are identical. Thus in thinking and knowing our minds take in, or take on, the structure or "forms" of the objects of thought and knowledge; in doing this our minds model or picture those objects. In *De Memoria* Aristotle drew the consequence that, since remembering is a kind of thinking, there is "in us" something that is "like an imprint or drawing" and which is "a sort of copy" of the remembered thing (450b).

10. In his paper "On Propositions: What They Are And How They Mean," [34] Russell sets forth a similar view. Thinking and meaning are essentially picturing; genuine remembering is a form

---

33. Aristotle, *De Anima*, 431a. Trans. J. A. Smith. *Basic Works of Aristotle*, ed. R. McKeon (New York: Random House, 1941).
34. Reprinted in Russell, *Logic and Knowledge*.

of thinking and requires that we have a picture of the past occurrence. In this paper Russell sets for himself the following problem:

It is obvious to begin with that, if we take some such word as 'Socrates' or 'dog', the meaning of the word consists in some relation to an object or set of objects. The first question to be asked is: Can the relation called 'meaning' be a direct relation between the word as physical occurrence and the object itself, or must the relation pass through a 'mental' intermediary, which could be called the 'idea' of the object? [35]

Russell's reflections lead him to the conclusion that a "mental intermediary" is required. It appears to him that the only alternative would be some form of behaviorism, to which he states no decisive objection but which he is inclined to think is inadequate as a theory of language. He is doubtful that a behavioristic view can account for a conspicuous feature of thinking and of language, namely, the feature of referring to "absent objects," and the feature of expressing anticipations of possible but nonexisting states of affairs. Russell says:

The phenomenon called 'thinking', however it may be analysed, has certain characteristics which cannot be denied. One of the most obvious of those is that it enables us to act with reference to absent objects, and not only with reference to those that are sensibly present. The tendency of the behaviourist school is to subordinate cognition to action, and to regard action as physically explicable. Now I do not wish to deny that much action, perhaps most, is physically explicable, but nevertheless it seems impossible to account for *all* action without taking account of 'ideas,' i.e., images of absent objects. If this view is rejected, it will be necessary to explain away all desire. [36]

As an example of a use of language to refer to an "absent object," Russell offers the case of a child who tells of some remembered event: "It is clear that, in so far as the child is genuinely remembering, he has a picture of the past occurrence, and his words are chosen so as to describe the picture; and in so far as the hearer is genuinely apprehending what is said, the hearer is acquiring a picture more or less like that of the child." [37] The use of words in

35. Ibid., p. 290.   36. Ibid., p. 297.   37. Ibid., p. 302.

thinking, Russell says, divides up into the use of words to refer to something we *remember* and the use of words to refer to something we *imagine*. In both cases the mediation of images is required in order to "bring us into touch with what is remote in time or space." [38] "Thus the problem of the meaning of words is reduced to the problem of the meaning of images." [39]

Russell goes on to say that "The 'meaning' of images is the simplest kind of meaning, because images resemble what they mean, whereas words, as a rule, do not." [40] He allows, however, that what an image means is "partly within the control of our will." For example, "In thinking of dogs in general, we may use a vague image of a dog, which means the species, not any individual." [41]

As noted previously, Russell distinguishes two types of "propositions," those composed of words and those composed of images. "As a general rule, a word proposition 'means' an image-proposition." [42] He further says:

The most important thing about a proposition is that, whether it consists of images or of words, it is, whenever it occurs, an actual fact, having a certain analogy of structure—to be further investigated—with the fact which makes it true or false. A word-proposition, apart from niceties, 'means' the corresponding image-proposition, and an image-proposition has an objective reference dependent upon the meanings of its constituent images.[43]

These remarks provide a rough intimation of the picture theory of the *Tractatus*. A proposition is structurally analogous to the situation it accurately represents. Russell's notion that the meaning of image-propositions is primary and the meaning of word-propositions is derivative is similar to the *Tractatus* view (as I have interpreted it) that a linguistic structure (a sentence) obtains its meaning from a psychical structure (a thought) that is isomorphic with the linguistic structure. Russell says: "The content of a belief *may* consist only of words, but if it does, this is a telescoped process. The primary phenomenon of belief consists of belief in images, of

38. Ibid., p 303.   39. Ibid.   40. Ibid.   41. Ibid.
42. Ibid., p. 308.   43. Ibid., p 309.

which, perhaps, memory is the most elementary example." [44] Russell does not explain what the nature of "a telescoped process" is. My guess is that Russell would say that if a person utters a sentence but has no image-proposition, it still may be true (in a secondary sense) that he "expressed a belief" and "meant what he said," *provided* that he is able, if pressed, to produce an image-proposition corresponding to the verbal sentence. The occurrence of thought, belief, and meaning in this secondary way is "a telescoped process."

Russell gives an example of how a proposition will be related to the fact which makes it true or false, called its "objective":

The simplest possible schema of correspondence between proposition and objective is affored by such cases as visual memory-images. I call up a picture of a room that I know, and in my picture the window is to the left of the fire. I give to this picture that sort of belief which we call 'memory'. When the room was present to sense, the window was, in fact, to the left of the fire. In this case, I have a complex image, which we may analyse, for our purposes, into (a) the image of the window, (b) the image of the fire, (c) the relation that (a) is to the left of (b). The objective consists of the window and the fire with the very same relation between them. In such a case, the objective of a proposition consists of the meanings of its constituent images related (or not related, as the case may be) by the same relation as that which holds between the constituent images in the proposition. When the objective is that the same relation holds, the proposition is true; when the objective is that the same relation does not hold, the proposition is false.[45]

11.   Russell is here giving a statement, both bold and crude, of the philosophical idea that in thinking and remembering there must be a pictorial structure. In declaring that Russell's statement of the picture theory is "crude," I have three points in mind.

In the first place, there is the obvious fact that no relevant imagery is present in much of our thinking and remembering. Suppose that a clerk in a grocery store is busily occupied with customers, hurriedly fetching articles from the shelves, rapidly adding figures, replying to questions, making change. In the midst of this activity

44. Ibid., p 308.   45. Ibid., pp. 315–316.

the manager calls to him, "Where did you put the package for Mrs. Casey?" Without a pause in his activity the clerk immediately replies, "Under the meat counter." Is it even likely, let alone necessary, that the clerk had at that moment an image of himself putting the package under the meat counter? If the clerk did not have that image, or anything close to it, Russell would be bound to hold that the clerk's utterance ("Under the meat counter") was a "telescoped process" which the clerk would have to be able to "cash" in the relevant image. But this seems arbitrary. Why should it not be just the other way round, namely, that the clerk's utterance was itself a *primary* expression of memory and that the image, if it occurred, would be an expression of memory only if *it* could be cashed in some appropriate words, or in some appropriate behavior such as swiftly fetching the package from under the meat counter?

A second criticism of Russell's view that "image-propositions" are the primary vehicle of thinking is that in many (indeed, in most) cases we do not know what images would correspond to a particular thought. Suppose that I tell someone, "I bought twelve books today." Would my image have to contain twelve books? Or would an image of one book and an image of the numeral 12 suffice? And what image would correspond with *I*, and what with *today*, and what with *bought?* If we do not permit ourselves to be hypnotized by sentences like "The cat is on the mat" or "The window is to the left of the fireplace," the theory of image-propositions loses all plausibility.

The third criticism of Russell's version of the picture theory was made clear to me by Goldberg.[46] In Russell's example of an "image-proposition" there is an image of a room, and in this image there is an image of a window to the left of an image of a fire. The complex image is supposed to be *the* proposition "The window is to the left of the fire." We see, however, that the same complex image could express a number of different propositions. If a person, A, were to make a drawing of the image and hand this drawing to

46. In an unpublished paper entitled "The Picture Theory: Memory."

someone, B, the following are some of the propositions that A could be asserting by means of the drawing, depending on what question was at issue:

There was only one window in the room.

The window was closed.

The fire was burning.

The window was too near the fire.

The window was higher than the fire.

The room needed a fire.

The room would be more attractive if it had a single window.

In the drawing the window is to the left of the fire: but this does not determine *which* proposition is represented by the drawing. The same is true of the mental image in which the window is to the left of the fire. The whole image is supposed to *be* a proposition: but the image is ambiguous in the sense that it cannot be discovered from the image itself which proposition it is. It is *not* a picture that *"shows its sense."* The image is supposed to be a thought; but the image itself does not determine which thought it is. The image is also supposed to provide the *content* of a memory, i.e., what was remembered. Russell says: "I call up a picture of a room that I know, and in my picture the window is to the left of the fire. I give to this picture that sort of belief which we call 'memory'." [47] From this description of the mental picture one cannot tell what was remembered: might it not have been that the room needed a fire; or that the window was too near the fire? If you could look into the mind of a person and see that picture there, you would still not know what he remembered. It might not even be true that he remembered that the window was to the left of the fire.

12.   Russell shared with the author of the *Tractatus* the conception that thinking and remembering require psychical structures that portray without any *possibility* of ambiguity what is thought or remembered. But Russell's specification of the elements of the psy-

47. Russell, *Logic and Knowledge*, p. 315.

chical structure was too simpleminded. For him the psychical structure was a complex mental image. The image he described in his example is, however, a potentially *ambiguous* picture. It is compatible with a large number of logically independent thoughts. As proposition, thought, memory, it does not have a *determinate* sense. Russell is trying to specify the thought-structure that corresponds to the sentence "The window is to the left of the fire." Consequently, he obtains a thought-picture that "shows *too much*." [48]

Wittgenstein, in the *Tractatus*, would take this as a proof that the words "window" and "fire" are not "names," that the thought-structure is something far more complex than the image that Russell described, and that the elements of this thought-structure have not been specified. If the sentence "The window is to the left of the fire" has sense, then it has an absolutely determinate sense. The thought-structure that corresponds to it can be a picture of *one and only* one state of affairs. What the precise thought-structure is and what its elements are, we cannot tell from the sentence. "Language disguises thought. So much so, that from the outward form of the clothing it is impossible to infer the form of the clothed thought" (4.002). The sentence-sign (*Satzzeichen*), which we perceive by the senses, may not reveal the structure of the thought, the proposition. But the proposition itself "must be completely articulated." [49] This complete articulation necessarily brings in *simple* objects and *simple* signs. Russell's so-called "image-proposition" was not completely articulated, as is disclosed by the fact that it does not have a single, definite sense. Only a structure composed of *simple* elements can have a definite sense. "The demand for simple things *is* the demand for definiteness of sense." [50] "The sense of the proposition must appear in the proposition as divided into its *simple* components." [51] "When the sense of the proposition is completely expressed in the proposition itself, the proposition is always divided into its simple components." [52]

48. As Goldberg puts the point, in the unpublished paper just cited.
49. Wittgenstein, *Notebooks*, p. 63.   50. Ibid.   51. Ibid.
52. Ibid.

A proposition *shows* its sense only when its sense is completely expressed in the proposition itself. The sense that the window is to the left of the fire is not completely expressed, nor even expressed at all, in Russell's image of a room with a window to the left of a fire.

13. A conclusion that emerges from our study of this example is that "the constituents" of a thought cannot be images, and that a thought cannot be a complex image. One may surmise that Wittgenstein realized this when he said, in response to Russell's query, that he did not *know* what the constituents of a thought are. It is even probable that he thought about this matter in the way that he thought about "simple objects" and "atomic facts," namely, that it was not necessary for him, as a *logician*, to determine which objects are simple and which facts are atomic: his job, as a logician, was confined to proving that there *have to be* simple objects and atomic facts.[53] Similarly, it was necessary for him to prove that behind or beneath a word-sentence that has sense there must be a thought-structure; but he did not have to determine the nature of its constituents or its composition.

This is not a tenable position. If images cannot be the final constituents of a picture that "shows its sense," neither can anything else. If a picture were composed of lines, dots, or colors, instead of images, this would not make it come any closer to Wittgenstein's former "ideal" of what a picture must be. One cannot understand a map of a certain terrain unless one knows the method by which the lines and points of the map are projected onto the terrain. The same arrangement of points and lines can be projected by different methods: different interpretations of the map are possible. This is very evident in geometrical projections: a method of projection is possible by which the projection of a circle would be a rectangle; by another method, a straight line. One has to know the "key" of interpretation, the "pictorial relationship," the method of projec-

53. See my *Ludwig Wittgenstein: A Memoir* (London: Oxford University Press, 1958), p. 86.

tion. This is so regardless of what the elements are that compose the map. The same holds true for any picture.

In the *Tractatus* Wittgenstein's conception was that a picture that *shows* its sense *includes* the "pictorial relationship" (2.1513). He adds that "the pictorial relationship consists of the correlations of the picture's elements with things" (2.1514). So the correlations are *already in* the picture. The way the picture applies to reality is thus supposed to be determined by the picture itself. No further interpretation is necessary or possible. In this way the picture succeeds in being a "meaning terminus," a structure that shows its sense.

An objection to this idea was already indicated in Chapter IV. We noted that a schema or key that is attached to a map in order to explain how the map is to be read may itself need to be explained. This explanation might take the form of a second key that is added to the map in order to explain the first key. This is why Wittgenstein imagined an arrangement of arrows that indicated the direction of pointing of a previous set of arrows. It would be possible for there to be a misunderstanding of the sense of the second set of arrows, which might be removed by still a third set of arrows, and so on. There cannot be an arrangement of arrows such that a question as to their sense could not, logically speaking, arise. The same holds for any key, or schema of interpretation, or method of projection. None of these things can be a meaning terminus. None of them can "show their sense," as required by the *Tractatus*. By parity of reasoning, no word-structure, or image-structure, nor any structure whatever can be turned into a "picture" that will satisfy the demands of the *Tractatus*, by attaching to it a key of interpretation or method of projection.

14.   Students of Wittgenstein are often in doubt as to whether the picture theory of the *Tractatus* is rejected in his later philosophical thought. It seems clear to me (my thinking here having been greatly assisted by discussions with Goldberg) that the answer is affirmative. There are paragraphs of the *Investigations* in which

Wittgenstein appears to be addressing himself directly to the idea of *Tractatus* 2.1513, that the picturing relationship belongs to the picture. I have in mind paragraphs 139 to 141 of the *Investigations*, in which Wittgenstein discusses the notion of *understanding a word*, his example being the word "cube." Wittgenstein puts the question, "What is it that happens in your mind, or comes before your mind, when you *understand* the word 'cube'?" He imagines someone giving the answer—a *picture*. Wittgenstein agrees to suppose that when you hear the word "cube" a picture comes before your mind, in the form of a drawing of a cube. But he notes that a cube is not the only thing that would *fit* that picture. According to an easily imagined method of projection a triangular prism, for example, would fit it. The same drawing, the same picture, can be taken in more than one way, can be applied to reality in more than one way. The drawing or picture does not of itself impose one and only one application of it.

In paragraph 140 Wittgenstein remarks that we are inclined to put the point like this: the picture or drawing exerted only a *psychological* compulsion, *not* a *logical* compulsion. But this comparison, says Wittgenstein, is a confusion; for it makes it seem as if there *could be* a kind of picture that *did* exert *logical* compulsion; it makes it seem as if we knew of two kinds of picture, one compelling us only psychologically, the other compelling us logically. Whereas we should realize that the *only* sense in which a picture can "force" a certain application on us is that a *different* application of the picture simply *does not occur to us!* This is what the so-called "logical compulsion" comes to! "Our 'belief that the picture forces a particular application on us' consisted in this, that only the one case and no other occurred to us" (para. 140). In paragraph 139 Wittgenstein remarks that the picture of the cube certainly does make a particular employment of it *natural* for us, but that nevertheless "I could employ it differently." And in a footnote he uses the following illustration: "I see a picture; it represents an old man walking up a steep path leaning on a stick.—How? Might it not have looked just the same if he had been sliding downhill in that position? Perhaps a

Martian would describe the picture that way. I do not need to explain why we do not so describe it." [54]

In paragraph 141 the attempt persists to conceive of a picture that, "logically speaking," *forces* a particular application on us. We are to suppose that "not merely the picture of the cube, but also the method of projection comes before our mind." Here Wittgenstein is clearly referring to the idea of the *Tractatus* that the picture will *include* "the pictorial relationship" that makes it into a picture. The notion of the *Tractatus* that a picture can "show its sense" entails the notion that there can be a kind of picture that picks out a certain state of affairs as the only state of affairs that will satisfy the picture. Surely we achieve this if *the method of projection* is contained in the picture—is a part of our total picture.

Wittgenstein then asks us to consider *in what way* "the method of projection comes before our mind." He asks: "How am I to think of that?—Perhaps I see before me a schema showing the method of projection: say a picture of two cubes connected by lines of projection.—But does this really get me any further? Can't I now think of different applications of this schema too?" [55] No matter how we amplify our picture, we do not come any closer to achieving something that can fit only one state of affairs.

There is an inclination to agree to this but at the same time to feel that what we do is nothing so gross as to see in our mind's eye schematic projection lines. Or, if we do, that this is not what is important. The essential thing to do is to *actually connect* the picture of the cube with reality. To connect it with reality *in our minds*. This is the idea that lies behind the question that comes next in paragraph 141: Can't *an* application of the picture of a cube *come before my mind?*

Here again Wittgenstein would seem to be addressing himself to a former idea of his own. In the *Tractatus*, after remarking that a picture as he conceives it contains the pictorial relationship (the method of projection) which makes it into a picture, he adds, "The

54. Wittgenstein, *Investigations*, p. 54.   55. Ibid., para. 141.

pictorial relationship consists of the correlations of the picture's elements with things" (2.1514). "These correlations are, as it were,
the feelers of the picture's elements, with which the picture touches
reality" (2.1515). These remarks express vividly the idea that in the
very process of framing a propositional picture I, as it were, apply
it to reality. The correct application of the picture of a cube to reality has already taken place *in my mind.* If subsequently I should
point with my finger to a cube, or go fetch one, this would be a
mere *consequence* of the previous mental act of connecting the picture with reality.

The criticism of this idea that occurs in paragraph 141 is typical
of the *Investigations.* Wittgenstein admits, laconically, that to be
sure an application of the picture of a cube can come before one's
mind; one can apply it to reality in one's mind. The question, however, is: When should we say that this has occurred? Suppose that
a person knew several methods of projection and that I asked him
to employ a certain one of them. When should we say that the one
I meant "came before his mind"? Wittgenstein remarks that we are
aware of two different criteria for saying this: one is the picture,
drawing, or model that the person may see in his mind or produce
on paper; the other is the subsequent *application* that he may make
of this picture or drawing.

Suppose I meant the person to use a method by which the projection of a cube is a triangular prism, and that he saw in his mind
or drew on paper a picture of a cube connected by projection lines
with a triangular prism. On the basis of just this fact, if I knew it, I
might think that the method I meant had come before his mind.
But suppose he went on to point to or fetch not prisms but cubes.
Should we say then that the method I meant had not come before
his mind after all, but a different method had? We could say different things, depending on how we want to use the expression,
"the method I meant *came before his mind.*" We could say that this
method *had* "come before his mind" but that it was there as "a *mere*
picture" and was not given any application. Or we could say that
the method I meant came before his mind but he *applied* it *incor-*

rectly. Or we might say that the method I meant "did not come before his mind at all," as proven by the fact that he proceeded to fetch cubes, not prisms. Whatever answer we give, we ought to see that we cannot make sense of the conception of a picture that "logically" (or "magically," we might say) forces us to employ it in only one way—that *cannot* be given a different application.

I do not want to give too much space to the question of whether Wittgenstein rejected the picture theory of *Tractatus* in his later thinking. But I cannot forbear calling attention to some striking remarks that he wrote in a manuscript (probably composed in 1936), which is included in the volume published under the title *Philosophische Grammatik*. [56] In these pages Wittgenstein is criticizing his previous notion of an "elementary proposition" and also his notion of "the complete analysis" of a proposition. He goes on to comment on the idea of a *picture* and of a *method of projection:*

One can say: a blueprint *serves as a picture* of the object which the workman is to make from it.

And here one could call the way and manner in which the workman has converted such a drawing into a piece of work, "the method of projection." We might now express ourslves in this way: the method of projection mediates between the drawing and the object, it reaches from the drawing to the piece of work. Here we are comparing the method of projection with lines of projection, which reach from one figure to another.—*But if the method of projection is a bridge, then it is one which is not built, so long as the application is not yet made.*—This comparison makes it appear that the picture *together with* the lines of projection does not permit different kinds of application, but that by the picture and the lines of projection the thing which is depicted, even if it does not actually exist, is determined ethereally, is just as determined *as if* it did exist. (It is "determined one way or the other; yes or no.") In that case we may call the "picture," the blueprint *together with* the method of its application. And by the method we imagine something that is attached to the blueprint, even if it is not employed. [57]

56. Wittgenstein, *Philosophische Grammatik*, ed. R. Rhees (Oxford: Blackwell, 1969), pp. 210–214. I have made use, with occasional deviations, of the translation into English by Anthony Kenny, *Philosophical Grammar* (Oxford: Blackwell, 1974).

57. Wittgenstein, *Philosophische Grammatik*, p. 213. The second and fourth emphases are added. The quotation in parentheses is a reference to *Tractatus* 4.023.

Wittgenstein goes on to remark that there is a confusion here of the *lines* of projection, which connect the picture with the object, with the *method* of projection. And he characterizes his new viewpoint in the following way: "One may say that I still consider the lines of projection to be part of the picture—but not the method of projection." [58]

In this manuscript Wittgenstein is quite clearly attributing to the *Tractatus* a failure to distinguish the lines of projection from the method of projection. The *Tractatus* says:

This is how a picture is connected with reality; it reaches right out to it. It is laid against reality like a measure. Only the end-points of the graduating lines actually *touch* the object that is to be measured. According to this conception there belongs to the picture the pictorial relationship, which makes it into a picture. The pictorial relationship consists of the correlations of the picture's elements with things. These correlations are, as it were, the feelers of the picture's elements, with which the picture touches reality (2.511–2.1515).

In the *Tractatus* it was imagined that the pictorial (picturing) relationship belonged to the total picture, and that it consisted of the lines of projection (the "feelers") that reached out to the depicted situation, and that therefore the total picture picked out, unambiguously, a uniquely determined situation in the world, *the* one and only situation that the picture depicts. This is how the picture could *show* its sense: for how the picture was to be applied was *already settled* by the picture itself. Even if there were no existing situation for the projection lines to catch hold of, it was determined "ethereally" (that is, "in the mind") exactly which situation, were it to exist, would fit the picture. The projection lines were certainly being imagined, in the *Tractatus*, as a *bridge* between thought and reality. This is why there is so much power in the remark of the *Grammatik* that this bridge is *not built*, not finished, *until* the application of the picture is made!

It seems to me that perhaps the most dramatic change in Wittgenstein's thought from the *Tractatus* to the *Investigations* lies in

58. Wittgenstein, *Philosophische Grammatik*, p. 213.

his brilliant diagnosis and complete rejection of the picture theory. In the *Tractatus* he had conceived that in order for thought and language to be possible there must be something (a picture, a proposition, a thought) that depicts a state of affairs in the world in so luminous a way that no room is left for differing interpretations. It would be something that, as it were, contained its interpretation, its application, *in itself.* In *The Blue Book*, the *Grammatik*, and the *Investigations*, Wittgenstein is saying that it is an illusion to think there might be such a thing. Now we are ready to acknowledge this if the thing were only a *physical* sign, or drawing, or sentence. But we imagine that the *meaning* of this physical thing will lie in something "mental," something in the mind or soul. This is like supposing that an arrow signpost *points* only because one joins to it an *image* of an arrow. But what would make the image-arrow point? Not another image-arrow. The attempt to provide meaning for a physical sign by means of a mental act of making correlations get us nowhere. In paragraph 454 of the *Investigations* Wittgenstein makes remarks which both repudiate and replace the picture theory:

"Everything is already there in. . . ." How does it come about that this arrow points? Doesn't it seem to carry in it something besides itself?— "No, not the dead line on paper; only the psychical thing, the meaning, can do that."—That is both true and false. The arrow points only in the application that a living being makes of it.

This pointing is *not* a hocus-pocus which can be performed only by the soul.

According to the *Tractatus* everything necessary to make a picture *say* something, to make it depict unambiguously one particular state of affairs, is already *in* the picture itself. For the mental act of correlating the picture with reality belongs to the picture: the picture is already correlated with reality "in one's mind." The *Investigations* retorts that this presumed "mental" act of making correlations is a hocus-pocus. It can do no more than can an image-arrow, which in turn is just as lifeless as an arrow drawn on paper. "The arrow points only in the application that a living being makes of it." The picture theory of meaning is here replaced by Wittgenstein's later conception that a sign has meaning only insofar as it is employed by living beings in a common practice, in a shared form of life.

15. In this chapter we have continued to examine the classical view that in remembering there must occur a representation, image, copy, or likeness of what is remembered. As I see it, there have been two different philosophical motivations for this view. One is the feeling that in recounting something from memory, or in acting on the basis of memory, one must be guided by the "memory-event" or "memory-experience." Otherwise our saying and doing the correct thing, in such a high proportion of cases, would be a "miracle." As Harrod puts it, the memory-event "must be in some sense a copy of the thing remembered"—for, he says, "how otherwise can we say how much of it is remembered?" In Chapter IV I pointed out that this idea is really inconsistent with the concept of memory: for just to the extent that in describing something one previously witnessed one must rely on, be guided by, depend on, some signs or indicators that are contemporary with the describing, just to that extent one does not *remember* what one witnessed. In addition, there is Wittgenstein's fundamental point that *being guided* has to come to an end. Even if one were presented with an image, or copy, or "cognitive map," or clue of some sort, one would have to respond to it *without* guidance. Thus it cannot be a requirement of reason that one's memory responses should be guided. The point is the same as the one that Wittgenstein makes against the assumption that in our employment of language to describe our observations and experiences we must be guided by *rules:* "Don't always think that you read off your words from facts; that you portray these in words according to rules. *For even so you would have to apply the rule in the particular case without guidance.*" [59]

59. Wittgenstein, *Investigations*, para. 293. Emphasis added. Also: "What use is a rule to us here? Could we not (in turn) go wrong in applying it?": Wittgenstein,

A second motivation for the classical view takes its inspiration from a conception of the nature of thinking in general, of which remembering is a special case, since if one remembers (in the "cognitive" sense) that so-and-so occurred, one has the *thought* that so-and-so occurred. The most sophisticated development of this conception occurs in the *Tractatus*. According to the *Tractatus*, a thought has a structure that is isomorphic with the state of affairs that exists if the thought is true. A thought and what it depicts must have the same "logical multiplicity." A thought mirrors an actual situation in the world by being isomorphic with it. A thought is a picture of reality. Since to remember something (in the "cognitive" sense) entails thinking of it, therefore in remembering there must be a picture, a copy, a representation, an "image," of reality. This picture or copy is the *content* of what one remembers. Without it one's thought would be, in Stout's phrase, "empty." [60] One would not be thinking or remembering anything. On this second conception, the picture or copy that must be present in remembering does not *guide* one's memory-thought, but *is* one's memory-thought. With a sentence, a drawing or painting, or a sequence of gestures, one can *express* a thought. But the thought itself cannot be identified with these perceptible signs. The perceptible signs clothe the thought, but are not the thought. The thought is the meaning of the signs. The signs are capable of various interpretations, but not the thought, not the meaning of the signs. It is "the last interpretation." [61]

When we try, however, to consider realistically what process or state or thing might have this property, we begin to realize that *nothing* could have it. Russell imagined that a complex of images might be a thought (an "image-proposition"). But we can see that there is nothing about a complex image that makes it refer to one and only one state of affairs. If we substitute a physical drawing for

---

Ueber Gewissheit—On Certainty, ed. G. E. M. Anscombe and G. H. von Wright; trans. D. Paul and G. E. M. Anscombe (Oxford: Blackwell, 1969), para. 26.

60. Stout, p. 367.

61. Wittgenstein, *The Blue and Brown Books*, p. 34.

the image, it is easily seen that it could mean different things—could be used to assert different propositions. This point comes across very clearly with Russell's "image-propositions." But this is not because he selected the wrong constituents of the thought. *Whatever* constituents were selected, the outcome would be the same. No wonder Wittgenstein did not "know" what are the "constituents" of a thought! No wonder Martin and Deutscher say that the nature of what *we do* when we "represent the past" in memory is a "difficult" question! [62] If one looks at actual cases, it would seem that it is not difficult at all to describe what we do. The grocery clerk, for example, merely said, "Under the meat counter." What is difficult about that? But when we look at the matter in a philosophical way, it seems that this cannot be *all* that happened. There must be some state or process, with a complex structure of unknown constituents, that lies behind the overt utterance and *is* the memory-thought. But nothing we can conceive of would satisfy this demand.

16. It should also be pointed out that isomorphism is neither a sufficient nor a necessary condition of thought. If a triangle is drawn in chalk at one end of a blackboard, to draw another triangle, isomorphic with the first one, would not make the second one the thought, nor a thought, of the first one; nor would the first one be the, or a, thought of the second. There could be a method of projection by which a circle was isomorphic with the first triangle; but the circle would not thereby be a thought of the triangle, not even if lines of projection were drawn between the two figures. A circle drawn at one end of a blackboard *could be used* to express the thought that there is a triangle at the other end. But in order for the circle to be given that meaning it would not be necessary for it to be isomorphic with the triangle. A dot at one end could be used to mean that there is a triangle at the other end. The word "circle," written at one end, could mean that there is a triangle at the other

62. Martin and Deutscher, p. 172.

end; but there need be no isomorphism between the triangle and the word "circle."

The general conception of the *Tractatus* that thought *mirrors* reality would seem to be a fundamental error. The only correspondence required is that the thought that p should be true if and only if p. There is not a further requirement that the thought that p and the fact that p should each be divisible into elements and that the elements of the one should be correlated with the elements of the other.

If we were asked whether this chair and my hand do or do not have the same structure, our answer should be that the question does not, so far, have any clear sense. What the constituents, elements, or parts of my hand are does not have a definite meaning. Are its elements the four fingers, the thumb, and the rest of the hand? Or are its elements the bones, skin, and flesh? Are the elements of this chair the legs, seat, and back? Or are they wood, nails, and glue? Or electrons and protons? We could make different decisions for different purposes. Structure could be assigned to hand and chair in different ways. By one determination they might have the same structure, by another not.[63]

Thus to say that the *thought* that there is a triangle on the blackboard and the *fact* that there is a triangle on the blackboard "have the same structure" does not have a definite meaning. Decisions would have to be made as to what are the components of the thought and the components of the fact, and what the relations are between the members of each group of components, and what is to be the method of correlating the two sets of components and their relations. It is meaningless to ask whether something, A, and something, B, have the same structure unless we have a method of *defining* "the structure" of A and B and a method of projecting one structure onto the other. But then such specifications can be made *differently*. If they are made in one way, the thought and the fact will have the same structure; in another way, not.

63. See Wittgenstein, *Investigations*, para. 47.

17.   The philosophy of memory has been dominated by the idea that when one remembers there must be, in either one's mind or one's body, or possibly in both, something which mirrors what one remembers. As Harrod says, "The memory must be in some sense a copy of the thing remembered." [64] As Martin and Deutscher put it, when a person remembers there must exist a state of that person which is "a structural analogue of the thing remembered, to the extent to which he can accurately represent the thing." [65] This "analogue" will contain "at least as many features as there are details which a given person can relate about something he has experienced." [66] There must be a "structural analogue of what was experienced." [67]

I find two things wrong with such remarks. The first is something to which I have already alluded, namely, that one cannot speak, in some absolute sense, of *the structure* of "an experience" or of "what was experienced," any more than one can speak, in an absolute sense, of "the structure" of a chair, a fact, or a thought.

My second criticism is aimed at the idea that the supposed "structural analogue" contains "as many features as there are details which a given person can relate about something he has experienced." The structural analogue is conceived by Martin and Deutscher to be a "memory trace." I shall later be considering at length the idea of a memory trace: what I am presenting now is an initial criticism of that idea. My point here is that one cannot speak, in an absolute sense, of *what one remembers* of some event or experience: there is *no absolute number of details* that a person remembers of something he experienced or witnessed. If this is true, it has the consequence that the memory trace or structural analogue will have to be perplexingly indefinite in nature. This makes it difficult to imagine what this trace would be like or how it would function. My point can be illustrated by the following example: Suppose that last month you met, for the first and only time, Mr. A. Today you are asked whether he was blond or dark. "Blond," you answer.

64. Harrod, p. 49.   65. Martin and Deutscher, p. 191.
66. Ibid., p. 190.   67. Ibid., p. 189.

You are then asked whether he was more or less blond than Mr. B., who is standing before you. "More blond," you say. You remember that A was more blond than B is. You could have been asked to compare A with an *indefinite* number of persons of different coloring, and in an *indefinite* number of such cases you could have given correct answers, from memory. We see from this that what you remember of A's coloring cannot be put down as a fixed sum.

There may be an inclination to think that, strictly speaking, you do not *remember* that A was more blond than B is: what you have is a mixture of knowledge, part of it being memory-knowledge and part present perception. Well, it is true that you see B right now. But it is wrong to think that your statement "I remember that A was more blond than B is" can be analyzed into two conjuncts, one a pure memory component, the other a component of present perception. How would the analysis go? Should we say that what you remember is that A was of a certain degree of blondness (call it f) *and* that you now perceive that B's degree of blondness is less than f? But in what way is this f degree of blondness present to your memory? Doesn't it come down to this: that you could say, correctly and confidently, that A was more (or less) blond than any number of other persons who might be presented to you for comparison? But, according to the proposed analysis, these judgments would themselves be conjunctions of memory components and nonmemory components. Thus, this analysis would never arive at a "pure" memory component.

Reports of what one remembers are often comparative. The object of comparison is often something presently perceived. It is a mistake to think that in such a case the remembering is reducible to a conjunction of memory and nonmemory components. Once this is realized, we can see at once that the number of possible present objects of comparison is entirely indefinite.

The same point emerges if we consider that there is an indefinite number of true accounts of what you *did* at a certain time. At 8 A.M. you "walked out the door," you "crossed the threshold," you "stepped like *this*," you "left the house," you "began walking toward your car," you "started for your office," you "began another working day" and so on. What you did at 8 A.M. could be related to many different contexts, thus yielding many different descriptions of what you did. It would be absurd to think that there are only ten or fifteen true descriptions of what you did at 8 A.M. The number is indefinite because the number of contexts and concepts in terms of which your action might be described is indefinite. But then, *what you remember* doing at 8 A.M. is, in exactly the same way, indefinite. How you will describe, from memory, what you did will depend on what is at issue or of interest, on what is assumed, known, believed, or suspected by your audience.

The philosophical idea that there must be a state of a person which has features that correspond one-to-one with the details that the person can relate, from memory, of what he did or experienced appears to assume that one's memory of something could, in principle, be enumerated in a closed set of items. Once we realize that there can be no final, exhaustive account of what one remembers doing or witnessing on a certain occasion, the idea of there being a state of the person that has the same structure as what he remembers ought to lose its appeal. For the assumed state cannot be thought of as having any definite structure. It will be *amorphous*. It will not be easy, therefore, to think of it as mirroring or picturing anything, nor to think of it as possessing *the structure* of a past experience or perception. For how can a memory trace of a past experience be identical in structure with that experience, if the trace has no definite structure? One might reply that perhaps the experience has no definite structure either; to which I would agree. But then my question is: How can two things, A and B, neither of which has any definite structure, be said to be "identical in structure"? What could this mean? I will go more deeply into the notions of "structure" and "isomorphism" in Part Two.

PHYSICAL
MECHANISMS
OF MEMORY

Intellectual man had become an explaining creature. Fathers to children, wives to husbands, lecturers to listeners, experts to laymen, colleagues to colleagues, doctors to patients, man to his own soul, explained. The roots of this, the causes of the other, the source of events, the history, the structure, the reasons why. For the most part, in one ear out the other. The soul wanted what it wanted. It had its own natural knowledge. It sat unhappily on superstructures of explanation, poor bird, not knowing which way to fly.

Saul Bellow, *Mr. Sammler's Planet*

I saw this man years ago: now I see him again, I recognize him, I remember his name. And why does there have to be a cause of this remembering in my nervous system? Why must something or other, whatever it may be, be stored up there *in any form?* Why *must* a trace have been left behind? Why should there not be a psychological regularity to which *no* physiological regularity corresponds? If this overturns our concept of causality then it is time it was overturned.

Wittgenstein, *Zettel*

CHAPTER VI

The Conception of a Memory Trace

1. The studies of mental mechanisms of memory undertaken in Part One will seem to many present-day philosophers and psychologists to have interest only as a recounting of historical curiosities. They will be quick to concede that the *mental* processes traditionally assumed in theories of memory are fanciful or fantastic. This contemporary viewpoint assumes that of course remembering requires a *memory-process*, but that the process is something that takes place in the *brain* rather than in the "mind."

There is a significant difference between these two viewpoints. Both want to give an account of "what happens" when we remember, what "the memory-process" is. But their aims are different. The mental mechanisms have been intended primarily to explain how memory can be a source of *knowledge* or of *justified* beliefs— that is, how the processes of memory can provide us with *grounds* for our memory-judgments and beliefs. In contrast, the physical mechanisms have been conceived primarily as *causal* mechanisms: they offer explanations of how memory responses are *caused*.[1] The mental mechanisms are composed of things of which we are frequently conscious, such as images and various feelings. The components of the physical mechanisms, in contrast, are neural states and processes of which we are never aware. But this gives

---

1. In Chapter IV, Section 13, we saw that the advocates of mental mechanisms do not always sharply adhere to the distinction between the *grounds* and the *causes* of memory judgments.

rise to no objection, since the physical mechanisms are conceived of as explaining the *causation* of our memory responses, not the *grounds* we are supposed to have for our memory-beliefs and judgments.

There is also an important similarity between the two types of theory. The central component of the mental mechanisms is the memory-image. In the physical mechanisms the same position is occupied by the memory trace. As we shall see, the physical theorists have been inclined to attribute to the trace some of the principal properties that the mental theorists have assigned to the memory-image—notably, the properties of serving as a *representation* of the remembered scene or experience, and of being *identical in structure* with it. To the extent that this is so, some of the criticism directed at mental theories in Part One will be relevant to our appraisal of the physical theories. Between the two types of theory there is, I believe, a striking continuity of thought.

2.   It is an ancient conception that the phenomena of memory are mediated by physical states and processes in the bodies of people and animals. The conception is that a certain perception, experience, or training produces a physical change in the organism, which persists for some time after the termination of the experience or training. The persisting state or process is called a "trace" or "engram." It is generally conceived that the right sort of stimulation will cause the trace to pass from a dormant condition to an active condition. The activated trace produces a memory response.

In recent years there has developed a huge amount of speculation and experimentation, by psychologists and neurologists, pertaining to the nature of the memory trace. Such problems as the following are considered: How long does it take for a trace to be established in the brain? Do traces decay and, if so, at what rate? Is there interference between traces? Does a particular trace have a fixed location in some region of the central nervous system? Are there "long-term" traces and "short-term" traces, differing in their dynamical properties?

In an extensive review of the history of thought about memory traces, Bronislaw Gomulicki says:

The phrase 'the trace theory of memory' may be understood in at least two senses. First, it may be taken in a literal sense and as referring only to one of the earliest and most tenacious views of the physical basis of memory, viz. that the brain may be likened to a wax tablet upon which, like a stylus, sensory impressions engrave physical traces which persist until effaced by time. The second sense—that which will be used in this study— is that 'the trace theory of memory' signifies nothing more specific than an acknowledgment that memory does have a physical basis and is not a disembodied product of a 'soul' or some other metaphysical entity. When the phrase is used in this latter sense, the word 'trace' itself is not to be interpreted too literally, but rather considered as a convenient synonym for the unwieldy, if more accurate, phrase: 'the as-yet-unknown substrate of a memory process'.[2]

The reference to a "wax tablet" reminds us of the following remarks that Socrates made to Theaetetus:

Imagine, then, for the sake of argument, that our minds contain a block of wax, which in this or that individual may be larger or smaller, and composed of wax that is comparatively pure or muddy, and harder in some, softer in others, and sometimes of just the right consistency. Let us call it the gift of the Muse's mother, Memory, and say that whenever we wish to remember something we see or hear or conceive in our own minds, we hold this wax under perceptions or ideas and imprint them on it as we might stamp the impression of a seal-ring. Whatever is so imprinted we remember and know so long as the image remains; whatever is rubbed out or has not succeeded in leaving an impression we have forgotten and do not know.[3]

Plato pursues this playful figure at considerable length. For example, if a man knows two people, A and B, and therefore has imprints of both in his block of wax, and then, seeing them at a

2. Bronislaw R. Gomulicki, "The Development and Present Status of the Trace Theory of Memory." *British Journal of Psychology*, Monograph Suppl. 29 (London: Cambridge University Press, 1953), p. vii.

3. Theaetetus, 191C–191E; trans. F. M. Cornford, *Plato's Theory of Knowledge* (London: Kegan Paul, 1935), p. 121.

distance, mistakes one for the other, this is like putting one's feet in the wrong shoes!

In Plato's humorous metaphor the wax is said to be in "the mind," instead of "the brain" as Gomulicki's "literal" view proposes. It appears that Aristotle did accept, in all seriousness, the idea that when we perceive something by the senses, an impression is produced in the body: "It is clear that one must think of the affection, which is produced by means of perception in the soul and in that part of the body which contains the soul, as being like a sort of picture, the having of which we say is memory. For the change that occurs marks in a sort of imprint, as it were, of the sense-image, as people do who seal things with signet rings." [4]

Aristotle seems to be saying that when a new perception produces in both soul and body "a sort of imprint of the sense-image," this is what we call memory.

Gomulicki's characterization of his own second sense of "the trace theory," would appear to commit one who held it to very little. It is no more than "an acknowledgment that memory does have a physical basis and is not a disembodied product of a 'soul' or some other metaphysical entity." Obviously, this characterization is extremely vague. If one were to admit (as I should) that the concept of memory would have no application to human beings if they did not manifest memory responses in the form of physical movements, actions, gestures, and utterances, one could be said to be acknowledging that memory does have "a physical basis." But would it be appropriate to say, on that account, that one held "a trace theory of memory"?

An almost equally vague characterization of the concept of a memory trace is J. Brown's remark: "By memory trace is meant only the neural substrate of retention, whatever this may be." [5] Brown is saying that what Gomulicki calls "the physical basis" of memory is neural. But suppose one agreed that the functioning of

4. Aristotle, *De Memoria et Reminiscentia*, 450a.

5. J. Brown, "Some Tests of the Decay Theory of Immediate Memory," *Quarterly Journal of Experimental Psychology*, 10 (1958), 12.

the central nervous system is a necessary causal condition for the existence of normal memory powers, but did *not* hold that there have to be any *specific correlations* between particular neural processes and particular memories; could such a one be rightly said to be committed to a trace theory of memory? I think it will be evident that the answer is no. It is imperative that we achieve a more adequate characterization of the concept of a memory trace.

3.   Presumably the reader will know that memory traces are not entities, states, or processes that neural surgeons have discovered in the course of their investigations of the brain, as dentists discover cavities. The memory trace is what may be called "a theoretical construct." It is something that is inferred to exist from the presence of things that unquestionably exist, such as learned skills, habits, and occurrences of recognition and remembering. The step of postulating traces gains plausibility when certain familiar phenomena are viewed in terms of a simple model. Let us suppose that a person witnessed some event or underwent some experience at a certain time. Let us express this by saying that an event, E, occurred at a time t_1. At a later time this person either relates event E, or in some other way manifests a memory of E. Let us call this second event "the memory response," M, which occurs at time t_3. The temporal interval between t_1 and t_3 might be an hour, a day, a month, or a year. A trace theorist assumes that the event E produced a memory trace of E (call it T) which persisted in the person, P, from t_1 to t_3.[6] Nowadays it is typically assumed that T is a state or process of the central nervous system. The occurrence of some stimulus, S, "excites" or "activates" the trace, T, and this causes the occurrence of M.

In what ways does the postulation of a memory trace give satisfaction to a trace theorist? For one thing, he thinks of it as bridging a temporal gap. He conceives of M as the final event in a causal sequence, of which E was the initial event. A considerable period

6. See Broad, *Mind and Its Place in Nature*, pp. 444–445.

of time elapsed between E and M. When M occurs E no longer exists, and perhaps has not existed for years. For the trace theorist it would be definitely "spooky" to suppose that E *directly* brought about M on the occurrence of S. Some intermediary must be postulated as filling out the temporal space between E and M. This is the trace.

Speaking in defence of his "field theory," Kurt Lewin makes a remark that expresses this part of the thinking of a trace theorist: "Field theory insists that the derivation of behavior from the past is . . . metaphysical, because past events do not exist now and therefore do not have an effect now. The effect of the past on behavior can be only an indirect one; the past psychological field is one of the 'origins' of the present field and this in turn affects behavior." [7] Lewin also remarks that "Any behavior or any other change in a psychological field depends only upon the psychological field *at that time*." [8] A trace theorist will agree with Lewin that "the past cannot have an effect *now*": at least the effect of the past on the present can only be "indirect." That which has a "direct" effect *now* can only be something that *exists now*.

This thinking is made explicit by K. Koffka in defending the assumption of the memory trace. He draws an analogy between the behavior of a piece of wire and the behavior of a person, where in both cases the behavior has been influenced by something in the past:

We clamp a wire at one of its ends and twist it clockwise through a certain angle, holding it in this position for a couple of minutes. We then release it and observe it turning back into its initial untwisted position, whereupon we give it a counterclockwise torsion of the same angle, and after a short time we release it again. The wire will slowly unwind, but it will not come to rest in its untwisted state but will go beyond it, and that the more, the longer we held it originally in its clockwise torsion. The event after the release is evidently here determined not only by the tension at the moment of release but by a previous tension which had ceased to exist. No less a

7. Kurt Lewin, *Field Theory in Social Science*, ed. D. Cartwright (New York: Harper, 1951), p. 64.
8. Ibid., p. 45.

physicist than Boltzmann has applied the name of memory to this, and it has been possible to treat such events mathematically with the help of a "memory function." Nevertheless, the physicist is not satisfied, he does not want to introduce effects between events which are separated by time, and therefore he turns to the molecular structure of the wire for a more satisfactory explanation.[9]

In explaining the behavior of the wire the physicist will assume that the original torsion produced a change in the molecular structure of the wire. Koffka makes the following comparison between the wire and a woman who had learned to use a typewriter:

Her present performance depends upon much earlier performances, and is therefore called an achievement of memory. And yet, if we follow the method of the physicist, we must interpret this macroscopic fact by microscopic ones. . . . Of course most psychologists have more or less followed the physicist's example. The concept of memory trace is an attempt at explaining the influence of the past by the condition of the present. Just as our wire has been changed in its molecular structure by being held in torsion, so the brain of our typist has been changed by her practice of typing. And just as the wire, when released, does what it would not do without the change of its molecular structure, so the typist when given copy will do what she could not do before her brain had been changed by her exercises.

In this explanation of memory events an event in time influences another event, which succeeds it after a finite interval, not directly but only through some effect which it has left behind and which, for brevity's sake, we will call a trace, without implying by that term anything about the special nature of this after-effect.[10]

W. Köhler puts forward the same argument for memory traces:

What has happened in our past life could hardly co-determine our present activities unless to some extent the past were preserved far beyond the time of its occurrence. We clearly mean this when we say that events of the past become conditions of the present mental processes. Much time may pass between an original experience and the moment in which there is unmistakable evidence of its delayed effect. Some authors seem to think

9. K. Koffka, *Principles of Gestalt Psychology* (London: Routledge & Kegan Paul, 1950), p. 428.
10. Ibid., p. 429.

that we need not assume an entity which survives during the interval as a representative of that previous experience, and which becomes effective when present circumstances are favorable. They ought to realize what this view implies: a first event would influence a second, even though between the two there is an empty period, no connection and no continuity, sometimes for hours and days, occasionally for years. I should hesitate to adopt this notion which is so strikingly at odds with all our fundamental ideas of functional interdependence or causation.[11]

Thus the first ingredient in the conception of a memory trace is the abhorrence of "action at a distance"—in this case, action at a temporal distance. There must, it is held, be a continuous series of neural states or processes intervening between the experience at t_1 and the memory response at t_3. It would appear, however, that to accept this requirement falls short of accepting the idea of a memory trace. For suppose there was no regular correlation between the experience, E, and the neural processes that intervene between it and the response, M. In other words, suppose that no neural process *corresponds* to the experience, E, but that E one time causes one neural process and one time another, and that there is no common pattern uniting the neural processes that intervene between different occurrences of E and different occurrences of the memory response M. If such were the case should it be said that the brain of the subject, P, contains a *trace* of the experience E? Does not the idea of a "memory trace" require *more* than that there should be some effect or other in the brain, perhaps a different one each time?

It would seem so. For *this* requirement would come to little more than the assumption that the central nervous system should not have "gone dead" between t_1 and t_3. Broad aptly remarks that the "*persistent* condition" required by trace theory is not merely "the general integrity of the brain and nervous system":

On the trace theory there is a *special* persistent condition, which was started by the past experience and would not have existed without it. . . .

11. Wolfgang Köhler, *The Place of Value in a World of Facts* (New York: Liveright, 1938), pp. 234–235.

On the trace theory, if you were to take a cross-section of the history of the experient's body and mind anywhere between the past experience and the stimulus you would find something, viz., the trace, which corresponds to and may be regarded as the representative of the past experience.[12]

Notice that the trace is not just something that persists between the past experience and the memory response; it is something that is *"the representative* of the past experience." Note that Köhler, too, declared (in his remarks just quoted) that we must "assume an entity which survives during the interval as *a representative* of that previous experience."

Thus the trace theory, as conceived by many of the thinkers who have endorsed it, demands more than the existence in the person, P, of a continuous causal process reaching from the experience, E, to the memory response, M. The typical viewpoint of trace theory is that a past experience can be remembered, or can produce memory responses, only by virtue of depositing in the organism "a neural representation" of the past experience, a representation that is continuously present in the person's brain as long as he remembers the experience or is influenced by it. How a neural state or process could "represent" a past experience, what this could *mean*, is a matter into which we must inquire. But first I want to draw out another implication of the thinking that supports the theory of traces.

4. Another aspect of the postulation of physiological memory traces is that it makes intelligible to the trace theorist the concept of *retention*—that is, the concept of retaining something in one's memory. It is clear that the ideas of memory and of retention are closely connected. In some contexts we are willing to use interchangeably the expressions "He remembers *x*" and "He retains *x* in his memory." This is so, of course, only when "remember" is used to refer to an ability or power, not when it is used in its so-called "occurrent" sense. Suppose that long ago I had acted a part in a certain

12. Broad, p. 458.

play. Years later it might be true that I "retained in my memory" some of my lines but did not "retain" the plot.

There is a tendency to assume that the concept of memory can be represented by the following schema: an experience occurs; the experience is *retained;* finally, the experience is *recalled.* William James provides an example.

Retention means *liability* to recall, and it means nothing more than such liability. The only proof of there being retention is that recall actually takes place. The retention of an experience is, in short, but another name for the *possibility* of thinking it again, or the *tendency* to think it again, with its past surroundings. Whatever accidental cue may turn this tendency into an actuality, the permanent *ground* of the tendency itself lies in the organized neural paths by which the cue calls up the experience on the proper occasion.[13]

In this passage James makes a distinction between the retention of an experience (which is a "liability" or tendency to recall it) and the "ground" of the tendency (which is some organization of neural paths). But he makes further remarks which suggest that he thinks of the "organized neural paths" as being the *same* thing as retention, and not merely the ground or cause of it. He says: "But be the recall prompt or slow, the condition which makes it possible at all (or in other words, the 'retention' of the experience) is neither more nor less than the brain-paths which *associate* the experience with the occasion and cue of the recall. When slumbering, these paths are the condition of retention; when active, they are the condition of recall." [14] This passage is somewhat ambiguous. The neural paths are said to be "the condition" of retention; but also they are said to *be* the retention. This latter identification becomes more prominent in the immediately following passage:

The *retention* of *e* [the experience], it will be observed, is no mysterious storing up of an 'idea' in an unconscious state. It is not a fact of the mental order at all. It is a purely physical phenomenon, a morphological feature, the presence of these 'paths', namely, in the finest recesses of the brain's

13. James, *Principles of Psychology,* I, 654.   14. Ibid., p. 655.

tissue. The recall or recollection, on the other hand, is a *psycho-physical* phenomenon, with both a bodily and a mental side. The bodily side is the functional excitement of the tracts and paths in question; the mental side is the conscious vision of the past occurrence, and the belief that we experienced it before.[15]

The habit-worn paths of association are a clear rendering of what authors mean by 'predisposition', 'vestiges', 'traces', etc., left in the brain by past experience.[16]

James is saying that the *retention* of a certain event or experience in memory just *is* the persistence of "paths" between certain nerve centers in the brain. He is not saying that the retention of experience, *e*, is one state of affairs, and the existence of certain paths in neural tissue a different state of affairs, and that the latter causes the former. No: he is saying that the retention of *e* and the existence of certain neural paths are one and the same state of affairs.

John Hunter says, "It seems reasonable to suppose that there is some correlate in our nervous system of every experience we have, that this correlate is causally responsible for our experiences and that the mechanism by which we remember an experience is not one of somehow storing the experience itself, but of somehow storing the neurological correlate of it." [17] As these writers see it, the only intelligible or reasonable way of rendering the notion that a person retains something, *x*, in his memory is to hold that a neurophysiological state or process that is correlated with *x* persists in the person from the time of his experience of *x* to the time of his recalling it. This requirement is stated more sharply by Martin and Deutscher. Speaking of "the idea of a memory trace," they say:

This idea is an indispensable part of our idea of memory. Once we accept the causal model for memory we must also accept the existence of some sort of trace, or structural analogue of what was experienced. Even if someone could overcome the many difficulties of various kinds surrounding the idea of action at a distance, it could not be true to say that someone was remembering an event if his past experience of that event caused him, over a temporal gap, to recount it. There is an inevitable recourse to meta-

15. Ibid.   16. Ibid.
17. John Hunter, "Some Questions about Dreaming," *Mind*, 80 (1971), 71.

phors about the storage of our past experience involved in our idioms and thought about memory. Furthermore, if our past experience could act directly on us now, there would no longer be any reason to suppose that we could remember only what we had experienced ourselves. So long as we hold some sort of "storage" or "trace" account of memory, it follows that we can remember only what we have experienced, for it is in our experience of events that they "enter" the storehouse.[18]

Although Martin and Deutscher do not explicitly say so, I think we can safely assume that they conceive a memory "trace" to be some physiological state or process. Their statement is interesting on a number of counts. For one thing they make it plain that a trace is required *not merely* because "action at a distance" is a repugnant idea. Even if causation across a temporal gap were an admissable notion, a persisting trace is still demanded by our concept of memory, as is shown by the "storage" metaphors that permeate "our idioms and thought about memory." Even if an experience of yours could "directly" cause you, at a later time, to relate the experience, this would not be a *memory* response. We should think that you were relating the experience *from memory* only if we thought that there had been *stored* in you, throughout the interval of time between the occurrence of the experience and the relating of it, some state or process that corresponds to the experience. These authors are saying, in effect, that the notion of *storage* is to be taken literally and not just metaphorically.

For another thing, they are saying that a persisting state is a "trace" of a previous experience only if there is a *resemblance in structure* between the two: the state must be a "structural analogue" of "what was experienced." This implies that even if an experience caused a certain state to persist in you, and even if this state played a part in subsequently causing you to give a correct description of the experience, still you would not be describing the experience *from memory* unless the state bore a structural resemblance to the experience. This conception, undoubtedly, is largely responsible for the strong tendency that philosophers and psychologists have,

18. Martin and Deutscher, "Remembering," p. 189.

when they are trying to give an account of the operation of memory, to speak of experiences as leaving "imprints," "impressions," "traces"—or as "stamping" or "engraving" themselves on the remembering subject.

Martin and Deutscher employ the expression "structural resemblance" in such a sense that, for example, there would be a structural resemblance or analogy between the grooves of a phonograph record and the music that is produced by playing that record. For each variation in the pitch, tempo, or volume of the music there would be variations in the grooves of the record. If there was a perfect structural similarity between something A and something B, this would mean that there was "a system of differences" in which changes in A would be "mirrored, one to one" by changes in B, and vice versa.[19]

In Martin and Deutscher's account the concept of a memory trace involves three features. I regard these features as constituting what might be called the "full-blown" conception of a memory trace. The three features are the following: First, a trace has *a causal role* in bringing about a memory response: without the existence of a trace there would be a gap in a causal chain and causal action would occur at *a temporal distance*. Second, enduring traces provide for the *retention* or *storing* in memory of experience and learning. Third, a trace possesses a *similarity in structure* to what is remembered. In the following chapters I will examine these ideas.

19. Ibid., p. 190

CHAPTER VII

Memory as a
Causal Process

1. It is widely assumed by writers on memory that the concept of memory either is, or at least involves, the concept of a causal process. B. S. Benjamin says: "I think it would be true to say that the everday view of remembering is simply that it is the final stage of a causal process and that the memory is some sort of causal device or mechanism. . . . The view that remembering should be thought of as part of a causal process is, of course, fundamental to psychology and to neurologists attempting to find the brain mechanism responsible for the phenomenon." [1] W. von Leyden asserts that genuinely recollecting something X "implies" that the recollection was "the result of a memory process or causal chain stretching continuously from the occurrence of X and the original experience of X up to the present recollection of X." [2] He adds, "The elusive causal chain between the event recollected and the recollection of it, form[s] part of what is asserted in every memory statement and yet [is] extremely difficult to verify in any given situation." [3] Martin and Deutscher argue explicitly for a causal interpretation of the concept of remembering: "If a person remembers what he saw, his recounting it must be due in part to seeing it. Anyone who rejects this causal interpretation must himself explain its force." [4] Their claim is: "There is a causal connection between A's past observation of X

1. B. S. Benjamin, "Remembering," *Mind*, 65 (1956), 323.
2. Von Leyden, *Remembering*, p. 42.   3. Ibid., p. 46.
4. Martin and Deutscher, "Remembering," p. 175.

and his present representation of it, and a logical connection between 'A's past observation of X is causally related to his present representation of it' and 'A remembers X' " [5] Suppose that a person gives a fairly accurate account of some event that occurred during his childhood. He himself might be in doubt whether he remembers the event, or whether his account of it is derived solely from hearing his parents tell about the event. This doubt might persist even when he was assured by his parents that he had witnessed the event. According to Martin and Deutscher, whatever facts would determine whether he actually remembers the event would be the same facts that would determine whether he *would have* produced his account of the event if he had *not* witnessed it. "To decide that he would not have done so is to decide that his past witnessing is causally necessary for his present account." [6]

Alvin Goldman says the following: "Remembering, like perceiving, must be regarded as a causal process. S remembers p at time t only if S's believing p at any earlier time is a cause of his believing p at t." [7]

2.   The idea that the concept of memory is the concept of a causal process adds much plausibility to the postulation of traces. We have seen (Chapter VI, Section 2) how Köhler and Koffka consider the trace to be required by our "fundamental ideas" about causation. One supposed fundamental idea is this: if A caused B, then a continuous causal process connected the occurrence of A to the occurrence of B.

A development in very recent contributions to the philosophy of memory is the appearance of a cautious attitude toward the conception of the trace as being either a "representation" or a "structural analogue" of past experience—basing, instead, the argument for the trace on purely causal assumptions. For example, D. Rosen defends the conception of a trace, but holds that "The trace theorist,

5. Ibid.   6. Ibid., p. 176.
7. Alvin Goldman, "A Causal Theory of Knowing," *Journal of Philosophy*, 64 (1967), 360.

while committed to certain causal notions, is not, or at least need not be, committed to the notion of structural analogy or representation." [8] The crucial causal notion on which the trace theorist should base his case, according to Rosen, is "the deeply embedded assumption that there can be no direct causes remote in space or time." [9] This assumption is so basic to "the framework of ordinary beliefs about the character of the universe" that, according to Rosen, no one seriously questions it:

> To my knowledge it has never been seriously argued that an event can effect another over a temporal gap. [10] . . . So convinced are we in a spatio-temporal contiguity thesis that we assume, even where we do not have direct empirical evidence, that between causally related but spatio-temporally remote events there is some continuous causal mechanism which carries the residual effects of the instigating causal event. . . . It is, I believe, a principle of spatio-temporal contiguity which has led scientists in the field of remembering, and philosophers interested in causal explanations of memory, to posit a memory mechanism or trace to span the gap between the remembering and the causally important learning event in the rememberer's past. [11]

3. It is true that, when we philosophize in large terms about space, time, causation, and "the character of the universe," the idea of "action at a distance" seems magical and irrational. This may be partly because we are influenced by primitive imagery: for example, we picture ourselves swinging an axe through the air and thereby causing a tree a mile away to fall! (Action at a spatial distance.) Or we imagine someone striking a tree with his fist and causing absolutely no change in the tree, and then a year later the tree falls *because of* the blow it received a year previously! (Action at a temporal distance.) In addition to such imagery, some philosophers are influenced by a theoretical assumption that I will discuss later.

8. Deborah A. Rosen, "An Argument For the Logical Notion of A Memory Trace," *Philosophy of Science* (March 1975), p. 2.
9. Ibid., p. 10.   10. Ibid., p. 7.   11. Ibid., p. 8.

In order, however, to obtain a true account of a concept, we must look away from philosophical pictures and assumptions and reflect on the way we speak and think in the situations of real life where the concept has its home. But, first, how does the idea of causation across a temporal gap arise? What comparisons are we making? Isn't it something like this: We imagine a case where something A causes something B, there being a continuous causal process intervening between A and B, e.g., I light a fuse attached to a charge of gunpowder, and the flame runs continuously the whole length of the fuse, finally detonating the charge. Now we compare this with an imagined case where the fuse is in two parts, separated by a gap of several yards; when the detached section of the fuse is ignited and consumed, then, after an interval of several seconds, the remainder of the fuse ignites and the flame travels to the charge, exploding it. Here would be a genuine gap in a causal process!

There cannot be a gap in a causal process, however, unless first there is a causal process. Why should it be supposed that the concept of memory is the concept of a causal process? Let us see how the idea of causation is involved in the concept of memory, and whether it warrants the assumption of a *process*.

There is no objection to thinking that the concept of memory involves *a* concept of causation. Suppose I tell someone about the capsizing of a boat in Lake Cayuga last week. For some reason he is surprised that I should know about that happening, and asks, "How is it that you know about it?" I reply, "I know about it *because* I saw it happen." This would be an application of the concept of memory. I am claiming to remember seeing the boat capsize. What I am claiming, or implying, could be put in various ways: I am saying that my present knowledge of the happening is *due to* my previous perception of it. I am implying that my present knowledge *depends on* my previous perception; that had I *not* witnessed the event I would *not* now know about it and would *not* now be in a position to relate it. In other words, I am implying that, the circumstances being as they were, my previous witnessing of the happening was a *necessary causal* condition of my presently relating it.

There is nothing wrong in saying all of those things. Yet where in them is the implication of a causal *process?* In calling something a "process," we imply that it is not an instantaneous event, but instead an event that extends over a period of time, an event that has duration: e.g., the burning of a fuse, the growth of a plant, the building of a house.

We often say, however, that *x caused y*, or that *y* occurred *because of x*, without meaning that there was a causal process. For example: Suppose I learn that a certain person is coming to visit my family. I announce that I refuse to see him. "What is the cause of your refusal?" "Because he lied to me." Suppose it was replied to me: "But that was two weeks ago. Are you sure there has been a causal process from then until now?" This would be an idiotic question. Its irrelevance shows that this use of the word "cause" did not imply a causal process. (In this example the cause of the refusal was my *reason* for the refusal.)

Another example: "What caused you to do such a dangerous thing as to climb up on the roof?" "I did it because I intended to get my hat which had blown up there." "What makes you think there was a causal process connecting your intention with your action of climbing up on the roof?" Another queer question. (Here, too, the cause of the action was my reason for the action.)

Another example: "What made you gobble down your dinner so rapidly?" "Because I was famished." "Are you certain that a causal process led from your hunger to your behavior of gobbling down the food?" (Here the cause of my behavior was *not my reason* for it; rather, the behavior was a manifestation or expression of my hunger.)

Let us return to the example of memory, wherein my relating a happening of last week was *due to* or *because of* my having witnessed it. Imagine it being asked: "Are you certain that during the entire week there was an ongoing causal process that connected your witnessing the capsizing with your eventually relating it?" (This cause of my relating the incident was again, *not* my reason for relating it.)

The strange, irrelevant character of these questions shows that there is a familiar use of causal language consisting of such ordinary locutions as "because of," "due to," "the cause of," and the more technical "necessary causal condition," which carries no implication of a causal process filling up the temporal space between the occurrence of a cause of x and the occurrence of x. We can agree with Martin and Deutscher that the language of memory does, in a sense, require a "causal interpretation," but not agree that memory as a causal concept entails the concept of a causal process. "Causality; therefore a causal process" is an illegitimate principle. Yet it is only by resorting to this unjustified inference that the concept of memory can seem to provide a basis, on causal grounds, for the assumption of a memory trace. Eliminate the assumption of a causal *process*, and *the causal argument* for a memory trace collapses.

This is not to deny, of course, that often there is a process of *trying* to remember. And often, too, there is a process of remembering some episode, in the sense of dwelling on it in one's memory, reliving it in memory, and so on. I hope, however, that in Part One it has been convincingly shown that a great many occurrences of remembering something do not involve trying to remember it, or reliving it, or dwelling on it in memory. Sometimes there is a phenomenological process of memory; sometimes not. What I am presently criticizing is the idea that underneath these variations in the phenomenology of memory there has to be, in all cases, a causal process of memory.

4.   Russell once surmised that the kind of causality involved in memory might be what he called "mnemic causation." This notion of causation would involve a temporal gap between cause and effect. Mnemic causation would be involved if there are responses of an organism which

can only be brought under causal laws by including past occurrences in the history of the organism as part of the causes of the present response. I do not mean merely . . . that past occurrences are part of a *chain* of causes leading to the present event. I mean that, in attempting to state the *proximate* cause of the present event, some past event or events must be included, unless we take refuge in hypothetical modifications of brain structure.[12]

On Russell's view there would be mnemic causation only if there were mnemic causal *laws*. Assuming that there were, the philosophical question of primary interest for him was whether mnemic causation is an "ultimate" form of causation. He was inclined to favor the hypothesis that past experience affects present behavior *only* by means of present physiological traces. If this hypothesis were true, mnemic causation would not be "ultimate." But Russell thought that the hypothesis of traces is "not quite conclusive," and so we ought not to reject entirely "the possibility that mnemic causation may be the ultimate explanation of mnemic phenomena." [13]

Broad draws a comparison between Russell's theory of mnemic causation and the trace theory, remarking that what is distinctive about the mnemic theory is that it postulates a *time-gap* between an event and one of its necessary causal conditions.[14] The trace theory, in contrast, "holds that such a gap cannot be an ultimate fact"—all of the causally necessary conditions of an event must either be temporally continuous with it or immediately precede it.[15] On Broad's view, the weakness of trace theory is that it postulates "persistent entities" that are "purely hypothetical." The mnemic theory, on the other hand, proposes "an unfamiliar kind of causal relation." Broad's chief criticism of the mnemic theory seems to be that it would be impossible, or at least very difficult, to formulate mnemic causal *laws:* apparently for the reason that in stating such a law one could not specify any *constant time-relation* between the past experience and the present stimulus.[16] Broad does not believe that

12. Russell, *The Analysis of Mind*, p. 78.   13. Ibid., p. 92.
14. Broad, *Mind and its Place in Nature*, p. 499.   15. Ibid., p. 450.
16. Ibid., p. 459.

this consideration decisively refutes "the possibility of mnemic causation as an ultimate fact in mental life," but he does think that we have "very little ground" for *accepting* it.[17] Broad criticizes Russell for presenting the theory of mnemic causation as if it implied that past experience and present stimulus were the *only* conditions required to produce a present memory response. Obviously, "the general integrity of the brain and nervous system" is also a necessary causal condition. As Broad puts it, both mnemic theory and trace theory assume *some* "persistent condition," in addition to past experience and present stimulus, but for mnemic theory this is a "general" condition, while for trace theory it is a "special" condition. In the case of mnemic theory:

This persistent condition is just the general integrity of the brain and nervous system, which existed before as well as after the past experience and was in no way modified by it. On the trace theory there is a *special* persistent condition, which was started by the past experience and would not have existed without it. . . . On the trace theory, if you were to take a cross-section of the history of the experient's body and mind anywhere between the past experience and the stimulus you would find something, viz., the trace, which corresponds to and may be regarded as the representative of the past experience. . . . On Mr. Russell's theory . . . these intermediate slices . . . would contain nothing which corresponds to and represents the past experience.[18]

5. I wish to defend the idea of mnemic causation, but without defending either a *theory* or the notion of *nmemic causal laws*. By "mnemic causation" I do mean causation across a temporal gap, and I do mean the kind of causation that is present in memory. Contrary to Broad, mnemic causation is not an "unfamiliar kind of causal relation." Everyday we observe instances of it. Once when I stooped to pick up a rock from my lawn I was surprised to see a nearby dog rush away at top speed with his tail between his legs, casting fearful looks back at me. Undoubtedly someone had pre-

17. Ibid., p. 462.   18. Ibid., p. 458.

viously thrown rocks at the dog and this is what caused him to run in fright when I stooped to pick up a rock. The incident is a perfect example of mnemic causation.

Consider another example, imaginary but plausible. Professors A and B are members of the same department in a university. At a department meeting a week ago, A made a comment about some of B's students, which B took as an insinuation that B was not giving his students proper training. B made no reply but was furious. A and B formerly had enjoyed cordial relations. On a Sunday morning each had the custom of walking to a nearby store to buy the Sunday paper. Frequently it happened that they met *en route*, and it was their custom to stop and engage in a friendly chat. But this Sunday morning, when B saw A walking toward him, he crossed quickly to the other side of the street and pretended not to see A. This is a case in which something that happened a week before caused B to do something he would not have otherwise done. Notice that an observer, who was familiar with the previous history of relations between A and B, could present different causal explanations of B's unusual behavior: "B did that because A insulted him last week." "Because B wanted to avoid meeting A." "Because B saw A coming towards him." But in the latter two explanations, a reference to B's previous humiliation would have to be supplied or assumed in order to provide an adequate understanding of B's behavior.

In both the foregoing examples the use of the word "cause" is natural. Nothing could be more familiar than this kind of causal relation. What is strange is that there should be a need to defend it against the charge of not being an "ultimate" explanation of the behavior of the dog or of B. There is a sense in which, if there are two explanations, E_1 and E_2, of a certain phenomenon, E_1 may be *more* basic or a more ultimate explanation than E_2, in that the laws assumed in E_2 presuppose the laws assumed in E_1, but not vice versa. Since mnemic causation (in my understanding of it) does not assume laws, another kind of explanation of mnemic phenomena cannot be "more basic," in that sense. Even if the theory of traces were a coherent conception, which I will try to show it is not, it would not be a more fundamental explanation of mnemic phenomena than is mnemic causation. It would simply be a *different kind* of explanation, catering to different interests.

It is a truism that people respond to experiences and perceived events, weeks, months, years, after the occurrence of those events. In ordinary life our thinking is not boggled by those temporal gaps. Mnemic causation begins to appear problematic when, first, we approach it with the assumption that temporal contiguity is the norm in causality and, second, when we try to weigh mnemic causation down with laws. A related reason why mnemic causation presents itself as a strange, "unfamiliar" conception is the common assumption of philosophers and psychologists that the phenomena of memory require a memory-*process*, going on continuously between a past experience and a subsequent response to it. I have already argued that the actual employment of the concept of memory, in ordinary language and thought, provides no warrant for this assumption.

6.   I want to reject the idea that mnemic causation is impossible or dubious because there could be no mnemic causal *laws*. I agree with G. E. M. Anscombe that the widespread assumption of philosophers that any singular causal statement, by its very meaning, implies a universal generalization of the form, "Whenever x then y," is a prejudice. The statement, "The snow on my boots caused me to slip on the stairs," does not imply any nontrivial universal generalization that *we can think of;* and there is no good reason to believe that a person who makes this assertion is thereby committed to the *existence* of a universal generalization. The same holds for the singular causal statement, "His death was caused by pneumonia." Sometimes pneumonia causes death, sometimes it does not. Someone may say, "This shows that we do not know *all* of the causal conditions." But, as Anscombe remarks, this comment con-

tains the unwarranted assumption "that there is such a thing to know." [19] Anscombe observes, correctly it seems to me, that "our primary knowledge of causality" derives from our learning to apply a great number of causal concepts: for example, those conveyed by such words as "push," "cut," "smash," "throw," "drop," and so on.[20] Our mastery of the application of those words does not presuppose the acquisition of any universal generalizations. We learn to distinguish cases in which someone, A, pushed the chair or the table from cases in which A did not do this. Our acquisition of this control of the word "pushed" did not ever require us to formulate a nontautological generalization about the conditions or effects of pushing, nor did it require us to *believe* that there is any such true generalization.

7. It seems to me that the impression of strangeness and absurdity created by the idea of mnemic causation is due to distortions in our philosophical thinking produced by our tendency to adopt the false assumptions that causation, in its very meaning, requires both causal *processes* and causal *laws*. Once we free ourselves from those assumptions, the idea of causation at a temporal distance, which to many philosophers is the epitome of absurdity, loses its ridiculous aspect.

Carl Ginet takes note of the claim of Martin and Deutscher that there are "many difficulties of various kinds surrounding the idea of action at a distance," and Ginet comments as follows:

I don't know what difficulties surrounding the idea of action at a distance these authors have in mind. Perhaps one of them could be that it is hard to see how the spatial or temporal parameters would be accommodated in *general laws* governing a causal connection that could cross spatiotemporal gaps of various, and haphazardly determined, sizes. But this is a difficulty only on the assumption that any sort of causal connection requires that there be true causal laws under which its instances are subsumable—that

19. G. E. M. Anscombe, "Causality and Determination," An Inaugural Lecture (London: Cambridge University Press, 1971), p. 7.
20. Ibid., pp. 9–10.

only a law can make a causal connection. But it seems that in the concept of memory we have a counter-example to this assumption.[21]

The fact that the hypothesis of persisting memory traces is "widely accepted or appealing," says Ginet,

> should not be confused with the non-fact that the very concept of memory requires some sort of continuous causal link between an experience and the memory of it; this is no more the case than the fact that the hypothesis of an intervening medium to explain the phenomena of gravitational attraction was once widely appealing (and, some tell me, still is) indicates that the very concept of gravitational force requires such an intervening medium through which it is exercised.[22]

We are familiar with cases of causation where there is indeed a continuous causal chain: for example, a flame is fed by the continuous flow of a gas through a pipe. When we philosophize about memory, which involves causation, an analogy such as this one seems to tell us what must be the case in memory. But this it cannot do. We have to look and see whether the word "cause" is used in the same way in the context of memory as in our analogy.

Our failure to do so is exactly like our failure to see differences in the use of the word "recognition." There is a use of that word in which we speak of recognizing a stranger by comparing him with a photograph; there is also a use of the same word in which we speak of recognizing an old friend, but *not* by comparing him with a photograph. Here there is the philosophical temptation to feel that the two sorts of case must be "essentially" the same; therefore, in the second sort of case, one must have compared (perhaps unconsciously) the face of the old friend with some kind of inwardly held likeness or copy. From such thinking emerge psychological theories about mental "templates" and "cognitive maps."

The fact that the belief in the necessity of a continuous causal link in memory is "widely appealing" *only* serves to illustrate how difficult it is in philosophy to *see differences* in the use of a word.

21. Carl Ginet, *Knowledge, Perception and Memory* (Boston: Reidel, 1975), p. 166.
22. Ibid., p. 167.

8.   The notion that a memory response may be "accurate" or "correct" plays a part in generating the theory of traces. Köhler says:

> What does recognition mean? It means that a present fact, usually a perceptual one, makes contact with a corresponding fact in memory, a trace, a contact which gives the present perception the character of being known or familiar. But memory contains a tremendous number of traces, all of them representations of earlier experiences which must have been established by the processes accompanying such earlier experiences. Now, why does the present perceptual experience make contact with the trace of the *right* earlier experience? This is an astonishing achievement. Nobody seems to doubt that the *selection* is brought about by the similarity of the present experience and the experience of the corresponding earlier fact. But since this earlier experience is not present at the time, we have to assume that the trace of the earlier experience resembles the present experience, and that it is the similarity of our present experience (or the corresponding cortical process) and that trace which makes the selection possible.[23]

> All sound theories of memory, of habit, and so forth, must contain hypotheses about memory traces as physiological facts. Such theories must also assume that the characteristics of traces are more or less akin to those of the processes by which they have been established. Otherwise, how could the accuracy of recall be explained, which in a great many cases is quite high?[24]

Köhler is emphasizing the *accuracy* of recognition, recollection, and memory in general, as warranting the assumption of a causal process (including a persisting trace) reaching from a past experience to a later memory response. But since Köhler is thinking within a scientific framework, he must surely believe that when a memory response is *in*accurate or *in*correct, it, too, is the effect of a causal process. For example, asked who was the author of *Sons and Lovers*, I say Turgenev, instead of Lawrence. Or, it seems to me that I remember leaving my gloves at Kaplan's house last night, when actually I left them in my office. These errors of memory will surely have been caused. The exponent of a causal process in memory

23. W. Köhler, *The Task of Gestalt Psychology* (Princeton: Princeton University Press, 1969), p. 122.

24. Köhler, *Gestalt Psychology*, (New York: Liveright, 1947), p. 252

must admit that whether memories are accurate, inaccurate, or even delusive, they are equally the effects of causal processes.

On Köhler's view, therefore, when a memory is correct, the *right* causal process occurred. We might also say, the causal process *functioned correctly*. In the case of inaccurate, incomplete, or delusive memories, there is (by implication) a malfunction in the causal process. Now, on this view, how would it be decided (indeed, what would it *mean*) that a memory causal process had functioned correctly or incorrectly? It would seem that the advocate of the causal process view of remembering, can say only this—that such expressions as "the right process occurred" or "the process worked correctly" would just mean that the resulting memory was accurate. That is to say, the causal theorist has no criterion for the occurrence of the correct causal process or of its normal or proper functioning, other than whether its outcome is accurate or inaccurate. It is not as if he had observed this process in operation and had become familiar with the mechanism of it quite apart from its normal result. No. The causal process in the brain, operating continuously from the occurrence of an experience until the occurrence of a memory-manifestation of that experience, is completely hypothetical. That the right causal process occurred, or that the mechanism of the brain operated correctly, will be true *by definition*, if the resulting memory is correct.

It is important to note that this is not true in other cases. A process of calculation, for example, can be erroneous although the correct result emerges from it. Two errors might be made that canceled each other. Of course I do not mean that whenever a person is asked, say, for the product of two numbers he obtains the result by a calculation. But a person *can* obtain the right result by means of an *in*correct calculation. This is possible because there are standards, rules, for correct calculation. Therefore a correct result does not logically imply a correct process of calculation. (Although an incorrect result does logically imply an error somewhere in the process.) We can monitor the progress of a calculation and determine that it is wrong, even if the result (its effect) is right. We can say that this process caused this correct result without implying that the process itself was correct. In other words, a correct process of calculation is not a necessary causal condition of a correct result. By analogy, a properly functioning process of remembering, if there is one, should not be regarded as a *necessary* causal condition for correct remembering. Yet this is what Köhler's emphasis on the *accuracy* of remembering, as an argument for the necessity of assuming the operation of traces in a causal process, seems to require.

Nor is a properly functioning neural memory process a *sufficient* causal condition of correct remembering. This is shown by Hintikka's example of the boy who was taught that Columbus discovered America in 1392. The boy's later report to someone that Columbus made this discovery in 1392 reflected no failure of either perception or memory on his part. Presumably, therefore, the neural memory process was functioning properly. Yet the boy cannot be said to have "remembered" that Columbus discovered America in 1392.

The foregoing criticism shows that the concept of memory does not justify the requirement of a causal process as being either a necessary or a sufficient condition of correct remembering. Köhler is mistaken in thinking that the "astonishing achievement" of correct recognition and accurate recall demands the hypothesis of a causal process in memory. The *concept* of an accurate memory is not the concept of an effect produced by a properly functioning causal process.

In summary, although the concept of memory does warrant a "causal interpretation" (meaning that the relation between past experiences and subsequent memory responses to those experiences is naturally expressed in causal language), it is an error to infer that this causal ingredient in memory requires the assumption either of causal laws or of a temporally continuous chain of causation. When this is seen, the notion that a proper understanding of the concept of memory inevitably leads us to accept the requirement of physiological memory traces loses all force. The "causal argument" for memory traces collapses.

CHAPTER VIII

Retention and Storage

1. In Chapter VI we saw that one ingredient of the full-blown conception of the memory trace is the notion that traces account for the retention of experiences and facts in memory. We saw a certain ambivalence in the conception of some thinkers of how traces are related to retention. William James, for example, said on the one hand that the retention of something in memory was the ability or tendency to recall it, and that the *ground or cause* of this ability or tendency was the persistence of neural paths "left in the brain by past experience." On the other hand, James also said that the retention of experiences and information is *identical* with the persistence of those neural paths: "The *retention* . . . is no mysterious storing up of an 'idea' in an unconscious state. . . . It is a purely physical phenomenon, a morphological feature, the presence of these 'paths', namely, in the finest recesses of the brain's tissue." [1] In these latter remarks James is equating retention with physical *storage:* the experience or idea that is retained is not itself physically stored, but what is stored is a neural representation of it. And this is what retention in memory *is*.

The relation between the ideas of retention and storage has been troublesome for many thinkers. In the first edition of his *Essay,* Locke wrote that memory "is as it were the storehouse of our ideas. For, the narrow mind of man not being capable of having many ideas under view and consideration at once, it was necessary to

---

1. James, *Principles of Psychology*, I, 655.

have a repository, to lay up those ideas which, at another time, it might have use of." [2]

Locke subsequently thought that there was a confusion in those remarks; for in the second edition he added the following sentences:

> But, our *ideas* being nothing but actual perceptions in the mind, which cease to be anything when there is no perception of them; this laying up of our ideas in the repository of the memory signifies no more but this,—that the mind has a power in many cases to revive perceptions which it has once had, with this additional perception annexed to them, that *it has had them before.* And in this sense it is that our ideas are said to be in our memories, when indeed they are actually nowhere;—but only there is an ability in the mind when it will to revive them again, and as it were paint them anew on itself. [3]

Leaving aside Locke's mistake of supposing that the objects of memory (and of perception) are solely "ideas," the difference between the two passages is that in the earlier one Locke was taking the notion of a memory "storehouse" literally, whereas in the later one he conceived that the notions of "storage," "storehouse," and "repository" were to be understood solely as metaphors.

The literal interpretation of "storage" is emphatically endorsed in these remarks by Ebbinghaus:

> Psychical states of every kind, sensations, feelings, ideas, which at one time were present and then disappeared from consciousness, have not absolutely ceased to exist. Although an inward glance may not find them, they are not absolutely denied and annulled, but continue to live in a certain way, retained, as one says, in memory. We cannot indeed directly observe their present existence but we infer it from their effects which we know, with the same certainty that we infer the continued existence of the stars under the horizon. [4]

One such "effect" is deliberate recollection. Ebbinghaus says that when we deliberately recollect something, "It would be absurd to

2. Locke, *Essay Concerning Human Understanding*, Bk. II, Ch. X, Sec. 2.
3. Ibid.
4. Hermann Ebbinghaus, *Ueber das Gedächtnis* (Leipzig: Duncker & Humblot, 1885), p. 1.

assume that our will has created it anew and so to speak out of nothing; rather it must have been somehow and somewhere present; the will has, so to speak, only found it and presented it to us again." [5]

We can perceive in the foregoing quotations four different philosophical conceptions of the relation between retention in memory and storage: first, that the objects of memory are *literally* stored; second, that "storing" is merely a metaphor for retention; third, that storage is to be taken literally, but that what is stored are not the objects of memory but rather neural representations of them in the brain, and that this storing is identical with retention; fourth, that retention in memory, rather than being storage, is the ability to do something, but that the storing of neural representations is a necessary causal condition of the ability.

It is interesting to note that Martin and Deutscher seem to take "storage" *both* metaphorically and literally: "There is an inevitable recourse to metaphors about the storage of our past experience involved in our idioms and thought about memory. . . . So long as we hold some sort of storage or trace account of memory, it follows that we can remember only what we have experienced, for it is in our experience of events that they enter the storehouse." [6]

2. What do we mean when we say that we "retain" something? We mean that we previously had, or owned, or possessed it, and that we still do. One might say of a woman whom one had not seen for several years that she retains her good looks. One would mean that she was previously good-looking and still is. There would be no implication that her good looks are in storage. It might be said of a man that despite the many hardships he has suffered he retains a sunny disposition. Has his sunny disposition been stored? Abilities are retained (the ability to read Japanese, or to run a mile in six minutes). Is there an implication that the abilities have been stored?

Retention and storage are different concepts. Of course, some-

5. Ibid., p. 2.   6. Martin and Deutscher, "Remembering," p. 189.

thing that is retained may also be stored. A man announces that he has replaced all his old furniture with new furniture: "The only piece I retained, and just for sentimental reasons, is grandpa's rocking chair; it is stored in the attic." If he had kept it for use in the living room, it would have been retained but not stored. Storage implies retention, but retention does not imply storage.

Among the things that can be retained are knowledge and beliefs. Indeed, as Sydney Shoemaker points out, "No sense can be given to the notion of a belief lasting no time at all," and the same holds for knowledge.[7] Belief and knowledge must have some duration; they have to be retained for some time. When memory is knowledge it is retained knowledge. Leaving aside fine qualifications, if you remember that so-and-so, then you previously knew that so-and-so, and you have retained the knowledge.

Does retention in memory imply storage? Suppose that A and B see someone, C, who looks familiar to them. A says, "Do you remember his name?" B replies, "I can't think of his name at the moment. But I'm sure I remember it. I'm sure that his name is stored somewhere in my brain." I am assuming that B is not a philosopher, psychologist, or neurologist, giving voice to a theory about the nature of memory-retention, but just a layman employing a natural turn of speech. This use of "stored" is pure metaphor. This is shown by the fact that what will determine whether C's name, or the knowledge of C's name, is indeed "stored in B's brain" will be, not neurosurgery, but whether B will sooner or later *come out* with C's name. The *use* of the words, "I'm sure x is stored in my brain," is in this example exactly the same as the use of the words, "I'm sure that I remember x."

Martin and Deutscher declare that our "recourse to metaphors about the storage of our past experience" is "inevitable." Whether or not these metaphors are inevitable, they are *natural*. Just as natural as exclaiming, when bitterly disappointed in love, that "my

7. Sydney Shoemaker, "Memory," *Encyclopedia of Philosophy*, ed. Paul Edwards, Vol. 5, 273–274.

heart is broken." To take the storage metaphors, as Martin and Deutscher seem to do, as giving some warrant to the assumption of *traces* (*literal* storage) is both humorous and saddening. It has the comical aspect of being deceived by a pun. But when one sees this pun playing a part in the creation of a mythology of traces, where theories and research are pursued in dead earnest, one cannot help feeling a kind of grief.

3. The confusing of the idea of retention with the idea of literal storage is conspicuous in the writings of theorists and researchers in the neuropsychology of memory. Let us consider some examples: "Memory implies that, in some manner, impressions can be stored. As the storing of individual replicas of the original impressions would be a physical impossibility, storing must involve the transformation, coding and assimilation of those impressions." [8] What the concept of memory implies, of course, is that a remembered impression has been retained in memory, not that it has been literally stored. Another writer speaks of "the element of retention" and goes on, in the same breath, to say that *retention* "has been described as the 'memory trace' or 'engram.' " [9] He accepts this without question as a correct "description" and regards "the nature of the engram" as the primary problem. Another writer says:

The capacity to recall the past to consciousness can certainly be expected to reside in a primary mechanism of general biological validity. A firm link to the genetic mechanism is important, and in this respect especially, the RNA molecule, with its many possibilities, would fulfill many requirements. [10]

8. Maryse Metcalfe, "Problems of Memory in Man," *Aspects of Learning and Memory*, ed. D. Richter (New York: Basic Books, 1966), p. 6.

9. Derek Richter, "Biochemical Aspects of Memory," *Aspects of Learning and Memory*, p. 73.

10. H. Hydén, "Biochemical Aspects of Brain Activity," *Memory Mechanisms*, ed. K. H. Pribram (London; Penguin, 1969), p. 45.

The outer world is consciously experienced through the sensory part of the nervous system, and the information received is stored by memory mechanisms for future use.[11]

The unquestioning identification of memory-retention with storage is illustrated by this statement: "The brain's unique power is in part due to its ability to store information, i. e. to store a coded representation of experience for future use." [12] The same assumption appears in the following remarks:

In the present state of knowledge any theory about the storage of memories must be speculative and is likely to appear improbable. Plastic nerve nets are, by their very nature, unsuited for the prolonged storage of memories. There must be some mechanism by which a record is kept in the brain of the patterns which have formed in the cerebrum. The amount of information is very large and it must be stored in some form of code.[13]

Another writer speaks of "the enduring property of learning," by which he presumably means its retention in memory:

It was recognized as early as the turn of the century that the enduring property of learning, the part commonly referred to as memory storage, must involve a structural change in the nervous system. Seventy years later, the neural repository of storage (the engram, as it has been called) remains an enigma. Some have sought its anatomical locus, others have worried about its form, and both endeavors have been complicated by the possibility that the engram changes with age.[14]

The unquestioned identification of retention with storage is also evident in the following remarks: "The encoding phase of learning has been characterized in terms of the fact that information has first to be registered in the nervous system before a record can be made. It is commonly accepted that during this encoding phase a certain

11. Ibid., p. 33.

12. K. H. Pribram, ed. *Memory Mechanisms*, p. 7, Prefatory Note.

13. J. H. Taddum, "The Neurological Basis of Learning," *Aspects of Learning and Memory*, pp. 68–69.

14. Allen M. Schneider, "Two Faces of Memory Consolidation," *Short-Term Memory*, ed. D. Deutsch and J. A. Deutsch (New York: Academic Press, 1975), p. 340.

fixation time, which may be of the order of half an hour, is required for the information to become consolidated and hence permanently stored." [15] A great deal of current theorizing engages in speculations as to *how many* storage systems memory-retention requires—in particular, whether both a "short-term" and a "long-term" system are required. But that retention is identical with storage goes without question. Buschke says: "While I am persuaded that it is useful, and probably correct, to distinguish between short-term and long-term or permanent retention processes, I do not know whether such retention *processes* involve distinct *storages* or whether both operate in a common permanent storage." [16] Speaking of recalling an item of information, he remarks, "It seems obvious that at some point the item must be found in permanent storage for information retained in either short-term or long-term storage to be recovered by actually recalling the item." [17] But apparently it seems even more obvious, so obvious as not to deserve mention, that recalling an item of information necessitates that it has been stored.

Diana Deutsch refers to an experiment intended to investigate the capacity of people to remember "the sensory attributes of speech sounds":

Cole (1973) required subjects to decide whether two spoken letters were the same or different when they were presented either in the same voice or in different voices. He found that even with a retention interval of 8 sec, the subjects took a shorter time to respond "same" when the letters were spoken in the same voice rather than in a different voice. *The subjects must therefore have been storing the acoustic attributes of the spoken letters during this period.* [18]

The same writer remarks:

15. B. S. Meldrum, "Electrical Signal in the Brain and the Cellular Mechanism of Learning," *Aspects of Learning and Memory*, p. 123.

16. Herman Buschke, "Short-Term Retention, Learning, and Retrieval from Long-Term Memory," *Short-Term Memory*, p. 74.

17. Ibid.

18. Diana Deutsch, "The Organization of Short-Term Memory for a Single Acoustic Attribute," *Short-Term Memory*, p. 109. Emphasis added.

Considering the ease and speed with which we recognize a familiar voice by its intonation, we must be capable of storing the accoustical properties of speech sounds on a very long-term basis.[19]

It is also striking how acutely aware we may be of a single error or distortion in the performance of a musical composition. It is clear from such considerations that musical information must be stored in a highly specific form for substantial periods of time.[20]

The "must" in these remarks is interesting. Is it a tautological "must," acknowledging the conceptual truism that these performances of recognition and memory entail memory-retention? Or is it a "must" that marks an unexamined transition in thought from the idea of retention to the idea of storage? It would seem to be both at once, thereby reflecting the confusing of retention with storage.

In a study of the memorization of lists or sets of items, Sternberg remarks that "subjects could recall the sets they worked with several days later. In this case the sets must have been stored in long-term memory." [21] Here again is a "must" that discloses the mistaken identification of retention with storage. Sternberg provides a picturesque "model" of the "process" of memorization and subsequent recall or recognition of lists of words that are divided into sublists of different "categories":

Words in the memorized list are stored in a set of bins, with one category per bin. Either because the bins are unmarked, or because the category of the test word is not ascertained, selective access does not occur. Instead, the bins are entered and searched successively in random order. The words in each bin are searched exhaustively, and at the standard rate, whether or not they are in the same category as the test word. However, when the bin containing the relevant category is entered, this fact is detected, and the search stops as soon as this bin has been scanned.[22]

Sternberg's model is nearly as attractive as the Pine Board Theory of remembering and forgetting that was once described to me. Ac-

19. Ibid., p. 110.   20. Ibid., p. 111.
21. Saul Sternberg, "Memory Scanning: New Findings and Current Controversies," *Short-Term Memory*, p. 201.
22. Ibid., p. 218.

cording to this theory, there is a pine board in the head, which is the repository of memories. Items of perception are deposited on this board. Since the board is of knotty pine, it contains knotholes. If an item falls through a knothole it is forgotten, but if it remains on the board it is retained in memory!

Only rarely does there occur, in that part of the vast literature of the neuropsychology of memory that I have read, any indication that there is anything problematic about the notion of storage. The following is one of those untypical examples: "If we could observe memory storage directly, our problem of analysis would be simplified, but unfortunately we cannot. Instead, we are forced to infer storage from overt behavior." [23] In contrast, *retention* is not problematic, and does not have to be inferred. If someone is given a list of words to memorize, and on the following day can repeat the list without aid, then he has "retained those words in his memory." This is how we use that expression! That performance was a demonstration of retention. But that the words were *stored* in the person's brain was not demonstrated, and indeed what this could *mean* is totally obscure. Some sensitivity to this *conceputual* obscurity is indicated by the following remark: "It is our present lack of theoretical understanding of how the cerebral storage system might operate that hampers us in the search for its physical basis, as *we do not have any clear idea of what type of phenomena to look for.*" [24] By and large, however, there is no awareness that the idea of storage presents a conceptual difficulty. In the following remarks by Wilder Penfield there is no worry as to what could be meant by "preserving the record of the stream of thought":

It has fallen to my lot, during explorations of the cortex, to demonstrate a mechanism in the human brain which preserves the record of the stream of thought.[25]

23. Schneider, p. 341.

24. J. A. Deutsch, "Higher Nervous Function: The Physiological Bases of Memory," *Annual Review of Physiology*, 24 (1962), 283. Emphasis added.

25. Wilder Penfield, "The Permanent Record of the Stream of Consciousness," *Proceedings*, *14th International Congress of Psychology*, June 1954, p. 47.

The evidence suggests that nothing is lost, that the record of each man's experience is complete.[26]

During any given period of waking time each individual forms a record of the stream of consciousness.[27]

Mild electrical stimulation of the lateral or, more frequently, the superior surface of either temporal lobe may cause the conscious patient to relive a sequence of experiences from his life, experiences of months or years past. It is apparent that there is an enduring record of the stream of consciousness within the brain of each man. . . . Evidently there is a sequence of facilitated neuron connections somewhere which, when activated, is capable of producing a "playback," like a wire recorder or a gramophone, when stimulated.[28]

In the appendix to Chapter X we shall see evidence that Penfield and others have misrepresented the results of temporal lobe stimulation, and that in fact the same stimulation applied to the same brain site does not produce the same memory or the same response.

4.   A great deal of current speculation and argument concerns the question of whether "the mnemonic trace" is "structural" or "dynamic" in nature. To say that it is "structural" means, roughly, that the trace is a physical imprint or groove in the brain: the word "engram" was coined in order to signify that an experience or perception *engraved* a record of itself in the brain. In contrast, to say that the trace is "dynamic" means that the record is kept by some activity of the brain, perhaps electrical or chemical. This issue is addressed in the following remarks:

It must be recognized that the nature of the mnemonic trace is a central problem for any psychological theory that postulates real cerebral events as the basis of behavior. Two sets of facts are apparently opposed to each other. On the one hand, the persistence of early learning throughout life even despite major cerebral disturbances—including coma, anesthesia, *grand mal*

    26. Ibid., p. 67.   27. Ibid., p. 68.
    28. W. Penfield and B. Milner, "Memory Deficit Produced by Bilateral Lesions in the Hippocampal Zone," *A.M.A. Archives of Neurology and Psychiatry*, 79 (May 1958), 493.

convulsions and deteriorative diseases—argues strongly that some permanent and unmodifiable change in neural structures is the basis of the trace.
On the other hand, the facts of perceptual generalization and the apparent
lack of specificity of most cortical tissues in learned behavior seem to show
that the trace cannot be a property of any particular set of cells; that is,
that the trace cannot be structurally determined. On this rock psychological theories have foundered, or for fear of it have hardly dared leave port.
The nature of the mnemonic trace is a question of the first importance.[29]

R. W. Gerard also addresses this problem. First, he makes a general remark about memory, which typifies the viewpoint of psychologists, and is apparently regarded as self-evident: "Memory involves the making of an impression by an experience, the retention
of some record of this impression and the re-entry of this record
into consciousness (or behavior) as recall and recognition."[30] He
goes on to ask the following question:

Does memory depend on a continuing activity or on some static residue,
some structural alteration, left behind by past activity? Is a river the water
flowing in it or the channel the water cuts? . . . The second question is: Is
the structural trace (or dynamic process) for each memory located in a particular region, or are memory traces suffused through the brain in some
way? Are memories marks placed on violin strings or are they wave trains
playing over these strings? The latter would imply dynamic memory, but
the trace could still be structural, like the wiggled groove on a phonograph
record. . . .
    A dynamic memory would depend on the continuous passage of nerve im-
pulses or on the maintenance of some active metabolic or potential change
in neurons, presumably reinforced by the repeated arrival of impulses. A
nerve impulse travelling around a closed loop of connecting neurons would
be a mechanism for such a dynamic memory, each remembered item depending on the activity of a particular loop or set of neurons.[31]

What the mnemonic record exactly consists of is a matter of considerable speculation. One of the most imaginative conjectures has

29. D. O. Hebb and Esme N. Foord, "Errors of Visual Recognition and the Nature of the Trace," *Journal of Experimental Psychology*, 35 (1945), 335–336.
30. R. W. Gerard, "What is Memory?", *Scientific American*, September 1953, p.
118.
31. Ibid., p. 121.

been proposed by N. S. Sutherland, in an article dealing with visual pattern recognition. An animal can be trained to make differential responses to, say, a square shape and a circular shape. Having learned to do this with shapes of a particular size, the animal will go on to make differential responses to squares and circles of different sizes. This is an example of what is called "perceptual generalization." Sutherland's theory of visual pattern recognition is intended to explain, among other things, the phenomenon of perceptual generalization. Sutherland remarks:

> It is clear that man has a capacity for perceptual learning. It is not merely that we learn to identify now one object and now another, we can also learn something about a general class of pictures which facilitates recognition of the relevant differences between new members of that class and previously experienced members. . . . With sufficient exposure to Chinese faces, it becomes as easy to remember new Chinese faces as Western ones. Some account of the capacity for this rather general kind of perceptual learning must be included in any adequate theory of pattern recognition.[32]

Sutherland's theory envisages a mechanism in the brain containing a "processor" or "analyzer" that extracts an abstract description of similar visual patterns, and a "store" in which the abstract description or rule is deposited and retained. "The visual input is analysed by a processor that extracts local features (mainly bars, edges and ends) simultaneously at all points on the input picture. When a picture is memorized, a rule is written into a store describing the output from the processor in a highly abstract language."[33] Sutherland gives examples of what these abstract descriptions or rules might be like:

> It is of course extremely difficult to get at the form of the descriptions used by the brain when a shape is "memorized" but to make it clear what we mean by an abstract description, let us consider a symbolism which provides a description of simple shapes free from size and retinal position.
> One expression describing an outline square is as follows:

32. N. S. Sutherland, "Outlines of a Theory of Visual Pattern Recognition in Animals and Man," *Proceedings of the Royal Society, B.*, 171 (1968), 301.
33. Ibid., p. 315.

$$w^{H(x)}e = n^{V(x)}s = e^{H(x)}w = s^{V(x)}n =$$

. . . In brief, the letters H and V refer to horizontal and vertical lines or to the output from horizontal and vertical bar detectors. The lower case subscripts refer to the retinal coordinates of the west and east ends of the horizontal lines (e and w) and to the south and north ends of the vertical lines (s and n). The equals sign joining the subscripts means that the retinal coordinates of one end of one line are to be the same as the retinal coordinates of the specified end of the next line. The variable x refers to the length of the lines and can take any value though it must be the same value for all lines. The expression is to be read cyclically—that is the final n has the same retinal coordinates as the initial w. In everyday language the expression reads—"A horizontal line of length x joined at its east end to the north end of a vertical line of length x joined at its south end to the east end of a horizontal line, etc." Such an expression could be regarded as a rule for generating an outline square of any size at any position on the retina, and correspondingly this description of a square could be matched by an input square falling on any retinal position.[34]

Another example:

Consider the description that might be written for an "L" shape

$$V(2x)_{s=w}H(x).$$

In ordinary language this says that there is a vertical line joined at its south end to the west end of a horizontal line and that the vertical line is about twice the length of the horizontal line.[35]

Sutherland conceives that these abstract descriptions of patterns will probably be arranged in the brain in a hierarchical order. He says:

Consider a complex shape like a face: it would clearly be uneconomical to hold in one part of the storage system a description of an eye, elsewhere a description of an ear and to repeat these and others in a location holding a description of a face. It would be much more economical when describing a face to use in the description terms like "eye" and "ear" and in order to obtain their descriptions to refer to other locations where descriptive rules for these items are held. It seems likely then that the storage system will be hierarchically arranged so that descriptive rules can occur at many different levels and high level rules will contain elements which refer to lower level rules.[36]

---

34. Ibid., pp. 304–305.   35. Ibid., p. 307.   36. Ibid., p. 310.

In this way different descriptions can be formed of the same input pattern. What we see corresponds to the description selected to match the input. The same type of process allows us to understand how it is that a picture can be ambiguous. The whole appearance of the Boring (1930) wife-grandmother figure changes when we switch from seeing it one way to seeing it in the other. When we are seeing the figure as an attractive girl we are matching the input to a rule describing a young girl seen in profile. When we switch to seeing an old lady we are matching to a rule describing an old lady seen full face. The part of the input that was matched to a rule for an ear is now matched to a rule for an eye and so on. This reversible figure dramatically illustrates our contention that what we see is not the pattern on our retina, but the rule or series of hierarchical rules to which we match this pattern: by this we mean that all that is available to determine our responses is the rule formed (or matched) to describe the input picture. . . . As in vision so in hearing, what we hear is not the actual waveform received by the ear but the descriptive rules to which that waveform is matched.[37]

Different descriptions of the same visual input may be formed and stored and this must be the key to perceptual learning. When we learn the capacity to individuate the members of a class of pictorial structures (such as individual Chinese faces), we presumably learn to modify our description-forming mechanism so that just that information is stored that readily differentiates one member from another.[38]

Sutherland says, "There is no physiological evidence either in favour of or against our postulated description of the store."[39]

5. This last remark is a glaring understatement. How could there be physiological evidence in this matter? Is it really possible that *the brain* should employ symbols, rules, descriptions? This is something that *people* learn to do in learning language. Such learning requires a lot of teaching and practice. Errors are made and corrected. A child, learning language, may mistake "right" for "left," or "eye" for "ear." Given correction and more examples, the child will begin to apply the words correctly. What does it mean to say that the child applies them *correctly?* It means that its use of those

37. Ibid., p. 311.   38. Ibid., p. 312.   39. Ibid., p. 314.

words conforms to the practice of the community of speakers in which the child is reared.

How does *the brain* of a person or animal fit into this picture? Is a brain a member of a community of speakers? Does it say things? Does it receive instruction? Does it apply words or other "symbols" to objects and situations? Does it share a common language with other brains? Does the brain, in the beginning, make mistakes; or is it always right?

We know what a mistake is like, in the case of a child. Told to hold out its right hand, it holds out the left one instead; asked to point to an ear it points to an eye; told to draw a square, it draws a circle. Did the child's brain make a mistake too? Presumably when the child heard the sound "right," something happened in its brain, and then the child held out its left hand. Was this event in its brain "correct," or was it "incorrect"? What nonsense!

6.   Sutherland supposes that since an Englishman can learn to identify a face as a Chinese face, therefore there must be an abstract rule or description that provides a general characterization of Chinese faces. But what can the Englishman do here? He might be confident that a face was Chinese and not English or Spanish, but uncertain whether it was Chinese and not Japanese or Korean. Certainly he could not *formulate* a rule that characterizes all Chinese faces and distinguishes them from non-Chinese faces, any more than he could give a general rule for distinguishing any young girl seen in profile from any old lady seen full face. Sutherland thinks that nevertheless those general rules must be there, *in* the Englishman; for how otherwise could he pick out Chinese faces with fair accuracy, or see an ambiguous figure now as the profile of a girl, now as an old lady seen full face? These capacities are *explained* by postulating the presence of abstract rules in the brain.

The same thinking is illustrated by Lenneberg. He says, "Understanding involves seeing the basis on which objects are categorized, thus enabling a child to name an object correctly that he has never seen before." [40] Again: "Knowing a word is . . . the successful operation of those principles, or application of those rules, that lead to using the word 'table' or 'house' for objects never before encountered." [41] And again: "Since every native speaker of English *can* tell a well-formed sentence from an ill-formed one, it is evident that some principles must exist." [42] Lenneberg, like Sutherland, assumes that these principles or rules are in, or are employed by, the human brain.

One should be struck by the similarity between the Lenneberg-Sutherland view, and the thesis of those philosophers (noted in Chapter V) that remembering a past event requires that we possess a "picture" or "copy" or "present mental content," which informs and guides our memory-judgments. Both the scientists and the philosophers think that the existence of an underlying mechanism (in one case "mental," in the other case physiological) can be deduced from the presence of certain *abilities*. Lenneberg assumes that the ability to name objects correctly that one has not seen before (e.g., tables) *requires* that one "see the basis" in terms of which the objects are categorized. Sutherland assumes that the ability of a person or animal to make differential responses to squares and circles, or to pick out Chinese faces from non-Chinese faces, *requires* that the human or animal possesses and employs highly abstract general rules or principles.

This is a nice illustration of how a philosophical assumption can control the thinking in what is supposed to be an empirical science. In the case of Lenneberg and Sutherland, the assumption is the Platonic conception that the ability to distinguish tables from non-tables (chests, dressers, benches) requires that one grasp, in some way, the "essential nature" of tables—that is, a principle that specifies the logically necessary and sufficient conditions for a thing to be a table. For Plato the essences (of table, bed, beauty, justice) were apprehended by "the mind"; for Lenneberg and Sutherland the essences are deposited in the brain.

40. Eric Lenneberg, "On Explaining Language," *Science*, 164, (May 1969), 639.
41. Ibid., p. 640.   42. Ibid., p. 641.

This kind of philosophical thinking receives a jolt if one sets out deliberately to try to specify a set of logically necessary and sufficient conditions for a thing to be, for example, a table. What size, what shape, how many legs, must it have; composed of what material; used for what purpose? One will find that any specifications are easily defeated by counter examples, real or possible.

Undoubtedly tables display what Wittgenstein calls "a family resemblance." [43] This does not mean (as some readers of Wittgenstein surprisingly take it to mean) that there is something, namely, a family resemblance, that characterizes each table and separates tables from all other things. No. Wittgenstein's point is that there need be *nothing* common and peculiar to all tables to account for our acquired mastery of the word "table." The same for "game," [44] "sentence," [45] "green," [46] "number," [47] "reading," [48] "understanding," [49] "being guided," [50] and so on. Wittgenstein remarks, "I am saying that these phenomena have no one thing in common which makes us use the same word for all,—but that they are *related* to one another in many different ways." [51] When we encounter new and different things that we call "tables," we are extending our application of the word "table" because of different and overlapping similarities with other things we have called by that name—"as in spinning a thread we twist fibre on fibre. And the strength of the thread does not reside in the fact that some one fibre runs through its whole length, but in the overlapping of many fibres." [52]

We cannot *say* what differentiates tables from all other objects, because there is no such property, and therefore nothing that can be captured by a principle, rule, or description. Contrary to Lenneberg and Sutherland, we do *not* "see the basis" for calling something a table or for identifying a face as Chinese. Even if it made sense to suppose that the brain operates with abstract rules or

43. Wittgenstein, *Investigations*, paras. 65–71.   44. Ibid., paras. 66, 69, 75.
45. Ibid., para. 108.   46. Ibid., para. 73.   47. Ibid., paras. 67, 68.
48. Ibid., paras. 156–171.   49. Ibid., paras. 143–155.
50. Ibid., para. 172.   51. Ibid., para. 65.   52. Ibid., para. 67.

descriptions, there is no warrant for believing that somehow and somewhere such rules *must* be present in order to explain the phenomena of recognition or of differentiated response. The conception of physiological memory traces and of a cerebral storage system is motivated, to a large extent, by this philosophical error.

CHAPTER IX

The Causal Role of the
Neural Representation

1. In Chapter VI we saw that what I called the "full-blown" conception of the memory trace endows the trace with three fundamental properties: first, it has a *causal* role in bringing about a memory response; second, it provides for the *storing* of experiences and information; third, by virtue of having the *same structure* it is a *representation* of what is remembered. In Chapters VII and VIII we examined the first two ideas, and in this chapter we turn to the third one. The notion that the trace of an experience has the same structure as the experience is often expressed by saying that the experience is "coded" into the trace. The following remarks by a neuropsychologist present all these features of the full-blown conception of the trace:

There seem to be four fundamental functions that a memory mechanism must perform: (1) the configuration of external and internal stimuli impinging upon an organism, which constitute an experience, must somehow be coded into a neural representation; (2) the neural representation of that experience (coded information about the set of stimuli) must be stored; (3) it must be possible to gain access to the coded information in order to retrieve specific experiences from storage; and (4) the retrieved data must again be decoded into neural activity, which somehow recreates the sensations and qualities of the original experience and thus constitutes a "memory." [1]

1. E. R. John, *Mechanisms of Memory* (New York: Academic Press, 1967), pp. 2–3.

These remarks provide a good summary of the thinking that lies behind the assumption of traces by psychologists, neuro-psychologists and philosophers. The thinking goes like this: You have an experience. The experience itself does not survive the passage of time, but the structure of the experience can be stored in the brain. The neural mechanism that performs this function is the trace. As long as the trace persists undamaged, you have a "dispositional" memory of the experience, since the experience is coded into the trace. If one knew the code, one could "read off" an experience from its trace. When the trace is subjected to the right sort of stimulus, an "occurrent" memory results, which is an active representation of the original experience. The process of memory is fundamentally the preservation and transmission through time of an identical structure, which is first the structure of an experience, then of its trace, then of an "occurrent" mental representation, i.e., a "memory," of the original experience.

2.   In Chapter V we undertook to show that genuine, occurrent remembering does not have to contain a representation of what is remembered. Let us revert to this point, making use of new examples. The following one I owe to Bruce Goldberg: A man, B, had a dinner engagement with a friend, C. Then C canceled the engagement. B wanted to take someone else to dinner and called up several friends of his. He finally succeeded with M. Now could it not be said that when B phoned these different people he remembered the canceling of his previous engagement? Yet what did he do which was a *representation* of it? And how many times did he do it? Each time he called another person? Did he do it each time he picked up the phone, or each time he said, "Can you have dinner with me this evening?" (He need not have mentioned, or even thought about the cancellation.) Did he represent the cancellation in the action of driving to the house of his friend M, with whom he had made the new engagement?

Consider another example (my own): Jones is a fireman who has been trained in the use of artificial respiration. In response to an emergency call he applied mouth-to-mouth respiration to a man who had received an electric shock. The man did not recover. Later Jones was asked why he had used the mouth-to-mouth method rather than the Schaeffer method. Jones replied, "I remembered that the mouth-to-mouth method is more effective for cases of electric shock." (Here we have moved from remembering an event, the cancellation of an engagement, to remembering a fact—that so-and-so.) Is there any reason to say that Jones, when giving artificial respiration, represented the fact (assuming that it is a fact) that the one type of artificial respiration is more effective for electric shock? He did not say anything about it at that time. He did not even think about it. As soon as he arrived at the scene of the accident, he began to apply mouth-to-mouth respiration. Yet it is right to say that "Jones remembered" that this type of respiration is more effective for electric shock. It would be absurd, also, to say that Jones had only a "dispositional" and not an "occurrent" memory of this fact. His action at the scene was surely a manifestation of that memory knowledge.

These examples should remind us that there is a multitude of cases wherein remembering occurs without a representation of what is remembered. The view (for example, of Martin and Deutscher) that remembering demands a representation is like the view that *meaning* something requires *thinking* of it. Of course this is false. I can ask the maid to clean the living room without having the thought that she should empty the waste basket, although I *mean* that she should do that. Consider Wittgenstein's remark: " 'When I teach someone the formation of the series . . . I surely mean him to write . . . at the hundredth place.'—Quite right: you mean it. And obviously, without necessarily even thinking of it. That shows you how different the grammar of the verb 'to mean' is from that of the verb 'to think'." [2]

Someone might object: "Even if it is true that occurrent remembering, at the phenomenological level, does not require a represen-

2. Wittgenstein, *Investigations*, para. 693.

tation, it does not follow that a representation is not required at the neural level." No; it does not *follow*. But surely this latter requirement is being undermined. For if a representation does not appear at the phenomenological level, why should a representation have to occur in the brain? One motivation for the assumption of a trace is the idea that when I remember something I picture or depict it, and that a trace must be there to make it possible for me to do this. But if no depiction occurs then *this* demand for a trace vanishes.

3.   Another point that may be briefly mentioned is that there can be a representation that is not identical in structure with what is represented. Think of how a cartoon or line drawing can represent someone (De Gaulle or Churchill) although there is a gross exaggeration of some facial feature such as the nose or jaw. This very distortion may convey something striking or typical of the character or personality of the person who is represented. (Levine's drawings in *The New York Review*.) The drawing will also omit many details. Yet when we see it we may exclaim, "What a superb representation of De Gaulle!" Here is representation without one-to-one correspondence.

In the New York Museum of Modern Art there is, or was, a representation in sculpture of the flight of a bird. (It is called, I think, *The Bird*.) It is a vertical, curved, smooth shaft of gold-colored metal, with no protuberances. It captures the idea of a bird's swift, effortless flight. Yet there is no one-to-one correspondence with any bird, or with any bird's flight. It is representation without structural identity.

This is a point worth noting, in view of the usual assumption of trace theorists that since a trace is supposed to represent a remembered past experience or event, therefore it must be isomorphic with it.

4.   Let us revert to the idea that the memory trace provides for *storage*, and let us ask: *What* is it that is stored? One answer, of course, is "memories." Another answer is "impressions." Metcalfe, for example, says: "Memory implies that, in some manner, impres-

sions can be stored. As the storing of individual replicas of the original impressions would be a physical impossibility, storing must involve the transformation, coding and assimilation of those impressions." [3] A more frequent answer is that "information" is what is stored:

The notion that learning and memory are a type of data sorting implies that at least three distinct phases are involved—encoding, storage, and retrieval of information.

The encoding phase of learning has been characterized in terms of the fact that information has first to be registered in the nervous system before a record can be made. It is commonly accepted that during this encoding phase a certain fixation time, which may be of the order of half an hour, is required for the information to become consolidated and hence permanently stored. . . .

Once information has been stored in the brain, it must be available to be able to affect behaviour. The retrieval of information from storage can involve either direct recall or recognition. [4]

It is notorious that writers on the neuropsychology of memory use the word "information" in two radically different ways. In one use "information" means some pattern of neural firings, which might be "stored" in the sense, for example, that the pattern would be continuously repeated in a reverberating circuit of neurons. In this use of the word "information," it is hard to understand how "the retrieval of information from storage can involve either direct recall or recognition," since no one recalls or recognizes any pattern of neural firings in his brain. In another use of the word, "information" means what it often means in ordinary language, namely, information *that* so-and-so (that Eisenhower was a President of the United States, that Lombardi coached the Green Bay Packers, that I left my watch in the bathroom). Information, in this sense, can be expressed in propositions; and there is a temptation to think that to remember information, in this sense, is *always* to remember it *in*

3. Maryse Metcalfe, "Problems of Memory in Man," *Aspects of Learning and Memory*, p. 6.

4. I. Steele Russell, "Animal Learning and Memory," *Aspects of Learning and Memory*, p. 123.

propositions. This is false, since if someone said to me, "Where is your watch?", my response might be just to go into the bathroom to get it, without my either saying or thinking to myself that I left it in the bathroom. I remembered that I left it in the bathroom, although when I remembered this I did not have the propositional thought, "I left it in the bathroom."

In Chapter V we saw how philosophical studies of memory have been dominated by the notion that every "genuine" memory involves a "representation." The representation turns out to be a propositional thought. Descartes held that all perceptions, and even bodily sensations, require propositional thoughts. This is the basis for his famous doctrine that the lower animals are unconscious automata. Since they are incapable of propositional thoughts, they do not possess perception or sensation in its full "human mode." [5]

The tendency to assume that perception, awareness, sensation, actually require propositional thoughts will be particularly strong when what one perceives, is aware of, or senses *can* be put into propositional statements. The same tendency will hold for "information," when the information can be stated in propositions. It is quite natural that the neuropsychology of memory should be influenced by this tendency. The common model of "the memory-process" is this: a human or animal organism receives, stores, and retrieves information. The very same information that comprises the "data" or the "input" is first stored, then retrieved. If the information is propositional, then what is stored is propositional. What could be more obvious! An equally obvious consequence is that if propositional information is stored in the brain then propositions, in some form, must be present in the brain!

One occasionally finds this consequence *explicitly* spelled out by neuropsychologists. For example:

Nerve cells receive, generate, and conduct excitations. These properties form the basic vocabulary, and neural connections determine the complex-

5. See my paper, "Thoughtless Brutes," *Proceedings of the American Philosophical Association*, 46 (1972–1973). Reprinted in Malcolm, *Thought and Knowledge: Essays* (Ithaca, N.Y.: Cornell University Press, 1977).

ity of the nervous system's language. Throughout the animal kingdom, from the most eloquent to the most reticent of nervous systems, from the brains of primates to the nerve nets of coelenterates, one can observe not only statements of the present but messages from the past. . . . The past, speaking the language of the nervous system, informs the present.[6]

Here the nervous system is said to contain language, vocabulary, messages, and statements! I will quote another writer who does not explicitly endow the nervous system with statements or propositions, but whose remarks seem to imply such a view:

Different items of information in the memory system are related to each other. Some people prefer to call these relationships associations, others call them bonds, some call them networks, and others markers, nodes, pointers, or links. Regardless of the names, the basic concepts are all similar. In retrieving information, one follows the path laid down by these associations through the network of stored information, until, finally, the desired information is retrieved. Just how one actually follows through the network is not known. Even the very basic question of how one recognizes when the correct answer has been retrieved has not been studied. This last point is extremely important. If you know the answer for which you are looking, then you wouldn't need to look. But if you don't know the answer, then how can you recognize it when you find it?[7]

To speak of the storage system as containing "items of information" certainly suggests that it is information in a propositional sense that is contained there. I might, for example, possess some items of information about a house that I was considering for purchase, e.g., that it has three bedrooms, that the furnace needs replacing, and so on. Norman's assumption that the storage system contains "answers" to "questions" conveys the same suggestion. If I put to someone the question, "What is your name?", I may receive the answer that his name is Robinson, i.e., an item of propositional information.

6. A. L. Leiman and C. N. Cristian, "Electrophysiological Analyses of Learning and Memory," in J. A. Deutsch, *The Physiological Basis of Memory* (New York: Academic Press, 1973), p. 126.

7. Donald A. Norman, "What Have the Animal Experiments Taught Us about Human Memory," *The Physiological Basis of Memory*, pp. 404–405.

It should be noted that Norman speaks misleadingly in saying that "one follows the path . . . through the network of stored information." For the word "one" here could only mean *a person*. But neither I nor any other person follows a path through a neural network. Neither does any person put questions to or receive answers from a mechanism in his brain. What Norman should be literally saying is that a mechanism of the brain puts questions to and receives propositional information from another mechanism of the brain! Incidentally, the puzzle that Norman raises about "retrieval" is indeed a grave difficulty for any conception of memory as an information-processing mechanism of the brain; but the problem is misleadingly stated. For it isn't a matter of how *you* (a person) "know the answer for which you are looking," but rather of how a neural mechanism recognizes a correct answer to a question it has put to another neural mechanism.

In the previous chapter we saw that Sutherland endorses the idea that the neural storage system preserves information in an "abstract symbolism," and that this information is "represented" in the storage system by "rules" or "descriptions." It is clear that Sutherland conceives these rules or descriptions to be propositions, since he gives sample translations of them into propositions of ordinary language. He is accepting in all seriousness the notion, which is inherent in the conception of memory as an information-processing mechanism, that the brain literally contains and employs propositions! He is making explicit what is implicit in the common doctrine that sensory information is "coded" into a "neural representation."

Here again we perceive the continuity between the traditional "mentalistic" theories of memory and recent physiological theories. In the traditional theories there is an insistence on an "image," or "something like an image," or a mental copy, picture, or representation of some sort. The function of this mental entity is to provide the propositional content for a memory-judgment. In short, the mental entity is a proposition. As Russell puts it, we address to the mental representation the assertion, *"This* occurred." The physiological theories have merely *transferred* the propositions, which are assumed to constitute the core of memory, *from a mental medium to a neural medium.*

5.   Let us return to a point that was touched on in Section 4 of the preceding chapter. The point was that what determines whether an expression of a language is understood or misunderstood is the common practice of a community of users of that language, i.e., of a community of people. Such a practice is a pattern of responses and actions. Language is embedded in actions—in deeds. Whether a child understands the word "chair" is a matter of how it responds to orders such as "Sit in a chair," "Push a chair up to the table," "Move the chair." Whether a certain process occurs in its brain whenever and only when there is a chair in its visual field, or whenever it hears the sound "chair," is not to the point. When a person *recognizes* another person, or some object, the recognition presents itself, in its most primitive form, in looks and acts of recognition.

The brain is not a kind of thing that could perform or fail to perform the actions that display understanding or misunderstanding of language, or recognition or lack of recognition. It cannot take a seat in a chair or push a chair up to the table; nor can it try and fail to do those deeds. Therefore, it literally makes no sense to think of the brain as understanding or misunderstanding a language. It is a conceptual absurdity to attribute to the brain the employment of symbols, rules, descriptions, codes. Nor can the brain exhibit a look or exclamation of recognition, or any of the other behavior that would determine whether or not recognition had, or had not, taken place. Therefore one cannot say that the brain recognizes, or fails to recognize, squares, patterns, Chinese faces, or anything else. Even if molecular changes in a piece of blotting paper corresponded to changes in the state of the weather, this would give no sense to the supposition that the blotting paper was aware of the weather changes or that it was *describing or recording* states of the weather. Teaching a child the names of objects, at the most primitive level, is a training that consists of giving examples, rewards, disapproval, encouragement. The aim of the training is to induce the child *to do* something, as in training a dog to retrieve.[8] The intent of the training is to produce a skill in acting and interacting with other members of that linguistic community. The emergence of the appropriate skill or skills in the employment of the word "chair" is the criterion of the child's understanding the word, not whether something goes on inside, regardless of whether this inner happening is the occurrence of the "idea," "concept," or "image" of a chair (as traditional, mentalistic empiricism would have it), or whether it is the occurrence of a "rule" or "generalization" in the brain (in accordance with current neuropsychology). The presence of an interior "representation," whether mental or physical, is irrelevant to the concept of understanding.

6. A memory trace is conceived of as having a role in a continuous causal process, the memory-process. The causal chain begins with an experience, which has a certain structure; the experience (or its neural correlate) produces a trace in which this structure is preserved; upon the occurrence of an appropriate stimulus, the trace causes the occurrence of a memory which, if it is complete and accurate, will contain the same structure that was present in both the original experience and in its enduring trace.

In considering this conception it is necessary to have a clear understanding of what *the effect* of the causal process is supposed to be. As I understand the conception, *if* a trace had not decayed or been subject to interference from other traces, then it would be identical in structure with both the initiating experience and with the occurrent memory: that is, the same structure would be present at the beginning, the middle, and the end of the causal process. Martin and Deutscher, for example, say that the trace is a "structural analogue of what was experienced." [9] Here the trace is said to have the same structure as the initiating experience. They also say

8. Cf. Wittgenstein, *The Blue and Brown Books*, p. 77.
9. Martin and Deutscher, "Remembering," p. 189.

that the trace "contains at least as many features as there are details which a given person can relate about something he has experienced." [10] Relating, or representing, is the final stage of the causal process; and here it is said that the trace must have a matching feature for every feature of the representation. Martin and Deutscher also use two analogies which show that they think of the trace as having the same structure as both the beginning and the end of the causal process. They say that the general requirements of a memory trace can be explained by the analogy of "a print of a coin in wax." In this analogy the print in wax (the trace) matches the structure of the coin (the initiating cause). The second analogy is the structural similarity between the groove in a phonograph record and the music. [11] In this analogy the groove (the trace) has the same structure as its effect in music (the occurrent memory representation). Thus the trace, as the middle term of a causal process, will match the structures of both the initial and the final terms of that process.

The same view is present in the writings of Wolfgang Köhler. His thinking is guided by "the principle of psychophysical isomorphism," which holds "that the structural properties of experiences are at the same time the structural properties of their biological correlates." [12] This means that when an experience occurs there will be a simultaneous, structurally identical, neural state or process. This neural correlate establishes a trace of the experience, and the trace (if it remains unchanged) will be isomorphic with its neural cause and (presumably) with the experience that is isomorphic with that neural cause: "So far as cortical correlates of experience are isomorphic with this experience itself, the same isomorphism obtains between those correlates and their traces. With one essential restriction, however: We cannot assume that such isomorphism will be strictly preserved far beyond the time at which the traces have been formed." [13] The restriction is a warning that

10. Ibid., p. 190.   11. Ibid.
12. W. Köhler, *Dynamics in Psychology* (New York: Liveright, 1940), p. 109.
13. Köhler, *The Place of Value in a World of Facts*, p. 243.

memory traces will probably undergo some alteration through time. It is, however, at least a theoretical possibility that a trace should undergo no alteration. In this eventuality, a perfect structural identity would be preserved throughout the causal process of memory: the initiating experience, its trace, and the memory representation would all possess the same structure.

My purpose, in this section, is to take a closer look at the presumed *effect* of the neural process of memory. It will be said that, at the phenomenological level, the effect will be a memory, or an act or event of remembering, or a memory experience, or a mental occurrence of remembering—and so on. But in Chapters II and III it was pointed out that we tend to have a confused conception about this effect. We tend to imagine that when, for example, Robinson suddenly remembered an appointment, there occurred, then and there, either in Robinson's mind or in some behavior of his, something that was identical with remembering that appointment, something that "intrinsically"—that is to say, in all circumstances whatever—would be an instance of remembering that appointment. On reflection, and as a result of describing different cases, we saw that this notion of an "intrinsic memory" event is unintelligible.

Let us, however, not concern ourselves at first with what the effect of the physiological causal process of memory would be at the phenomenological level. Let us first take note of what the effect would be at the neural level. The prevailing neurological schema, we have seen, is that information is taken in, then stored, then subsequently activated. Or put it like this: information is taken in, then stored in a neural representation that remains in a latent state; and later this neural representation is activated by a suitable stimulus. The occurrence of an activated neural representation (activated trace) would be the final effect, at the neural level, in this three-stage model of the working of the memory process.

Now let us consider what the effect of the activated trace is supposed to be at the phenomenological level. Suppose that Jones planted a dogwood tree in his garden, and that when he finished the job he leaned the shovel against the trunk of another tree. Later his wife wants to do some transplanting, and she asks her three boys, who are standing there, "Where did Daddy put the shovel?" The three boys (Tom, Dick, Jerry) had seen their father lean the shovel against that tree, and they remembered that he had done so. This is surely an example of taking in and retaining information. In response to their mother's question, Tom replied, "Daddy leaned it against the tree by the dogwood"; Dick pointed at that tree; Jerry ran to the tree and fetched the shovel for his mother.

All three boys had noticed what Jones did with the shovel, and all three had retained that information. Thus the same (structurally the same, numerically different) neural memory trace should have been produced in all three, namely the trace that is a representation of that information. In all three that trace was activated by the same stimulus, namely their mother's question. But note how different, at the phenomenological level, was the effect of the same stimulus applied to the same trace. One boy uttered a sentence, one pointed, another ran and fetched. This seems surprising. The activation of an identical trace by an identical stimulus, produced entirely different behaviors in the three cases!

Of course one will want to say that there must have been other differences at the neurological level among the three boys: differences of personality, motivation, or what not, would be represented neurally; and these neural differences would cause the speech mechanism to be activated in one boy, the pointing mechanism in another, and the running (and politeness?) mechanism in the third.

Still, the question remains: Disregarding these other supposed neural differences, what was the effect of the application of the stimulus to the trace? Allowing that the differences in the behavior of the three boys would have to be caused by different neural factors, what was the *common* effect of the *common* cause in all three cases? For the boys were alike in having the same memory trace activated by the same stimulus. What was the common effect of *that* in all three?

We are trying to learn more about the nature of the memory trace. We know that in our example the trace, in its latent or dormant condition, is supposed to be a representation of the information that Jones leaned the shovel against a particular tree; and we know that the activated trace is supposed to be an activated representation of the same information. What I want to know is: What is *the point* of there being a neural representation of that information? What is its function? What effect does it have, when activated, in the life of the individual? Surely it cannot be that one and the same activated trace caused one boy to utter a sentence, another boy to point, another boy to run. What *is* the one and the same thing that it caused in all three cases?

Did it cause, in all three boys, a mental representation of the fact that Jones (their father) leaned the shovel against a particular tree? But why suppose that a mental representation occurred in any of the three boys? Did each boy, for example, *think to himself* that his father had leaned the shovel against that tree? Surely that need not have happened. One boy did utter aloud the sentence, "Daddy leaned it against the tree by the dogwood." Must he have thought this silently to himself in addition to saying it aloud? Must the silent thought have accompanied the spoken sentence? If so, did it occur at the beginning of the sentence, or at the end, or was its duration simultaneous with the duration of the sentence? When Jerry ran to the tree, did he, too, have the silent thought just before he began running? Or did he have it all the while he was running?

Silent thoughts do occur, *sometimes*. To insist that all three boys *must* have had a silent thought is to depart from the ordinary criteria for the occurrence of silent thoughts (normally, the subject's own subsequent testimony), without providing any other criteria, thereby revealing that one doesn't know what one is talking about!

Would the mental representation be an image? Must all three boys have had an image of their father leaning the shovel against a tree? Enough should have been said in Part One to obliterate this temptation.

It could rightly be said that all three boys *meant* the same thing by their three different overt performances, namely, that their father leaned the shovel against that particular tree. But could it be said that their *meaning* this was the common effect of the activated trace? This would be to conceive their meaning this as an event that accompanied each of the three performances. Which is wrong. As Wittgenstein remarks, you can *mean* something without even *thinking* of it.

We are unable to specify the common effect of the common activated trace. This is damaging to the very conception of the neural trace, since the trace is conceptualized as, defined as, something that fulfills a supposedly necessary causal role in memory.

I believe that Martin and Deutscher would want to say that the common effect of the trace on the three boys was that all three depicted, portrayed, or represented the same fact, namely, that their father leaned the shovel against a particular tree. They do say, "Nobody actually remembers anything until he comes to the point of representing in some way what he has observed or experienced." [14] Did each of the boys give a representation of their father's leaning the shovel against that tree? This would seem to be a natural thing to say only if they had *pantomimed* his action. Did each boy represent his father *as* having leaned the shovel against that tree? But what does this come to other than their having *meant* that he did this? This does not give us an event that can be regarded as caused by the trace. Did each boy represent *that* his father placed the shovel against the tree? This would be an odd use of "represent." If we do decide to use that word here, what would this amount to other than to say again that each boy *meant* this?—which again does not yield a candidate for an effect of the trace.

Here are three boys presumed to have structurally the same memory trace. The same trace cannot explain the occurrence of three quite different sequences of behavior. What occurrence does it explain? Did it cause an identical "representation" in all three cases? What was this identical representation? One boy spoke; one

14. Martin and Deutscher, p. 172.

pointed; one ran and fetched the shovel. But since they *remembered* the same thing, then, according to Martin and Deutscher, there must have been some one and the same thing that they all *did*.[15] Yet, apparently, this common thing is not out in the open, but is *hidden* in, or behind, the three pieces of behavior. But if it is hidden, what is the warrant for holding that it occurs at all?

My argument in this section has been to show that the conception of a neural memory trace is highly confused. A neural trace is postulated, in part at least, to provide a causal explanation for the occurrence of a certain effect. Traces are not states or processes that have been picked out and identified in the brain; they are postulated entities. A trace is *defined*, in part, as the cause of a certain effect. If critical reflection reveals that we do not really have a conception of what this effect is supposed to be, then at the same time it reveals that we do not really have a conception of the postulated entity that is defined as the cause of this effect.

The memory trace is not a scientific discovery, nor a required postulation of scientific thought. It is a product of philosophical thinking, of a sort that is natural and enormously tempting, yet thoroughly muddled. I am inclined to believe that Martin and Deutscher exhibit the key temptation when they say: "On anyone's account of memory, it is not enough that someone should have observed or experienced something in the past. He must do something in the present. 'What sort of thing must he do in the present, in order to be said to remember?' is a difficult and very general question."[16] Actually it is neither a difficult nor a "very general" question. We know what the three boys did. Clearly different things; not something "very general." The idea that something "very general" occurred is the idea that some one and the same thing is *concealed* in, or behind, their three different performances. This common thing is a *representation*. This common thing is the presence of *the proposition*—that so-and-so. Neuropsychological theorizing about memory is infected with this same overintellec-

15. Ibid.   16. Ibid.

tualizing of memory. The memory trace, a "neural representation," is, in both its dormant and its activated state, the proposition that so-and-so, embodied in a neural medium. The activated neural representation performs the same role as does the memory-image in traditional philosophical theories of memory. From here the thinking becomes vague. Does the neural representation itself present a proposition for the memory-judgment, "This occurred" (Russell)? Or does it *cause* a *mental* representation (perhaps "unconscious") of the proposition? But where thinking is imprecise, it is probably idle to speculate in which direction precise thinking would turn.

CHAPTER X

The Principle of Isomorphism

1. In Chapter IX it was argued that it is nonsensical to suppose that the brain could contain or employ language, propositions, statements, messages, descriptions, rules, representations, symbols, codes. There would be many who would agree with me on this point, but who believe that this supposition is only a matter of stating things in misleading metaphors. Behind the metaphors is a literal truth, namely, that which Köhler calls the Principle of Isomorphism, and which he equates with the proposition that "the structural properties of experiences are at the same time the structural properties of their biological correlates." The word "experiences" is presumably taken vaguely to refer to all of those perceptions, sensations, desires, feelings, emotions, thoughts, and so on, of which we are in some sense "conscious." The "biological correlates" of experiences would be states, events, processes, in or of the central nervous system. Acceptance of the principle of isomorphism, either explicit or implicit, clearly has been influential in generating and supporting the hypothesis of memory traces and also the idea that remembering is a process that occurs in the brain. In previous chapters I have done some sniping at the notion of an isomorphism between experiences and neural processes, but in the present chapter I want to undertake a more thorough study of this topic.

2. Between entities of what sorts could isomorphism hold? Would it be intelligible to assert that China is isomorphic with France, or

that Beethoven's Quartet, Opus 132, is isomorphic with *The Brothers Karamazov*, or that chess is isomorphic with ice hockey?

I think it is convenient to regard isomorphism as holding, in the first place, between *domains* of things, objects, events, states, or processes. Suppose there are two domains, D and D'. D is composed of the things a, b, c, . . . , and the relations R, S, T, . . . (I omit mention of properties, for the sake of simplicity). D' is composed of the things a', b', c', . . . , and the relations R', S', T', ... Suppose that $a\ R\ b$ holds if and only if $a'\ R'\ b'$ holds, and likewise for all other combinations in the two domains. We then say that D and D' are "isomorphic."

To illustrate: Suppose that D consists of boys at Eton, a, b, c, . . . , and the relation $x\ S\ y$ (which means: x is socially superior to y at Eton). D' consists of the male parents of the Eton boys, a', b', c', . . . , and the relation $x\ S'\ y$ (which means: x is wealthier than y). Each male parent is the father of one and only one Eton boy. Suppose it has been observed that $a\ S\ b$ if and only if $a'\ S'\ b'$, and so on for all other combinations. In that case D and D' are isomorphic. Note that in terms of this schema, it would have no meaning to ask whether one Eton boy was or wasn't isomorphic with another Eton boy. Nor would it have any direct meaning to say that the *fact* that $a\ S\ b$ was or wasn't isomorphic with the *fact* that $a'\ S'\ b'$, although one could give meaning to this by defining these facts as themselves being domains. One could obtain the same result by stipulating that when two domains, F and G, are isomorphic, then each pair of correlated facts of the two domains, comprised of the specified things and relations, is isomorphic in a secondary sense. This is probably how Köhler is using the expression "isomorphism" or "same structure," when he holds that *an experience* and its correlated neural process or state have the same structure.

The concept of isomorphism between two domains involves the concept of what Eric Stenius calls "a *key* of isomorphism." Each domain is composed of "elements"—that is to say, is composed of some things (e.g., Eton boys) *and* of some *relation* between those things (e.g., social superiority), *and*, perhaps, of some *property* (e.g., having blond hair). What a key of isomorphism does is to make one-to-one correlations of the elements of one domain with the elements of another domain. (The "picturing relationship" of the *Tractatus*, which "consists of the correlations of the elements of the picture with things" (*Tractatus* 2.1514), would be a key of isomorphism). If you undertook to establish whether or not there is an isomorphism between two domains, you would have to employ a definite key of isomorphism; otherwise the undertaking would be senseless.

A key of isomorphism could be said to *define* what are the "elements" of each of two domains, as well as to specify the one-to-one correlations between domains. The key thus establishes what a "configuration of elements," or an "elementary state of affairs," is in each domain. Given a particular configuration in one domain, the key also determines what the *corresponding* configuration would be in the other domain. Suppose, for example, that, at Eton, Tim is socially superior to Nick. The key of isomorphism specifies that the male parent who corresponds to Tim is Hornblower, that the one who corresponds to Nick is Weatherbottom, and that the relation corresponding to *socially superior* is *wealthier*. Thereby it is determined that what corresponds to the state of affairs, "Tim is socially superior to Nick," is the state of affairs, "Hornblower is wealthier than Weatherbottom." If empirical inquiry establishes that both of these states of affairs exist, this is a piece of evidence in favor of isomorphism between the two domains. If *whenever* and only when a state of affairs, as specified by the key, exists in one domain, the *corresponding* state of affairs, as specified by the key, exists in the other domain, then the two domains are isomorphic; otherwise not.

3. If someone wonders whether the domain of experiences is isomorphic with the domain of brain processes, but is not in command of a key of isomorphism, his question is not very meaningful. But his wondering may not be totally without meaning, for he may be vaguely asking whether it would be *possible* for a key of isomor-

phism to be devised, such that it would turn out that the domains of experience and brain process, as defined by the key, were isomorphic. When philosophers ask whether it may not be the case that experiences and brain processes are isomorphic, I think this is usually the kind of sense that their question has. They do not have in mind any definite key; nor do they even assume that any key has so far been devised. What they seem to be asking is whether there *could be* a key, in relation to which isomorphism would turn out to hold.

The situation might seem analogous to the following: someone asks whether the top of this table is isomorphic with the floor of this room. Since no key of isomorphism has been devised, the question is meaningless. But it would be possible to invent a key such that the question of whether the surface of the table and the surface of the floor were isomorphic, *relative to that key*, would have a definite answer, affirmative or negative. For example: I draw rectangles on the table top and also on the floor, the same number in both cases. I give rules according to which each rectangle of either domain is correlated one-to-one with a rectangle of the other. I give the name T to the domain of table rectangles, and the name F to the domain of floor rectangles. I add to the domain of table rectangles the relation $x \, D \, y$ (which means: x is darker than y), and to the domain of floor rectangles the relation $w \, S \, z$ (which means: w is smoother than z), and I stipulate that these two relations are counterparts. The rectangles of T constitute the range of values for the relation D, and the rectangles of F make up the range of values for the relation S. We now have a key of isomorphism that defines and correlates the elements of the two domains, T and F. The question of whether the domains, T and F, are isomorphic, is the following question: Is it the case that for all values of x and y, and for all values of w and z, $x \, D \, y$ if and only if $w \, S \, z$? (Actually, some restriction would have to be placed on allowable combinations, i.e., some ordering relation would have to be included in the key— otherwise, contradictions would result; but I omit this for the sake of simplicity.) An empirical investigation would be required to determine whether one of any pair of table rectangles is *darker* than the other one, if and only if the corresponding one of the corresponding pair of floor rectangles is *smoother* than the other one.

It is perhaps a natural assumption that just as the originally meaningless question, Is the table isomorphic with the floor?, was converted into a meaningful question by virtue of the invention of a suitable key of isomorphism, so too the presently meaningless question, Is there an isomorphism between experiences and neural processes?, can be converted, by the same means, into a meaningful question that would have an empirically ascertainable yes-or-no answer. I will argue that this natural assumption is false, for the reason that no satisfactory key of isomorphism *can* be devised for the domains of experiences and neural processes. My point will not, of course, be based on any surmise about technical difficulties, but will be a conceptual point.

4.   First, however, it will be useful to mention that two radically different types of "correlation" may be involved in different keys of isomorphism. In the preceding example of table and floor, the correlations were stipulated: they were conventional, not natural. The relation between the English language and the language of Morse code is one of isomorphism, based on one-to-one correlations, settled by arbitrary stipulation, between letters of the Latin alphabet of English and configurations of dots and dashes. This is quite unlike a correlation between smoke and fire, or between tides and phases of the moon. Conventional correlation and natural correlation are such different concepts that it is probably misleading to use the same word, "correlation," in both cases.

If we are to conceive of an isomorphism between experiences and neural processes, we must conceive that not only have "elements" been designated for each of the two domains, but also that there are one-to-one correlations connecting the elements of one domain with the elements of the other one. But *these* correlations cannot be correlations by stipulation. They must be natural correlations. An isomorphism between experiences and neural events, if there were one, would be an isomorphism in nature, not an isomorphism by convention. The function of a key of isomorphism is different in the two cases. For both conventional and natural isomorphisms a key will stipulate what are the "elements" of each domain. A key for a conventional isomorphism will also stipulate what the correlations are between elements. But the key of a natural isomorphism cannot do this. It can only *propose the hypothesis* that such and such correlations hold. Whether they do or do not hold can be determined only by observation of what occurs in the world, not by the mere looking up of stipulations.

5.   We are now to consider whether there could be a key of isomorphism for the domains of experience and neural events or states. The key will have to stipulate what are to be regarded as elements of each of the two domains. I do not know whether there is any *conceptual* difficulty pertaining to the selection of elements in the neural domain. Perhaps there is; but I will assume that there is none. The key might specify that individual neurons are elements; or that an element is not just a neuron but instead the emitting of an electrical impulse by a neuron; or that an element consists of an "assembly" of neural cells firing in a certain order; or that the relation, "x is firing more rapidly than y," is an element; or that the property of "increasing in protein concentration," which an area of the brain might have, is an element; and so on.

Let us suppose that a satisfactory selection of elements from the neural domain has been achieved. Can the same thing be achieved for the domain of experiences? We need to bear in mind that a key for a natural isomorphism will try to specify elements for each domain that are related by one-to-one correlations with elements of the other domain. Assuming that neural elements have been specified, could any experience element be selected that would stand a chance of being related one-to-one with any neural element? Suppose that an element in the neural domain had been specified to be the simultaneous firing of a set of neurons in a certain region of the brain. Let us call this element "N." Now the domain of experiences consists of desires, thoughts, sensations, memories, and so on. Let us pick out a particular desire, e.g., *wanting to catch a bus*, designate it as an element, and call it "E." Is it reasonable to suppose that there might be a one-to-one correlation between E and N? Is it likely that E occurs if and only if N occurs? We need not go so far as to consider whether this might be so for *all* human beings. Let us limit the problem to a *single* human being. We will ask whether it is reasonable to suppose that whenever and only when a particular person, Fred, wants to catch a bus, the neural event or process, N, will occur in Fred's brain. We need to reflect on the variety of cases in which it will be true that Fred wants to catch a bus. Let us note a few cases:

1) Fred normally takes a bus to work every day. The bus goes right past his front door and stops at 8 A.M. at a bus stop two blocks away. Fred has to board that bus in order to arrive at his job on time. Usually he eats his breakfast in ample time and walks to the bus stop. But one morning, unknown to him, his watch is slow, and while still seated at the breakfast table he is shocked to see the bus go past his house. He leaps up from the table, struggles into his coat, frantically looks for his brief case, and rushes out of the door in hot pursuit of the bus. He runs down the street at full speed with heart pounding and lungs straining. He is terrified by the thought that if he misses the bus he will lose his job, since his boss has recently reprimanded him several times for being late. Fred has an image of his boss's angry face, his legs and chest hurt from the violent exertion, and the fearful thought fills his mind, "What if I don't catch it!" Someone looking out of a window asks, "Why is that man running so hard?", and receives the true and informative reply, "Because he wants to catch the bus."

2) Compare the foregoing with the more normal case, where Fred finishes his breakfast and saunters to the bus stop with time to spare. As he stands there his attention is absorbed by the sports page of the newspaper he is reading. He is not thinking about the bus, his job, or the boss, but about the Green Bay Packers. Someone looking out of the window asks, "Why is that man standing

there?", and receives the true and informative reply, "Because he wants to catch the bus."

3) Fred is eating breakfast in ample time. His wife says, "I don't need the car today. Do you want to take it?" Fred replies: "Finding a parking space is such a nuisance. I prefer to take the bus." Here the only behavior indicative of his wanting to catch the bus is his remark. He is not moving toward or standing at the bus stop, nor having thoughts about the possibility of missing the bus. It is true that he will go to the bus stop at the appropriate time.

4) On this occasion Fred overslept without realizing it. He is in the bathroom shaving when he sees the 8 A.M. bus go by. He says, "Damn!" Then he shrugs his shoulders and calmly returns to his shaving. His wife calls out, "Fred, don't you want to catch the 8 o'clock bus?" Fred replies with irritation, "Of course I want to catch it. But what can I do about it?" On this occasion Fred wants to catch the bus, since he himself says so. But here there is no behavior, either actual or potential, of running after or waiting for the bus; nor any thoughts about the possibility of missing it. It is true that Fred *would* have gone out to the bus stop *if* he had not overslept.

Many other differing cases of Fred's wanting to catch the bus could be described, but these four will suffice to make my point. There are striking differences between these four cases in respect to Fred's behavior, thoughts, images, sensations, and so on. Any believer in psychophysical isomorphism will of course hold that there would be differences in neural processes matching those differences in behavior and experiences. For the moment let us grant that this would be so. What needs to be asked is, Why should the neural process, N, have been present in each of the foregoing cases of Fred's wanting to catch the bus? Why should the simultaneous firing of all the neurons in that specific cell assembly have occurred in all four cases? With *what* is N correlated? Certainly not with Fred's behavior of running; nor with Fred's image of his boss's angry face; nor with a pain in Fred's chest; nor with Fred's utterance, "I prefer to take the bus"; and so on. For none of these phenomena occurs in all four cases; and yet N is supposed to be present in all four cases; therefore N is not correlated one-to-one with any of the particularized phenomena that we mentioned in describing the four cases.

I can imagine someone protesting, with indignation, that since we are trying out the hypothesis that Fred's neural state, N, stands in a one-to-one correlation with Fred's wanting to catch the bus, then *that* is what N is correlated with—*Fred's wanting to catch the bus!* Quite right. That is the hypothesis. But my question is whether it is a *reasonable* hypothesis. To assume that it is would be to assume that there is some factor that is common to all occasions of Fred's wanting to catch the bus, and that it is that common factor with which N is universally correlated. This is to adopt the Platonistic conception that was criticized in Chapter VIII, Section 5. According to this conception it is necessary to assume that there is some property (other than being called a "table") that every table has and that only tables have—otherwise it would be unintelligible that all tables are called by the same name. But nothing in our observation of tables confirms this assumption. And the fact that the same name, "table," is applied to many objects, differing widely in their properties, is satisfactorily accounted for by Wittgenstein's suggestion that tables constitute "a family" of objects that are united by various similarities—not *one* similarity that is present in all of them, but different similarities that "overlap." Despite the presence of many dissimilarities, the similarities are distributed among these objects in such a way that we find it natural to call them by the same name, even though there is no "essential nature" of tables.

If this is a satisfying account of our use of common nouns, we can think of particularized psychological descriptions, such as "Fred wants to catch the bus," along the same lines. There is "a family of cases" in which we apply this description as a matter of course and without hesitation, because of criss-crossing similarities, not because of a common property or nature present in all cases. In the four cases that I described there was the same common background of Fred's needing transportation to his job and habitually taking the 8 A.M. bus; but of course there could be cases of Fred's wanting to catch the bus where those circumstances did not hold.

In our four cases there are striking differences in Fred's behavior, thoughts, feelings, sensations, utterances. According to the thesis of psychophysical isomorphism, there is a neural activity that occurs if and only if Fred is having the experience of running frantically in pursuit of a bus. There will be another, different neural activity that occurs if and only if Fred is having the experience of quietly standing at the bus stop and reading with avid interest about the fortunes of his favorite football team. Fred cannot have these two experiences simultaneously (unless Köhler and others are using the word "experience" in some outlandish way), and therefore the two respectively correlated neural activities cannot occur simultaneously. Thus, the hypothesized neural state, N, which is supposed to occur when and only when Fred wants to catch the bus, cannot be identical with either of those complete neural activities. It could only be identical with some common *part* of those two neural activities. But with *what* common part? Not with the neural activity that is correlated uniquely with Fred's running; nor with the neural activity that is correlated uniquely with his standing; nor with the neural activity that is correlated uniquely with his uttering the sentence, "I prefer to take the bus"—and so on. If someone supposes that the neural state or activity, N, occurs when and only when Fred wants to catch the bus, that person must be supposing that N is uniquely correlated with a state or experience of Fred's that is *common* to all the cases of Fred's wanting to catch the bus. But what is this common aspect? Do we know what we are talking about? What could one say in support of there being a common aspect other than to repeat the truism that all of them are instances of Fred's wanting to catch the bus? It would appear that the scientific-looking Principle of Isomorphism is nothing other than an offshoot of the traditional philosophical outlook of Platonistic essentialism.

6. Let us recall that our problem was whether it is possible to formulate a key of isomorphism for the two domains of experience and neural activity. One who formulates a key will try to specify an element of one domain that is uniquely correlated with an element of the other domain. I have been arguing that this is a hopeless undertaking, since if we specify an element of experience by means of a descriptive word or phrase of English (or of any other natural language), it will turn out that the element of experience thus referred to *fragments* into "a family of cases" that have no common aspect with which a specified, fixed, neural element *could* be uniquely correlated.

Now there will be a temptation to think that this difficulty only shows that it is necessary to select elements from each domain that are *simple*. The trouble with using the description, "Fred's wanting to catch the bus," to select an element in a key of isomorphism is that this description refers to something *complex*, not to something simple. Pick elements for each domain that will not dissolve into a myriad of different cases, and then there will be a fair chance that an element from one domain will be uniquely correlated with an element from the other domain!

Some remarks of the distinguished neurologist, Ewald Hering, are representative of such a viewpoint:

The soul does not move unless, simultaneously, the brain moves. Whenever the same sensation or the same thought recurs, a certain physical process which belongs to this special sensation or thought is repeated; for both are inseparably connected. They are conditioned by and productive of each other. Accordingly, from the course of our sensations we can draw inferences concerning the simultaneous and corresponding course of processes in the brain. The resolution of our sensations into their various elements is at the same time an analysis of the involved interactions of the various elementary cerebral functions or irritations.

For instance, let us suppose that the great variety of the sensations of light and color can be reduced to a few simple or elementary sensations, to those of the principal colors, which by combining in different proportions can produce innumerable different sensations. This fact, if proved, would justify the conclusion that different kinds of elementary irritations can take place also in the nervous substance of the visual organ. Each of them corresponds to one of the elementary sensations, and the elementary irritations can be arranged in a manner analogous to that of the elementary sensations. Or similarly, if we succeed in reducing all the many and various gustatory sensations to a few simple sensations, we may again justly infer that a corresponding number of elementary irritations can be produced in the nerve-substance of the tongue.[1]

The knowledge of the tools alone does not suffice to ascertain what work is performed by the tools. The anatomist, therefore, will never understand the labyrinth of cerebral cells and fibres, and the physiologist will never comprehend the thousand-fold intertwined actions of its irritations, unless they succeed in resolving the phenomena of consciousness into their elements in order to obtain from the kind and strength, from the progression and connexion of our perceptions, sensations, and conceptions, a clear idea about the kind and progression of the material processes in the brain. Without this clue the brain will always be a closed book.[2]

Hering is here presenting the view that not only are there one-to-one correlations between certain phenomena of consciousness and certain neural processes, but also that within each of these two domains there are events or states that are "simple" or "elementary." The idea is that every phenomenon in each domain either is simple or else is a complex of simple phenomena. If we could learn what the simples are in each domain, and what are the one-to-one correlations between simples in one domain and simples in the other, and what the laws are by which the simples in each domain combine to form complex configurations within that domain, then the brain of a person would be an open book to science, in the sense that scientists could, theoretically at least, determine what phenomena of consciousness are being experienced by a person solely from observation of his neural processes.

7.   The idea we are now considering is that in order to frame a satisfactory key of isomorphism it is not adequate to designate, ar-

1. Ewald Hering, *On Memory and The Specific Energies of the Nervous System*, (Chicago; Open Court, 1902), pp. 39-40.
2. Ibid., pp. 46-47.

bitrarily, just any thought, feeling, sensation, or experience as being an element for the purpose of the key. What one must do is to designate as an element something that *really is* an *element*— something that is *intrinsically* "simple" or "elementary," and has not merely been given the role of an element by stipulation within the framework of a certain key. In this way it will be guaranteed that what has been selected as an element will not fragment, or dissolve, into a "family" of phenomena.

The conception that the world divides into the simple and the compound, the simple not merely being simple relative to some choice, purpose, or contrast, but being simple "intrinsically" or "in an absolute sense," has of course been an important influence in Western philosophy. It is hardly necessary for me to undertake a criticism of that conception, after Wittgenstein's brilliant attack upon it.[3] Wittgenstein's criticism is that there are different kinds of complexity and that, therefore, whether something is to be called "simple" or "complex" depends on the kind of complexity one is talking about. A chair might be called a "simple" piece of furniture in contrast with a chest of drawers, since the latter has moving parts. The leg of a chair might be called "simple" because it is composed of a single type of wood, in contrast with a chair leg composed of several types of wood. The visual appearance of a tree might be said to be "simple" if one saw only the trunk, in comparison with seeing branches as well as trunk. You can say that white is a simple color in comparison with a mixed color such as orange; or you can say that white is complex because it consists of the colors of the rainbow. To see that the words "simple" and "complex" are used in many different ways, refer to many different kinds of contrast, makes one realize that there is no "absolute" sense of simplicity or complexity.

I will comment on Hering's suggestion that sensations of light and color "can be reduced" to some "simple" sensations and their combinations. Hering assumes that the simple sensations would be

3. Wittgenstein, *Philosophical Investigations*, paras. 46–51.

sensations of the principal or primary colors. Remember that the project is to select a sensation that will stand a reasonable chance of being correlated one-to-one with some fixed neural process. *Red* is usually considered to be a primary color. Is it plausible that the sensation of red might be universally correlated with some constant neural process? One wonders *which* sensation of red this would be. There are many *shades* of red. Are we to suppose there is a red that is *common* to all shades of red? As Wittgenstein notes, if we are asked to say or point out what is common to a light red and a dark red, we don't know what to do—as contrasted with the case where there are two paintings of different landscapes, but with an identical-looking bush in both, and when asked what the two paintings have in common we point to that bush.[4] This difference between the cases shows that to ask what is common to different shades of red is a question without any clear meaning.

Would there be a better probability of finding a one-to-one correlation if we fixed on a single shade of red? Will a single shade of red yield a constant sensation? Hardly. If we use linguistic descriptions, such as "orangish red" or "purplish red," it is obvious that there are many different shades of orangish or purplish red, each one presumably yielding a different color sensation. Could we specify a single, specific shade of red and expect it to yield a constant, one-and-the-same color sensation? No, for we know that the same pigment or the same combination of pigments *looks* different when placed in settings of different color. Could one specify *"this sensation of color that I have right now"* and hope that there might be a one-to-one correlation between *this* sensation and a constant neural process? The difficulty here would be in arriving at an objective measure of *this* sensation. It would be unsatisfactory to designate *this* color sensation as *the* sensation produced by light of a certain wavelength, since we know that light of the same wavelength can produce colors of different appearance when the surrounding colors are different. Could we stipulate that *this* color sen-

4. Wittgenstein, *The Blue and Brown Books,* p. 130.

sation is *the* color sensation correlated with some specified neural process? The trouble with this procedure is that, first, it would yield a *defined* correlation, not an empirically discovered one; and, second, it would beg the question of whether there is in fact a constant correlation between a certain neural process and one and the same sensation of color.

Hering's program of reducing all color sensations to a few simple sensations, in the hope of discovering correlations between the latter and simple neural functions, loses its appearance of intelligibility when one considers Wittgenstein's point that one and the same thing may be called "simple" or "complex," depending on what comparison one is making—that nothing is simple in any absolute sense, but that simplicity (and complexity) are relative to human choices and human ways of dividing up things. There is the further point, which I have been making, that when it comes to color sensations, which seemed to Hering to provide examples of "simple" sensations, there seems to be no way of specifying some one-and-the-same sensation in such a way that the sensation would stand any chance of being found to be uniquely correlated with one and the same neural process. Of course the same holds for "gustatory" sensations, sensations of sound, and so on.

8. The thesis of psychophysical isomorphism is that an experience, or a perception, or a feeling, or a thought, has a definite structure, and that for each of these structures there is a matching neural structure. But just as nothing is simple or complex in any absolute sense, so also nothing has a structure in any absolute sense. Structure is a relationship between parts or elements. There can be different decisions as to what are the parts or elements of a thing (see Chapter V, Section 16). The parts or elements of a human hand could be said to be *six*—the four fingers, the thumb, and the rest of the hand. Or the elements could be said to be *three*, namely, bones, flesh, and blood. Given these two different ways of analyzing the hand, what is going to be meant by "the structure" of

the hand will obviously be different. There is no such thing as *the* structure of the hand, in any absolute sense. The same holds for experiences, thoughts, events, facts, and everything else. Take the event of my walking across this room and opening the door. What is its structure? One doesn't know what to say, because this question has no meaning in the abstract. It could be *given* a meaning by virtue of a decision as to what are to be called "the elements" of that event.

An exponent of psychophysical isomorphism might declare that he is perfectly aware of the relativity, in this sense, of elements and of structure, but also that nothing prevents him from choosing "elements" in the domain of mental states, and doing the same in the domain of neural states, and then determining by empirical investigation whether elements of one domain are correlated with elements of the other one. In the present chapter I have proposed a serious difficulty for that project, namely, that if we employ expressions of ordinary language to specify elements in the domain of experiences, desires, thoughts, and so on, then we find that any such expression ranges over a family of cases, comprising many different phenomena. A believer in isomorphism would and should consider it absurd to suppose that one and the same neural state could be correlated with each one of such widely different phenomena.

I will add that there appears to be no intelligible alternative to employing descriptions of ordinary language to specify elements in the domain of mental states, using those descriptions in accordance with the normal criteria that govern their application. Certainly there can be no recourse here to "private, inner, ostensive definitions." Even if this idea were intelligible, it would be useless for the purpose of ascertaining whether there are scientifically verifiable correlations between mental states and neural states.

9.   The notion that a mental state has a structure strongly appeals to the imagination of philosophers and psychologists. Such a view

is put forward in a recent philosophical work by Gilbert Harman.[5] Harman designates as "mental states" what some philosophers have called "propositional attitudes," although Harman prefers to speak of "sentences" rather than of "propositions." He says: "The names of certain mental states are formed by combining the name of a type of state—belief, desire, hope, fear, or whatever—with a sentence. For example, we speak of 'the belief that snow is white' or 'the hope that war will end'." [6] Harman makes a distinction, however, between the "inner sentences" of thought and the "outer sentences" that we utter:

I will speak of a "language of thought" and will speculate on the relations between the inner language of thought and the outer language we speak. In particular I will try to say how the meaning of the outer sentence can be in part a matter of the representational character of the inner sentence.[7]

Let us speak as if there were a "language of thought" and that mental states essentially involve "sentences" of this language. Then, to believe that Benacerraf is wise is to be in a relationship to a sentence of the language of thought, and to desire that Benacerraf be wise is to be in a different relationship to the same sentence. Representational characteristics of mental states derive from representational characteristics of sentences of the language of thought.[8]

Harman *seems* to be adopting the dualistic, metaphysical view that, when a person declares to someone that he believes the war will end, there occurs an inner sentence of thought, namely, "I believe the war will end." He says that *the meaning* of the outer sentence depends in part "on the role in thought" of the corresponding inner sentence: "What a sentence used in communication means depends in part on the role of a corresponding sentence in the language of thought. Outer language is used to express beliefs and other mental states. . . . Since the state expressed is an instance of a sentence of the inner language of thought, the meaning of an outer sentence is at least partly a matter of the role in thought of the inner sentence

5. Gilbert Harman, *Thought* (Princeton: Princeton University Press, 1973).
6. Ibid., pp. 54–55.   7. Ibid., p. 54.   8. Ibid., p. 57.

it expresses." [9] In holding that there is an "inner language" of thought Harman does not just mean, of course, that people sometimes say things silently to themselves or sometimes have inward thoughts. This is a truism, not a matter for philosophical conjecture. What Harman seems to be holding is that whenever a person believes or desires or hopes that p, the sentence "p" is present as an inner sentence. Furthermore, the *meaning* of an outwardly spoken sentence expressing a mental state is based (as we have seen) in part at least on "the role in thought" of "the inner sentence" that the outer sentence expresses. I am surprised by Harman's assertion that the existence of such an inner language of thought can readily be verified:

This suggestion that there is a language of thought is easy to verify. We can simply take mental states to *be* instances or "tokens" of appropriate sentences. The belief that Benacerraf is wise will then be the appropriate sentence of the language of thought stored as a belief; and the desire that Benacerraf be wise will be the same sentence stored as an end. We can take these states to be instances of sentences because they have structure and representational characteristics that depend on their structure. . . . Just as various speech acts—promises, threats, warnings, and so forth—can involve instances of the same sentence of the outer language, various mental states—beliefs, desires, hopes, and so forth—can be instances of the same sentence of the inner language of thought. [10]

This is a remarkable kind of "verification." Harman "verifies" that there are inner sentences by *stipulating* ("We can simply take . . .") that a mental state *is* an instance of an inner sentence! One could prove many wonderful things in that way.

Although Harman holds that a mental state is an inner sentence, it is not clear whether he thinks that the inner sentence is composed of *words:*

Of course, I do not suppose that the relevant thoughts and mental states are just strings of words. My claim is that they are tokens of sentences under analysis. In other words, I suggest that mental states can be taken to be structures of elements that are isomorphic to structures that are sen-

9. Ibid., p. 160.   10. Ibid., p. 58.

tences under analysis, where the representational properties of the mental states correspond to those of the sentences under analysis.[11]

Harman's view may be like that of Wittgenstein in the *Tractatus*, namely, that thoughts are composed, not of words, but of "psychical elements" that correspond to the words of spoken language. The expression "sentences under analysis" is puzzling. I think it is probably supposed to mean the same as "sentences undergoing analysis" or "sentences in the process of being analyzed." If so, Harman is accepting another view of the *Tractatus*, namely, that when you hear and understand a sentence, or when you utter a sentence and mean something by it, you are actually engaged in a process (perhaps unconscious) of analyzing the sentence (see *Tractatus* 4.002). Harman's conception, if I understand him correctly, is that as you read, speak, hear, perceive, you are always engaged (usually unconsciously) in forming representational structures, composed of elements of some sort (let us call them "thought-elements"), which structures are isomorphic with word-sentences that are either completely analyzed or are at least in some stage of analysis.

This conception is highly relevant to the topic of an isomorphism between mental states and neural states, since if there are structures of thought-elements when a person perceives, desires, believes, understands, or remembers something, then there could be neural structures that were isomorphic with those mental structures. Let us test the conception against an example of discourse. Suppose that three friends of mine normally come to my house one night each week to play poker with me. After they arrive on this particular evening one of them says, "Where is the pack of cards?" I reply, "The pack of cards is on the table." In uttering this sentence I could be said to express a belief. On Harman's view there will be a mental state of belief which is a structure composed of elements. How many elements are there in this structure? Would

11. Ibid., p. 89.

there be a thought-element corresponding to each word of the spoken sentence—thus *eight* thought-elements? Or would there be one thought-element corresponding to the subject phrase "The pack of cards," one corresponding to the verb "is," and one corresponding to the predicate phrase "on the table"—a total of *three* elements? Or would there be one thought-element corresponding to "The pack," another to "of cards," a third to "is," a fourth to "on," and a fifth to "the table?" Suppose I know that there are 52 cards in a pack—would there have been a thought-element corresponding to that number when I spoke? Suppose I know that $4 \times 13 = 52$—would there be thought-elements corresponding to "4," to "times" and to "13"? Suppose that I have both a coffee table and a dinner table, and I *meant* that the cards were on the former: In that case would there have been an element in my thought process corresponding to "coffee," or to "coffee table"?

I might have replied to the question by saying "On the table," instead of uttering the full sentence. Would the number of thought-elements have been the same, or different? I might have responded to the question by pointing at the coffee table, without words. Would the same number of thought-elements be present as when I spoke the full sentence? Suppose that I was in the habit of keeping the pack of cards on the coffee table, and that in reply to the question I said, "In the usual place." Would the thought-elements be the same as they were when I uttered the full sentence, or when I pointed?

My aim in asking such questions is, of course, to induce the realization that we have no idea of how to answer them, and that this is because we don't know what we are talking about. We don't know how to count thought-elements and we don't know how to identify them. What we can do is to make stipulations as to what we are going to call the "parts" or "elements" of spoken or heard sentences (and we can make *different* stipulations for the same sentence); and then we can further stipulate that for each such sentence-element there is a thought-element. But such a procedure of definition can-

not yield the result that there are actually occurring thought processes (consisting of structures of thought-elements) in addition to
the actions and utterances of my examples.

Harman actually assumes that whenever a person responds ra-
tionally, intelligently, appropriately, to a question, there is a mental process occurring in the person that is a logically separate thing
from the person's response. Oddly, this is because Harman wants
to regard a person as an automaton. He says, "To have a theory of
another person's psychological makeup is to have a model of the
workings of his mind." [12] Here "workings" is meant quite literally,
in the sense of something actually going on. Such a model will
describe input, internal states, output—and how they are related to
one another. Harman says:

A psychological model represents a more or less rigorously specified device
that is intended to be able to duplicate the relevant behavior of a person. If
the device is sufficiently described, it should be realizable as a robot or, as
I shall say, an automaton. [13]

A detailed psychological model could be identified with an individual psychology. Anything that instantiates the associated automaton would have
that individual psychology; and vice versa. Thus a person instantiates the
automaton that serves as the model of his individual psychology. Given
sufficient technology, a robot could be constructed that would also instan-
tiate that individual psychology. [14]

An automaton is a mechanism with internal states and processes
connected causally to its output. But why should we suppose that
the "mental states" of a person (that is, his belief, desire, intention,
understanding, memory, and so on) are "internal states and processes" in that sense? When my friend asked, "Where is the pack of
cards?" one appropriate response would have been for me to point
to the coffee table. That might have been the *only* relevant thing
that occurred! Why this insistence on a mental *process?* Of course, I
understood the question; I *wanted* to give the desired information; I
remembered where the cards were; I pointed with the *intention* of

showing their location; my pointing gesture *meant* that the cards were there; and so on. But none of these psychological terms are used in ordinary language to stand for "internal states and processes," in the sense in which this latter expression applies to an automaton. The ordinary criteria of understanding, desire, memory, intention, or meaning have nothing to do with determining the presence of internal states, in that literal sense of "internal" in which an automaton has internal states.

Wittgenstein remarks: "In philosophy one is always in danger of creating a myth of symbolism, or of mental processes. Instead of simply saying what anyone knows and must admit." [15] This is what we see in Harman's book—a myth of mental processes. There is also a myth of *explanation*. He is going to explain, for example, what it is to *understand* a sentence that one says or hears. Harman says, "To understand what is said is to perceive it as having an appropriate analysis." [16] Thus when my friend said, "Where is the pack of cards?" and I understood his sentence, this understanding of mine was a process of perceiving that sentence as having such-and-such an analysis.

What are we talking about here? My friend asked the question, and I responded by pointing, or by saying, "On the table," or by saying, "The pack of cards is on the table," and so on. I did not speculate to myself as to what his question might mean; nor did I go through an "analysis" of it, whatever that might be. I merely pointed, or said those words. Harman would say that if the mental process of analyzing my friend's sentence, or of perceiving it as having a certain analysis, was not conscious then it was unconscious.[17] Such a contention is, of course, impossible to refute or to verify. But why should Harman be tempted to posit hidden, unverifiable, mental processes, instead of trying to describe what we know?

Here I can only conjecture. My conjecture is that Harman is strongly influenced by the notion (which is correct in itself) that

15. Wittgenstein, *Zettel*, para. 211.   16. Harman, p. 89.
17. Ibid., p. 31.

my friend's sentence was not for me a mere sequence of sounds but was a *meaningful* sentence, and by the further notion (which is incorrect) that its being for me a meaningful sentence required that it evoked in me a process of thought. Wittgenstein acutely characterizes this latter temptation in the following way: "The sentence is like a key-bit whose indentations are constructed to move levers in the soul in a particular way. The sentence, as it were, plays a melody (the thought) on the instrument of the soul." [18] He goes on to make an equally acute criticism of this idea: "But why should I now hypothesize, in addition to the orderly series of words, another series of mental elements running parallel? That simply duplicates language with something else of the same kind." [19] Harman is clearly conceiving of the thought as an order, a structure, of elements, "running parallel" with the spoken and heard sentence. This is implied by his remark that "Mental states can be taken to be structures of elements that are isomorphic to structures that are sentences under analysis." [20] The futility of postulating an inner structure that matches the outer one should be obvious. For suppose it could be verified that the postulated inner structure was there in me when I heard my friend's question, but that *by the ordinary criteria* of understanding I did *not* understand his words? The ordinary criteria would consist of facts such as the following: first, that I was brought up in an English-speaking community; second, that I made an appropriate response; third, that *if* someone had asked, "Why are you pointing?" (if that is what I did), I *would* have replied, "Because he asked me where the cards are and I am pointing to where they are"—and so on. None of these criteria implies anything about the occurrence of some inner process or structure. Consider these remarks by Wittgenstein: "Think of putting up one's hand in school. Must one have rehearsed the answer silently in himself, in order to have the right to put up his hand? And *what* must have gone on inside him?—Nothing. But it is important that he usually knows an answer when he puts up his hand; and that is

18. Wittgenstein, *Philosophische Grammatik*, para. 104.   19. Ibid.
20. Harman, p. 89.

the criterion of his *understanding* putting up one's hand." [21] Harman's basic idea, I believe, is that an outer sentence or gesture is meaningless in itself. In itself it is "dead." It gains meaning and "life" by being connected with something inner, which is a "thought." The thought is itself a symbol: "if it is a thought we can call it a symbol." [22] It is a "sentence" in the inner language of thought: "the meaning of an outer sentence is at least partly a matter of the role in thought of the inner sentence it expresses." [23] Thus an outer sentence derives its meaning from an inner sentence.

We should be struck by the resemblance between this idea and Russell's conception, which we examined in Chapter V, Sections 10–13. Russell said that a spoken or heard "word-proposition" obtained its meaning from an inner "image-proposition." Although Harman maintains that a thought is an inner sentence, he does not hold that the constituents or elements of the inner sentence are images. He does not specify the ontological nature of the elements of a thought. Probably, like Wittgenstein of the *Tractatus*, he does not know *what* they are. But his basic contention is that an outer sentence derives its meaning from an inner process, which is a structure of elements of some sort. Now note Wittgenstein's remark, previously quoted: "That simply duplicates language with something else of the same kind." What does he mean by saying it is "of the same kind"? Partly he means that if the outer symbol is in itself "dead," so is the inner symbol. Wittgenstein speaks of this matter in *Zettel*. He is talking about an *intention*, which for Harman would be an example of "thought"; and Wittgenstein uses the term "picture," which is the equivalent of Harman's term "representation." Wittgenstein begins by describing a temptation he feels, and then goes on to comment on it:

If I try to describe the process of intention, I feel first and foremost that it can do what it is supposed to do only by containing an extremely faithful picture of what it intends. But further, that too does not go far enough, because a picture, whatever it may be, can be variously interpreted, hence

21. Wittgenstein, *Zettel*, para. 136.   22. Harman, p. 59.
23. Ibid., p. 60.

this picture too in its turn stands isolated. When one has the picture in view by itself it is suddenly dead, and it is as if something had been taken away from it, which had given it life before. It is not a thought, not an intention; whatever accompaniments we imagine for it, articulate or inarticulate processes, or any feeling whatsoever, it remains isolated, it does not point outside itself to a reality beyond.

Now one says: "of course it is not the picture that intends, but we who use it to intend something." But if this intending, this meaning, is in turn something that occurs along with the picture, then I cannot see why that should involve a human being. The process of digestion can also be studied as a chemical process, independently of whether it takes place in a living being. We want to say "Meaning is surely essentially a mental process, a process of conscious life, not of dead matter." But what will give such a thing the specific character of what takes place?—so long as we think of it as a process. And now it seems to us as if intending could not be any process at all, of any kind whatever.—For what we are dissatisfied with here is the grammar of *process*, not the specific kind of process.—One could say: we should call any process "dead" in this sense.[24]

What will give life and meaning to an outer sentence is not an inner process that occurs along with it, no matter how articulated, but the function of the outer sentence in a situation of human discourse. The same for a gesture. My pointing gesture, or my words, "On the table," had a quite specific meaning in that setting where my friend asked where the cards were. Isolated from that setting they could mean anything, or nothing. The same would be true of any parallel process you might imagine. Wittgenstein once said to me, "An expression has meaning only in the stream of life." The situation in which my friends came to play poker with me and asked where the cards were was in the stream of life; and so was my response. There the meaning of my response in words or gestures was evident and out in the open. No parallel process, whether conscious or unconscious, was needed to give it meaning; and none could do so.

10.   I hope that in the long discussion of this chapter we have not lost sight of our principal topic, memory. Memory is a psycholog-

24. Wittgenstein, *Zettel*, para. 236.

ical or mental concept. To remember something (at least in the "occurrent" sense) would be to have a *thought*, in Harman's broad use of the word "thought." In the example of my friends who came to play poker, my response to the question asked, whether it consisted of a pointing gesture or of words, was a memory response, a manifestation or expression of remembering where I had put the cards. Harman would call my remembering a "mental state" or "mental process"; and he holds that it is a structure that is isomorphic to a "sentence under analysis."

In this chapter my concern has been to criticize the notion of isomorphism, as applied to the relation between "mental states" and neural states. I have pointed out that it makes sense to say that there is or is not an isomorphism there only if one has in one's possession, or in the offing, a "key" of isomorphism; and I have argued that it is impossible to devise a key of isomorphism that could provide any reasonable prospect for the discovery of a one-to-one correlation between any mental state and any neural state.

It might be supposed that although Harman adopts a kind of dualism between "inner" sentences of thought and "outer" sentences of communication, he does not hold to a *dualism* of mental states and neural states (as does, for example, Köhler), but instead opts for an *identity* between mental states and neural states—and that, therefore, my criticism of the possibility of *correlations* between mental and neural states is not applicable to the views of Harman and of other exponents of the so-called "identity theory." It is true that Harman favors "a kind of identity theory." He says, "Instances of mental states and processes are instances of physical states and processes, although different instances of the same mental states and processes need not be instances of the same physical states and processes." [25] I must confess that I cannot see how this can be regarded as an "identity theory." On Harman's view, on two different occasions of my remembering that I put the pack of cards on the coffee table, there might be two, numerically different, neural states. What could be the justification for holding

25. Harman, p. 43.

that the mental state on one of those occasions was *identical* with the neural state that occurred on that occasion? All we have is the occurrence of a mental state and the simultaneous occurrence of *some neural state or other*. Who would want to deny that? That a certain mental state is *identical* with a certain neural state ought to be a thesis that could, in principle, be *verified*. Certainly, the finding that when a certain mental state, M, occurred there also occurred a certain neural state, N, would not constitute the discovery that M and N are numerically identical. A logically necessary condition, although not a sufficient condition, for verifying that M and N are numerically identical, would be the finding that the same state, M, occurs when and only when the *same* state, N, occurs. Thus what Harman calls "a kind of identity theory" is not an identity theory at all. Of course, Harman can *stipulate* that whenever the same mental state, M, occurs, it is numerically identical with *whatever* neural or other physical state occurs at the same time. Such a stipulation would be of no philosophical interest, being merely an abuse of the concept of numerical identity.

A legitimate use of the concept of numerical identity requires, as a *minimum* condition, constant correlation. If a process, A, and a process, B, are genuinely identical, there is, in a trivial sense, a *correlation* between occurrences of A and occurrences of B: if A and B are numerically identical, then A is present whenever and only when B is present. This being so, my criticism of the possibility of a one-to-one correlation between a certain mental state (such as my remembering that I put the cards on the table) and a certain neural or other physical state strikes against any monistic, identity theory, just as much as against any dualistic theory, such as Köhler's.

11.   Philosophers tend to use the expression "mental state" in an all-encompassing way (as does Harman, for example). Such diverse things as wanting to catch the bus, believing that the train will be late, remembering where one put the keys, fearing that the cat will knock over the vase, hoping that the war will end, are all listed as "mental states." Of course this is not the ordinary use of the ex-

pression "mental state." Of a person known to suffer from severe, persistent depression, you might ask, "What is his mental state now?", and you might receive the reply, "He is still depressed," but not the reply, "He believes that the train will be late." To inquire about a person's mental state is to inquire about such things as moods or emotions that make a major contribution to his ill- or well-being, his happiness or unhappiness. Thus, the all-encompassing philosophical use is "technical." This might be thought to be all right, as long as we are aware of it. I think, however, that this "technical" employment of the expression is an important source of confusion, especially in the context of philosophical discussions of psychophysical isomorphism and of putative correlations between "mental states" and "brain states."

I want to compare the way in which the concept of *duration* applies to "mental states" with the way in which it applies to "brain states"; or, rather, I want to show that *different concepts of duration* have to be employed in the two cases. This will constitute another argument against the possibility of psychophysical isomorphism.

Suppose a young man has the intention to pursue a career in the army, and this has been a long-standing intention—in other words, an intention of long duration. Wittgenstein in *Zettel* says something curious about intention, namely, that intention "is not a state of consciousness. It does not have genuine duration." [26] What does he mean? My young man's intention is a conscious one—that is, he is aware of having it; so why not call it "a state of consciousness"? And since it is an intention of long standing, surely it has duration. What can Wittgenstein mean by saying that it does not have "genuine duration" (*echte Dauer*)?

A clue as to what he means is contained in the following remarks:

Where there is genuine duration (*echte Dauer*) one can say to someone: "Pay attention and give me a signal when the image, the thing you are experiencing, the noise, etc., alters." [27]

26. Wittgenstein, *Zettel*, para. 45.   27. Ibid., para. 81.

Think of this language game: determine how long an impression lasts by means of a stop-watch. The duration of knowledge, ability, understanding, could not be determined in this way.[28]

Indeed one scarcely ever says that one has believed, understood or intended something "uninterruptedly" since yesterday. An interruption of belief would be a period of unbelief, not for example the withdrawing of attention from what one believes—e.g. as in sleep.[29]

Wittgenstein is calling attention to *different concepts* of duration. Of course beliefs, intentions, knowledge, understanding, have duration: we can say that someone had such-and-such a belief or intention "for a long time"—or that he has known or understood so-and-so "for more than a year." Wittgenstein is not denying that this kind of duration is *genuine:* that would mean nothing. He is using the expression "genuine duration" (*echte Dauer*) to indicate a different kind of duration. And, I think, he is also using the expression "state of consciousness" in a technical sense, such that something is a "state of consciousness" *only* if it has genuine duration.

It is easy to illustrate the distinction Wittgenstein is calling attention to. Suppose you have a pain in your leg that comes and goes. Your doctor wants to find out how long each spasm of pain lasts. He asks you to pay attention and give a signal at the beginning and at the end of each spasm of pain. You can even time the spasms by means of a stopwatch. Wittgenstein says, "I can pay attention to the course of my pains, but not in the same way to my belief, my translating, or my knowledge." [30] Suppose I believe that the war will end in the present year. It would make no sense to ask me to time the duration of this belief with a stopwatch. Or suppose I know (remember) that I put the car keys in the kitchen drawer. Again, it would be absurd to ask me to determine the duration of that knowledge or memory with a stopwatch. In the case of the pain I could make this kind of report: "Now it has begun; yes, I still have it; now I no longer have it." But I could not pay attention, in *that* way, to my belief that the war will end this year. I

28. Ibid., para. 82.   29. Ibid., para. 85.   30. Ibid., para. 75.

could report that a spasm of pain lasted for three seconds; then for two seconds I had no pain; then for five seconds I had another spasm of pain; and so on. To speak in that way about my belief would be idiotic. One could describe the distinction in this way: in the case of pain there is a "content of consciousness" to which I can pay attention, but in the case of a belief, or knowledge, or memory, or intention there is not. This is the ground for saying that the pain in my leg is "a state of consciousness," whereas my belief, memory, or intention is not.

Many physical events, states, or processes have duration in the sense of genuine duration. The rolling motion of a ball across the floor could be observed and clocked in the same way as the pain. "Now it is rolling; it has stopped; now it is rolling again." One could continuously observe in this way the temperature of a metal that was being heated: "Now it has reached 200 degrees; it still is at 200; now its temperature is falling."

Let us apply this distinction between kinds of duration to the conception of psychophysical isomorphism. Those who espouse a mind-brain isomorphism are usually assuming what might be called "a simultaneous isomorphism." This is certainly true of Köhler. He thinks that *all* "psychological facts" have "brain-correlates." [31] He thinks that for each "mental event" or "mental state" there is a correlated neural event or state. For each "experience" there is a "cortical correlate" that is "isomorphic" with that experience.[32] Köhler believes that a correlated neural event "underlies" each "mental event." He believes that the mental event is present whenever and only when its correlated neural event is present. If the neural event ceases, so does the mental event. In short, Köhler supposes that for every "psychological fact," or "experience," or "mental event," there is a neural event, state, or process of *simultaneous duration*. I believe the same is true of those philosophers who speak, undiscriminatingly, of "mental states," and who suppose that for each "mental state" there may be a correlated

31. E.g., Köhler, *Dynamics in Psychology*, p. 47.
32. Köhler, *The Place of Value in a World of Facts*, p. 243.

brain state, whether or not they suppose that the correlated states would be numerically identical or numerically distinct.

Now a "neural state" would presumably be some electrical or chemical condition of one or more neurons. The emission of electrical impulses by neurons would be something that could, in principle, be continuously observed by means of instruments and continuously measured by some sort of timing device. The protein balance of a certain region of the brain would also be something that could be continuously observed and metered. In other words, neural states will have *genuine duration*. But the same is not true of most of the things that philosophers tend to group together under the broad and vague heading of "mental states." Some sensations, such as bodily pains, have genuine duration. But memories do not; beliefs do not; intentions do not; thoughts do not. These "mental states" do not have the kind of duration they would have to have were they to be simultaneous correlates of certain neural states.

Thus we have noted another respect in which the doctrine of psychophysical isomorphism is conceptual nonsense. Loose talk of "mental states" and "brain states" helps to conceal the differences in the modes of duration that are applicable within the two categories. If a belief, or thought, or memory, on the one hand, and a neural state, on the other, do not have the same *kind* of duration, then what could it mean to suppose that they might have *simultaneous* duration?

Appendix to Chapter X

I imagine that some readers will be of the opinion that recent work in neurology and neuropsychology has confirmed that there are one-to-one correlations between various brain states on the one hand, and on the other hand various moods, emotions, sensations, memories, thoughts, or actions. Having this opinion, they will feel that the conceptual arguments I have brought to bear against the possibility of there being any such correlations must contain some error or errors, even if they are unable to specify what these errors are. They will be disposed to believe that my book merely offers one more vain attempt by philosophy to impose limits on empirical science.

Popular presentations, in newspapers and even in scholarly journals, have grossly misrepresented what has actually been learned about the connections between brain states and mental states. Accordingly, in this appendix, I am going to cite evidence of such misrepresentations, taken from a recent book by Dr. Elliot S. Valenstein,[33] which provides not only much factual information, but also a critical evaluation of many of the claims that have been made about the possibility of producing and controlling mental states by brain stimulation. My justification for quoting from Valenstein's work at considerable length is that many philosophers and psychologists have a *prejudice* in favor of the possibility of brain-mind correlations, due in part to the influence of exaggerated or distorted accounts of the actual results of neurosurgery and of electrical or chemical stimulations of the brain. This prejudice is an obstacle to any serious consideration of the conceptual points I have made and, more generally, promotes undeserved attention for "wild" conjectures and theories in the philosophy of mind and body.

Valenstein remarks:

Most people have a grossly exaggerated impression of the omnipotence of various brain manipulations, a distorted view of the way specific brain regions are related to behavior, and an uncritical attitude toward suggestions of application of brain technology to social problems. It is easy to understand how this came about. Professional writers are encouraged to provide dramatic accounts that stimulate interest in as large an audience as possible. Unfortunately, this is easiest to accomplish by selecting unrepresentative experimental results, describing them with a minimum of context and qualifications, and ignoring major technical and theoretical obstacles blocking practical applications. While scientists tend to shudder at popular

33. Elliot S. Valenstein, *Brain Control: A Critical Examination of Brain Stimulation and Psychosurgery* (New York: John Wiley, 1973). I will place page references to Valenstein's book in the text instead of in footnotes. All page references in this appendix are to Valenstein's book.

reporting in their own field, there certainly have been cases where they have not been above reproach. Scientists also succumb to the same incentives as other people and there are many examples where the practical implications of preliminary investigations have been exaggerated in an attempt to gain notoriety and increased financial support for their work (pp. 7–8).

This is not to deny, of course, that there have been many remarkable findings about artificial brain stimulation. In the 1950s it was observed that cats that had been stimulated in certain brain areas would be disturbed and fearful when later they were placed in the same test chamber where the previous stimulation had occurred. The cats would even try to escape from the stimulation of those brain sites (p. 34). But it was also discovered, accidentally, that there were other brain sites which, when stimulated by a short burst of electrical current, seemed to give "pleasure" to an animal. Some rats learned to stimulate their own brains by pressing a lever, and would press the lever at a rate of more than 100 times a minute, for hour after hour (pp. 36–37). Subsequently, scientists discovered many examples of brain stimulation triggering various behaviors, such as eating, drinking, hoarding, nest building, and aggressive behavior (p. 44). Valenstein says:

The trend during the major part of the 1960s was to describe as many behaviors as possible that could be elicited by brain stimulation. As the list of responses that had been elicited grew larger, the potential for controlling behavior and motivation seemed greater and greater. Often there was a rather uncritical acceptance of the significance of these reports, which characteristically claimed to have tapped an anatomical circuit regulating specific motivational states (p. 46).

Neurosurgeons were encouraged to undertake various brain manipulations as a means of treating emotional and behavioral problems, by a number of reports of dramatic changes in animal behavior following experimental destruction of parts of the nervous system (p. 47). Valenstein says:

There can be no doubt that our observations of animals and humans have indicated that brain stimulation can produce very rewarding and pleasant

sensations that evoke a desire to repeat the experience. It has been demonstrated many times in laboratories that animals will display a seemingly in-
satiable desire to operate a switch over and over again to stimulate their
own brains (p. 66).

Valenstein reports that he observed a rat for twenty-one days, dur-
ing which time it operated the switch about 850,000 times (p. 67).
The animal was not, however, totally obsessed by self-stimulation.
Valenstein says.

The fact that there exist many demonstrations illustrating that brain stimulation can be a very compelling reward has been interpreted by a number
of people to indicate that it is irresistible to the point of self-destruc-
tiveness. That this is not true can be seen by behavior of the rat we described which self-stimulated for 21 days. This animal stopped to eat,
groom, sleep, and even explore the environment and in fact did not even
lose any weight during this three-week period (p. 69).

It is possible to misinterpret the experience that is produced by
brain stimulation. Dr. Carl Sem-Jacobsen employed brain stimulation on a female patient who responded by smiling and laughing
with apparent enjoyment. Sem-Jacobsen and several colleagues
were convinced that the electrode was in a "pleasure region." Sem-
Jacobsen says:

Because of the patient's uniform reactions in repeated sessions, the author
took it for granted that she liked it and discussed the significance of this
response in her presence without eliciting any comment from her. Suddenly one day the patient became angry and told us that she was 'fed up'
and 'did not enjoy these stimulations at all.' She asked us to stop and
refrain from any further stimulation of this contact. She said she 'had had
enough!' The stimulus did not give the patient any pleasure. Instead it
created in some of her pelvic muscles a rhythmic contraction which tickled
her and caused the laughter. It was evident that the author had not been
stimulating either a "pleasure center," nor a center dealing with sensation.
He had simply been stimulating muscles which contracted and caused the
tickling and, in turn, forced the patient to smile and laugh (pp. 71–72).

An important observation was that stimulation at the same brain
site in the same patient did not produce invariably the same re-

sponse, but instead the responses varied with the emotional and physical condition of the patient. Dr. Robert Heath says:

When the same stimulus was repeated in the same patient, responses varied. The most intense pleasurable responses occurred in patients stimulated while they were suffering intense pain, whether emotional and reflected by despair, anguish, intense fear or rage, or physical, such as that caused by metastatic carcinoma. The feelings induced by stimulation of pleasure sites obliterated these patients' awareness of physical pain. Patients who felt well at the time of stimulation, on the other hand, experienced only slight pleasure (p. 72).

Some experimenters have supposed that a certain stimulation might evoke a constant behavioral response pattern. Valenstein says:

Dr. José Delgado, for example, described a monkey who stopped what it was doing every time it was stimulated in a brain area called the red nucleus, circled to the right, walked on two feet to a pole which it climbed, and then, after descending to the floor, made an aggressive attack on a subordinate monkey. Although it has been reported that such complex sequential responses can be elicited repeatedly in a given animal, *there is no known way of predicting what behavior sequence, if any, will be obtained from a given electrode.* There are many reasons for doubting that complex sequential responses are directly elicited by stimulation at one neural site. It is likely that the responses are at first partly based on the individual animal's pattern of coping with an emotional state such as that induced by the brain stimulation. It moves about, climbs a pole, attacks another animal. It is quite possible that the exact sequence is maintained because of the so-called superstitious tendency of animals to repeat any responses accidentally occurring at the same time that a positive reward was presented or an aversive stimulus was terminated. It is as though the animal concluded that the way to get rid of the disturbing sensation caused by the brain stimulation is to repeat what it last did just before the stimulation was turned off (pp. 76–77; my emphasis).

Valenstein comments on another but similar idea about the relation between stimulation and response:

Another approach to the same problem that has seemed particularly seductive to science fiction writers and also to a few scientists involves stimulating areas of the brain with their own characteristic electrical pattern. It is a very tantalizing thought to be able to record the electrical pattern from a specific brain region and then to play back this same pattern through the implanted electrode from which the recording was obtained. The idea would be to record the electrical pattern from critical sites in the nervous system while a person engaged in a particular activity and then to play it back into the nervous system to reproduce the activity. Superficially, this seems to be an ideal solution to the problem of producing an electric stimulus that duplicates the natural physiological processes. Unfortunately, the glamor of this possibility quickly fades under close scrutiny. The electrical pattern that is recorded is both a distortion and a selection determined by the methods and apparatus used. (A high-fidelity tape recordings of the sound of rain on a tin roof does not contain all the information needed to make rain.) Even though there may be consistent electrical correlates of certain movements, this does not mean that there is any causal relationship between the electrical pattern in a given brain area and a particular behavioral pattern. There is absolutely no reason to believe that a playback of recorded electrical patterns through a brain electrode will reinstate either a response or, for that matter, any physiological state that was prevalent at the time the pattern was recorded (pp. 83–85).

Concerning the widespread notion that a specific stimulation is correlated one-to-one with a specific behavioral response, Valenstein says the following:

The impression exists that if electrodes are placed in a specific part of the brain, a particular behavior can inevitably be evoked. Those who have participated in this research know that this is definitely not the case. In a large percentage of cases, animals do not display any specific behavior in response to stimulation, even though great care may have been exerted to position the brain electrodes with as much precision as possible. Even in rats, where the behavior is more stereotyped than in monkeys and man, brain stimulation produces very variable results. In my own laboratory, we have provided a large amount of evidence indicating that electrodes that seem to be in the same brain area in different animals often do not produce the same results at all. . . . the impression that specific behaviors can be reliably manipulated by electrical stimulation of anatomical areas that have been precisely defined is not in accord with the evidence. The experimental data clearly indicate that electrodes that seem to be in the same brain locus in different animals often evoke different behavior, and electrodes located at very different brain sites may evoke the same behavior in a given animal. Such findings reported from stimulation studies conducted in my own laboratory forced me to conclude that *some characteristic response tendency of the animal makes a significant contribution to the obtained results* and that *the behavior that can be elicited by stimulation cannot be predicted accurately from knowledge of the anatomical location of the electrode* (pp. 87–89; my emphasis).

Valenstein quotes a conclusion of Dr. Detlev Ploog from his brain stimulation studies in socially grouped squirrel monkeys:

. . . one and the same electrical stimulus applied at the same brain site in the same animal at different times does not necessarily elicit the same response. Rather, the animals' response depends on the composition and disposition of the group, and on the rank, role, and sex of the stimulated and the interacting animal (p. 92).

Dr. Bryan Robinson makes the following observation about the stimulation of rhesus monkeys:

One strange fact was that the response of the animal when it was unrestrained and with the other monkeys could not be entirely predicted from the response obtained when the animal was confined to a restraining chair. And, the best aggressive responses came from loci which did not produce particularly convincing aggressive behavior in the chair (p. 93).

Valenstein recounts an interesting experiment with rats carried out in his own laboratory. A chamber was so arranged that the rats would receive brain stimulation on one side of the chamber, and when they ran to the other side the stimulation would be terminated. Food pellets were placed in the chamber. It was observed that when stimulated a rat would pick up a food pellet and carry it to the other side of the chamber, dropping it there when the stimulation was terminated. This at first produced the impression that a food hoarding neural circuit had been tapped. When rat pups were placed in the chamber, the rats carried the pups in the same way, giving an initial impression that a brain site governing maternal behavior had been located. But then it was observed that the rats would carry any objects whatever, including inedible ones, under those stimulation conditions. If there was no other object present, a rat would even pick up its tail or a foreleg and carry it across the chamber. Valenstein says:

It is fairly obvious that if only food pellets or pups had been placed in the test chamber we might have been convinced that the stimulation was tapping into a maternal behavior or food hoarding neural circuit. Some additional information made it clear that this was not the case. First, *all* of the animals that we tested in this chamber carried objects as long as the electrodes had been placed in an hypothalamic site that produced a positive reward. That is, as long as the animal would self-stimulate, it carried the objects placed in the chamber in spite of the fact that the position of the electrodes varied considerably. Furthermore, if we varied the conditions so that the animal received the *identical* brain stimulation, but independent of its location in the chamber, it stopped carrying objects even when the objects were directly under its nose.

Apparently, for the rat any condition that motivates it to move back and forth and at the same time produces a parallel alternation of arousal and calming is very likely to produce the carrying behavior. It is well known that rats carry objects in situations related to hoarding, nest building, and retrieving of young. They also carry objects that have no utility for them. The pack or "trade" rat, for example, may even leave the object it is carrying in order to pick up an apparently more desirable, shiny object. This transporting of objects by rats is invariably from a more open and vulnerable location that is known to increase their arousal level to a hidden home or nest site that is safer and therefore calming. There is something about the alternation of arousal and calming when it is regularly produced in two different locations that is a potent stimulus for encouraging the rat to carry objects. In spite of our first impressions, it now seems clear that the behavior elicited by the stimulation should not be considered either maternal or hoarding (pp. 93–95).

Valenstein's conclusion is that the carrying behavior was dependent on the circumstances. It was "situationally dependent." He says:

The carrying of objects could only be elicited when the stimulation was delivered under conditions consistent with the environmental arrangements that encourage this behavior (p. 96).

When we turn to the results of brain stimulation of human beings, the variability of response to the same stimulation is even more striking than in animals, and the dependence of the response on the personal history of the patient and the circumstances at the time of stimulation is very prominent. Valenstein says:

There is little convincing evidence that human brain stimulation produces a specific and predictable response from the same anatomical structure in different individuals (p. 105).

The evidence is not completely conclusive, but it strongly suggests that the contents of the experiences evoked by stimulation are greatly determined by the personal reactions of the patients—reactions which are influenced by their past history and the present setting. The interpretations given by a patient to the state induced by brain stimulation may even be shaped by the content of an interview an hour before stimulation was started (p. 106).

A number of researchers testify that the responses of patients are "highly individualized." For example, Dr. Robert Heath makes the following report:

It has been possible to stimulate each patient several times and in several different regions. The immediate effects differ in many respects, and individual patients have differed somewhat in their responses to the same type of stimulation to the same region at different times. There were, however, some consistent findings in the sphere of affectivity. . . .

Stimulation to the amygdaloid nucleus resulted in an intense emotional reaction. The nature of the response varied from one stimulation to the next in the same patient, although parameters of stimulation were constant. On some occasions the patient became enraged and attempted to strike out, on other occasions she became fearful and felt an impulse to run (p. 107).

Another report by Dr. Heath and his collaborators, Drs. Monroe and Mickle, draws the following conclusion:

Our studies, as well as the reports in the literature, *seemingly suggest that it is impossible to make a one-to-one correlation between stimulation of this nuclear mass* [the amygdala] *and the behavioral response. Apparently the dynamic physiological-psychological state of the total individual is of the utmost importance in effecting the final response, even though the parameters of stimulation are constant.* The same observation has held with our stimulations to other regions, regardless of the type of stimulation, whether electrical, psychological, or pharmacological (pp. 107–108; my emphasis).

Valenstein refers to the well-known reports and conclusions of Dr. Wilder Penfield:

An impression of precise replicability of the results obtained from brain stimulation has been derived in part from some of the descriptions of the auditory and visual hallucinations and memories that have been evoked by stimulating temporal lobe structures. Dr. Wilder Penfield, whose studies of epileptic patients at the Montreal Neurological Institute are very well known, stimulated the brains of aware patients during temporal lobe surgery. . . . Penfield reported that temporal lobe stimulation may repeatedly evoke the same memory, sometimes complete in minute details, and that these evoked memories were analogous to tape recording "playbacks" of past, forgotten experiences (pp. 108–109).

Valenstein makes the following comment:

Not generally appreciated is the fact that most of the patients' responses evoked by stimulation were very abbreviated and sketchy fragments (p. 110).

He quotes from a report by Drs. Paul Fedio and John Van Buren:

We would also like to mention that, in our patients, cortical stimulation did not elicit reports of personal memories or experiential responses like those described by Penfield (p. 110).

He also refers to an investigation by Dr. George Mahl:

Electrodes were implanted in the brain of a patient and a series of interviews was conducted during which time the patient's brain was stimulated at different neural sites and at different intervals. The use of the interview technique made it possible to reconstruct the origin of many of the responses reported by the patient. There seems to be little doubt that the stimulation can evoke brief hallucinations that often surprised the patient, but these hallucinations were frequently related to the present situation in obvious ways. Even when the hallucinations evoked by the stimulation had been momentary re-enactments of the past, the interview method often revealed that there was an ideational association with the patient's mental content at the moment of stimulation (pp. 110–111).

Referring to Penfield's reports, Valenstein says:

The fact that temporal lobe stimulation often evokes memories that are related to the prevailing thought processes suggests that these memories may not be elicited from the same brain site as reliably as some authors have implied. Indeed, Penfield reported: "If we went back to some point with the lapse of a few seconds or a minute or so, we usually had the same experiential response. If, on the other hand, we waited a little longer time and then went back to the same point, another experience would appear." . . . *It is unrealistic to think that the same stimulation would invariably evoke the same response.* Part of the problem is that even among researchers who should know better, there is a tendency to think of the nervous system within too static a framework. It is not realistic to conceive of all nerve cells responding without variation to the same stimulus and being arranged to convey impulses in a fixed direction and sequence (pp. 111–112; my emphasis).

The point that response to stimulation *depends on the situation*, is stressed by Valenstein:

Responses depend upon who is present, what has just happened, and whether it is a hospital (or laboratory) as contrasted to a life (or field) situation (p. 114; my emphasis).

I will end this summary with some comments by Valenstein about brain manipulations by means of drugs:

The effect of any drug can vary enormously in different individuals. Alcohol will put one person to sleep and make another aggressive, while a third person may become the "life of the party." Similarly, amphetamine may be a stimulant for one individual, it may help a depressed person to get sleep, and it is prescribed as a means to reduce hyperactivity in others. . . . A drug that might speed up mental processes could lead to increased productivity in one person while producing an increase in frustration and aggression in another and an exacerbation of anxiety in a third.

It has been argued that much more specific effects could be obtained if pharmacological agents could be supplied directly to critical brain sites. The administration through more common routes (mouth and injections) results in the drug affecting many areas and producing numerous "side effects." The hope is that more precise control could be exerted by the direct application of a drug to a discrete brain site. Is there any place in the brain where a drug will have a precise control over aggression? Unfortunately, the answer seems to be clearly, *No!* The brain is simply not organized so that all of one function is localized in one area. As already noted, even though aggressive behavior can be triggered by electrical stimulation of some areas of the hypothalamus, the destruction of these areas does not change the normal aggressive responses of animals to those stimuli which provoke them in natural settings. There is no reason to believe that the results would be any different following chemical manipulations of discrete areas. Furthermore, *it is unlikely that the brain is organized into systems that fit our labels* [my emphasis]. There are probably no neural circuits that are exclusively involved with the regulation of aggression. Responses that are part of aggressive behavior in one setting may be incorporated into sexual behavior under other conditions. For all of these reasons, it has to be considered highly unlikely that a drug modifying neural activity at a specific brain site would be very effective in eliminating aggression and no other behavior (pp. 129–131).

Although the material I have summarized out of Dr. Valenstein's informative book is not philosophy, it has philosophical significance. I have presented conceptual arguments against the possibility of psychophysical isomorphism and against the possibility of one-to-one correlations between certain mental states and certain brain states. This is likely to evoke the reply: "Such correlations must be *possible*, since they have actually been demonstrated; therefore your reasoning must be unsound." But many philosophers and psychologists, as well as the general public, have a mistaken view as to what has been demonstrated by neuropsychological experiments. Valenstein's survey shows that there is no evidence of any one-to-one correlations between neural circuits on the one hand and, on the other hand, any emotions or moods, such as fear, anger, or anxiety, or even any behavioral sequences, let alone any particular thoughts, desires, or memories. Thus the inference from supposed actuality to possibility is undermined. Brain stimulations do indeed "trigger" various psychological and physical responses, but the empirical evidence does not indicate one-to-one correlations, and it shows that the responses are "situationally dependent," which is just what one should expect.

Index

MEMORY AND MIND

Designed by R. E. Rosenbaum.
Composed by Vail-Ballou Press, Inc.,
in 10 point VIP Janson, 2 points leaded,
with display lines in Janson.
Printed offset by Vail-Ballou Press
Warren's No. 66 text, 50 pound basis.
Bound by Vail-Ballou Press
in Joanna book cloth
and stamped in All Purpose foil.

Library of Congress Cataloging in Publication Data
(For library cataloging purposes only)

Malcolm, Norman, 1911–
    Memory and mind.

    Includes bibliographical references and index.
    1. Memory.   I. Title.
BF371.M339   153.1'2   76-28017
ISBN 0-8014-1018-5